D1301975

Authors by Profession

This book is dedicated to my colleagues at
The Society of Authors, but in particular to

Elizabeth Barber OBE

who spent all her working life in the
service of writers. After taking Honour Mods
and a degree in law at Oxford, she was called
to the Bar in 1935. Next year she joined
The Society of Authors as Assistant-Secretary,
and directed the organisation as General
Secretary from 1963 until her retirement in 1971

Authors by Profession
Victor Bonham-Carter

How authors and dramatists have practised
their profession; their contractual and personal
relations with patrons, publishers and promoters; their situation under the law of copyright; their standing with the public; their part in
the trade of books and periodicals and presentation of stage plays; their professional
organisations

Volume One

From the introduction of printing until the
Copyright Act 1911

William Kaufmann Inc.
One First St./Los Altos, CA 94022

Published by WILLIAM KAUFMANN, INC One First Street Los Altos, CA 94022

ILLUSTRATION

The jacket of the hardcover edition and the cover of the paperback edition was designed by Diana Gardner, who has incorporated the cartoon of Walter Besant published in the *Chicago Herald*, when he attended the International Exhibition in that city in 1898.

Printed in Great Britain at The Spottiswoode Ballantyne Press by William Clowes & Sons Ltd, London, Colchester and Beccles

CONTENTS

Other Books by
VICTOR BONHAM-CARTER

The English Village
Dartington Hall (with W. B. Curry)
Exploring Parish Churches
Farming the Land
In a Liberal Tradition
Soldier True
The Survival of the English Countryside

2

ACKNOWLEDGEMENTS

First, I wish to express my most sincere thanks to the Trustees of the Alistair Horne Research Fellowship, St. Antony's College, Oxford, who awarded me a two-year Fellowship 1974–6; also the Committee of the Phoenix Trust for a grant in 1976–7. The emoluments from these Trusts provided me with the means to write the major portion of this book.

Secondly, I wish to acknowledge my debt to all who gave me personal aid and encouragement, and to those authors, publishers, and copyright owners, who allowed me to make extended quotations from their works:

The Committee of Management of the Society of Authors for permission to use the archives, and my colleagues, Philippa MacLiesh and George Astley, who gave me valuable criticism of the text.

For allowing me to quote contributions to *The Author* by Arnold Bennett and H. G. Wells, I am indebted respectively to the Executors of the Estate of the late Mrs Dorothy Cheston Bennett, and the Executors of the Estate of H. G. Wells.

Ian Campbell for information about Thomas Carlyle.

Mrs. Evelyn Elwin, who allowed me to use and quote from the biography of Charles Reade by her husband, Malcolm Elwin; and who gave and lent me books.

Miss Diana Gardner, who read and helped me revise every chapter, and spent many hours on research. Her own work on the Archives of the Society of Authors was invaluable. She also designed the jacket and cover of this book.

Michael Holroyd for much personal and professional help, including advice on Bernard Shaw, on whose authorised biography he is at present engaged.

Dan H. Laurence, Literary and Dramatic Advisor to the Estate of Bernard Shaw, who gave me invaluable assistance on the chapter devoted to Shaw and the Society of Authors.

Dr. Gavin McFarlane for access to his thesis on dramatic and musical copyright.

Miss Robin Myers for advice on the book trade and for the loan of books.

3

Oxford University Press and the Clarendon Press in respect of works written or edited by James J. Barnes, Dorothy Blakey, Gordon S. Haight, Phyllis Hartnoll, James Hepburn, Simon Nowell-Smith, and the Editors of the Pilgrim Edition of *The Letters of Charles Dickens*. Detailed references in the Notes.

Professor Robert L. Patten of Rice University, Houston, Texas, for an explanation of 19th century part and serial publishing, and for data about the finances of various works by Dickens and Thackeray.

Mrs. J. M. Patterson, Secretary of the Royal Society of Literature, for information about that body.

Miss D. E. Proctor, Hon. Librarian of the Theatre Museum, for information about the Dramatists' Club.

Routledge and Kegan Paul Ltd in respect of works by James J. Barnes, Kegan Paul, and J. W. Saunders. See the Notes.

Dr. A. L. Rowse and Professor David Daiches for information about Shakespeare.

Hallam Tennyson for checking the section on his forebear, Alfred Tennyson; and Dr. J. S. Hagen of Brooklyn, New York, for a sight of some of her research on Tennyson.

Professor Kathleen Tillotson for information about early attempts to form societies of authors.

The University of Chicago Press in respect of *The English Common Reader* by Richard D. Altick. See the Notes.

Dr. D. P. Waley, Keeper of Manuscripts at the British Museum, for access to early records of the Society of Authors.

Others who helped me include: John Coleby, Nigel Cross, Mrs. Pauline Dower, Richard Findlater, Benjamin Glazebrook, Mrs. Cynthia Hollie, Miles Huddleston, John Murray, Ian Parsons, Mrs. Cynthia Sanford, G. W. Trevelyan, Ian Willison, also Mrs. Anne Clarke and Miss Jane With of the National Book League; and Miss M. J. Stoneburg of Bucknell University, Lewisburg, Penn.

Finally, I wish to express my gratitude to all other authors and publishers whose works I have consulted for the purpose of reference or brief quotation, as recorded in the Notes and Select Bibliography.

V. B-C.

INTRODUCTION

W HAT IS an author? Someone who makes a living by writing? That would seem the logical answer although, as we all know, it is not the right one. Definition defies simple solutions; and that is one reason why I have conducted this search into history—not for the purposes of literary assessment, but in terms of economics, society, and the law.

I start about the year 1500, soon after the introduction of printing and long before writers were paid for writing. I then pick out authors in a variety of *genres* in order to illustrate the theme: how certain poets, novelists, essayists, historians, biographers, dramatists, and other sorts of writers, made their way within the circumstances of their day. One important qualification. I make no arbitrary distinction between authors and journalists, partly because the categories overlap, partly because journalism can hardly be identified as a separate profession before, say, the 1700s; but journalism as such is not the subject of this book.

A living? Some writers in every age have certainly lived by writing, but not many. Most have had to rely on patronage or on some occupation ancillary to, or outside, literature; and must do so today. Economics have always bedevilled authorship, often to the point of extinction. The explanation is complex and varies with each generation, which underlines the value of history in writing about the subject. In his *Calamities of Authors*, published by John Murray in 1812, Isaac d'Israeli included a chapter called 'Authors by Profession', which I have borrowed for the title of this book, though d'Israeli barely attempted analysis. What then is the yardstick for measuring authorship? Is writing a real profession? There have always been doubts about it.

Oddly, the case is different with other artists—composers, choreographers, painters, sculptors, and performing artists—partly because most of them have undergone some formal training or have had the opportunity to do so, passing an examination or securing a diploma or degree. Professionalism implies that kind of passport, at least at the outset of a career.

The public is aware of the existence of colleges of music and art and of schools of acting and dance: that they produce men and women who have achieved acknowledged standards of proficiency, comparable to those required for lawyers, architects, surveyors, and doctors. It is all part of the process of recognition.

Not so with writing which, until recently, was not regarded as a subject for instruction. Whereas schools, or departments of writing at universities, are fairly common in the USA, they are rarities in the UK. In the last few years the climate has begun to change. Certain British universities now award scholarships or appoint 'writers in residence', while a few authors are being attached to schools and even to public libraries. Also a handful of colleges and private institutions—such as the Arvon Foundation[1]—run informal courses in 'creative' writing or organise 'workshops', and are receiving positive support. Even so this is a new phenomenon for Britain and is still treated with reserve: not surprisingly since, in the past—with one or two exceptions—schools of writing have been suspect or revealed as plain bogus. It remains to be seen therefore whether the American practice will make real headway in Britain, for the general belief has been that—apart from studying syntax and the elements of style at school, and reading English at the university—the art of writing can only be learned by practising it. You learn as an apprentice does, except that you have no master to work for except yourself and the market.

> The fact is that as writing is an empirical art, which can only be learned by doing it, there is no formal way of graduating in authorship and no way of enumerating its practitioners. For them independence is of the essence, and this includes the freedom to practise without formal qualification, without regimentation, without the pressure of collective action. The price of that independence is the lack of identity in the public mind.[2]

This fact is no reflection on the art of writing. Because skill is acquired in a seemingly haphazard way, it is none the worse, indeed sometimes the better, for it. As in every art you must have at least the foundation of a gift, without which it is useless to proceed; but if the foundation exists, then success—not merely economic—is largely a matter of persistence and of making the most of opportunities. Experience is a hard school. Wastage among aspiring writers is high and, as noted, most survivors have to rely on another job. The pros and cons of that situation are debatable. Working out in the world is not solely a form of insurance; it can also be a vital source of material and incentive, particularly for the fiction writer. Many well-known authors mentioned in this book laboured away at other jobs for part or all of their lives, and either profited therefrom or made their names notwithstanding. Obvious examples include Fielding, the magistrate, in the 18th century; and Trollope, the civil servant, in the 19th.

Economic security frees the mind from worry, but a routine job also consumes mental energy which might otherwise be harnessed to creative output. This applies as much to freelance journalism and other ancillary activities of authorship as to non-literary employment. A regular stint of reviewing, reading MSS for publishers, broadcasting, lecturing, and the like, may oil the machinery of the mind, but it may also use up horsepower to the point of exhaustion. Moreover continuity of creation is often vital—whether for the construction of a work of fiction or for historical research or, indeed, for any idea that has to be digested into literary form. Interruptions nowadays however are a professional hazard that all authors have to contend with, but they are not insuperable and not the worst threat to a living literature.

A more insidious danger is concealed in the fact that writing is *par excellence* our national art. Whereas the British contribution to the other arts is considerable, it has nevertheless been spasmodic. In music, for instance, we can point to the Elizabethan and Jacobean composers; in painting, to the portraitists and landscapists of the 18th and early 19th centuries; not to mention contemporary composers and artists whose rating we must leave to the judgement of history. The record in these other arts does not however compare with that in writing, for there have been battalions of authors of the first rank—in every age from Chaucer onwards—and whole armies of the second and third ranks, who have made English one of the two greatest literatures of the world, French being the other.[3] And that leaves to one side the part played by writers of English in other continents—America, Africa, Australasia, India; likewise the fact that, thanks to trade, politics and diplomacy, English has become the *lingua franca* of international affairs. It all means that English is now the main means of communication for a huge segment of the world population. Where then lies the danger?

It lies in the paradox that the universality of English and its long literary tradition have blinded the British themselves to the fact that, without recognition and reward, no such tradition can continue, however marvellous and massive its past achievements. It is taken for granted that numerous authors of talent, and a few of genius, will always appear, whatever the prospects. The assumption is reinforced partly by success stories—the handful of writers who do make large incomes or write a bestseller; but partly and more importantly by the sheer volume of print, evident in publishers' profits and the production of over 30,000 titles annually in Britain alone, by the quantity of periodicals always on sale, and by free borrowing from public libraries. The word is indeed a common article, and authors are still two a penny. Sheer abundance tells the tale, implying that authorship cannot be regarded as a real profession, such as surveying or accountancy. It requires no formal training, no regular attendance at office or factory, it is as easy and everyday as putting on your clothes, anyone can do it and plenty do. Indeed as surveys[4] show, most authors do write in their spare time—not merely as a means of earning extra money or as a by-product of some other vocation—but because they have no alternative. This unpalatable fact has been turned round as an argument against the status of authorship, and the low rewards of writing used to denigrate the art which has placed Britain in the forefront of literature and language.

The point was forcibly illustrated in the debate on Public Lending Right in the House of Lords on 5 April 1976, when Lord Willis said:

> He [Lord Paget] actually said that there is no harm in authors being authors part-time, and he went on to say that it would not do authors any harm if they did normal work besides writing, or some phrase of that description. I am sure he did not mean it in that sense, but I find it deeply offensive. In my view, professional authorship is a dignified and honourable profession, and nobody in this House or anywhere else can tell me that it is less arduous to be a writer than it is to be a miner or a solicitor or a Member of Parliament, to none of whom is it suggested that they should get a 'normal job' in addition.[5]

The author therefore faces a dual problem. On the one hand he has to overcome the indifference of the public. On the other he must anticipate the virtual impossibility of living by the

8

profession in which he gains a reputation by talent and hard work. In what other walk of life outside the arts, but outside authorship in particular, does this happen? Does a dentist have to run a restaurant, or a state registered nurse take in washing, to get by?

It is not my purpose to suggest solutions in this volume, which has a strictly defined aim: namely, to record the changing situation of authorship within a specific span of time—the 400 odd years between the end of the 15th century and the beginning of the 20th; or more precisely between the introduction of printing by William Caxton in 1476–7 and the Copyright Act of 1911. This Act, a visionary piece of legislation, constituted the greatest single advance in protecting the rights of the creator up to that date. Not only was it the culmination of nearly 70 years of effort at reform since the earlier Act of 1842, but it also represented a boundary in artistic copyright. In other words it could be said to mark the end of an era, in which literary communication was restricted to print and the stage.[6] It is true, of course, that both these media continued to play a vital role, and have themselves experienced significant changes since 1911. It is also true that the Act took account of film rights (and for the composer, mechanical music rights); but these new media were still in their beginnings, and were to make no critical impact until after the 1914–18 war, when they were joined by radio, talkies, television and, later still, by tapes, cassettes, and all the new technical resources for storage and communication.

One clear lesson emerges from this early period—that authors' best aid sprang out of their own efforts. Self-help on any scale came late in the history of authorship. The first successful move towards collective action followed the foundation of the Society of Authors in 1884. Thus the greater part of the last five chapters of this book is based on material contained in the Society's archives—correspondence, minutes, and publications, especially *The Author* which not only records events but acts, as it does today, as a forum for discussion of subjects relating directly to authorship as a business. Before 1884 I have drawn on the scholarship of other writers, to whom I have acknowledged my debt elsewhere in the book.

Waterrow   VICTOR BONHAM-CARTER
Wiveliscombe
Somerset   May 1978

9

CHAPTER ONE

The evolution of authorship as a business, 1500–1800

BEFORE PRINTING, copyright presented few problems, for medieval law recognised virtually no distinction between a literary work and the material upon which it was written. The underlying Common Law principle that a man should be allowed undisturbed enjoyment of his property applied equally to both. The invention of printing however made possible the multiplication of copies of a work, the first English printer being William Caxton who set up his press at Westminster in 1476. This meant that a literary work could be appropriated without theft of a manuscript, and thus presented new problems for the protection of literary property which, in due course, found solution in the abstract legal concept of copyright.[1]

Printing, publishing and bookselling were at first all one business, and publishing and bookselling remained so for at least 300 years. Publishing—to apply a generic title to the process of book production—gained ground rapidly in the 16th century, thanks to the spread of literacy under the impetus of the Renaissance and the Reformation. Nevertheless it was subject to restraints, not so much technical and commercial as political, due to the influence of the Crown which:

> began to assert prerogative rights in the printing of books and to make a practice of granting monopolies to interested parties in the form of 'the sole privilege' to print certain titles or certain categories of books . . . This was not mere venality on the part of the sovereign . . . It was much more an attempt to curb publication of seditious or blasphemous books by controlling the source of supply; in short by operating an indirect form of censorship.[2]

It was not possible however to sustain absolute control in an age characterised by a growing and passionate interest in religion and the arts. While retaining Crown prerogative, powers were delegated under the Royal Charter of 1557 to an agency, the Stationers' Company, which acquired two functions.

First, it maintained a Register in order to record publication and inhibit the duplication of titles, so that the words 'Entered at the Stationers' Hall' virtually constituted notice of a claim to copyright. Secondly, it created a monopoly for, unless publication was separately authorised by the Crown, a work could only be issued by a publisher who belonged to the Company. There was opposition of course, both above and under ground; but essentially it was a fight over the freedom to publish, or the means to do so, and in that sense it affected publishers more closely than authors.

For at least 150 years after the introduction of printing, few—if any—authors made a living by writing. Instead they survived by means of patronage or, as is still the case with the majority of writers, supported themselves from the proceeds of other kinds of employment. In the 16th and early 17th centuries patronage was not primarily concerned with the giving and receiving of money, but formed part of the social system. Writing was not yet regarded as a profession to which you devoted your life, hoping that it would yield you a livelihood. Rather, it was a form of civilised communication that, among educated people, was quickly replacing the oral traditions of the past. To write lyrical poetry and elegant prose was a refined accomplishment. The Tudor nobles practised it, and it pleased them to support writers of humbler origins as befitted the cultural climate of the day. The influence of the Court was paramount—in refining and stabilising the language, in finding outlets for the new literature by the presentation of masques, plays, and addresses for ceremonial occasions, and generally in stimulating the writing of poetry, drama, and belles lettres. Publication in this field was incidental. The custom of circulating work in manuscript continued far longer at Court than elsewhere, for it was considered *infra dig.* to have any truck with a publisher. What the writer received by way of reward, apart from acclaim, was security: a job as a secretary, tutor, chaplain, actor, librarian, or political agent. Sinecures, or profits from monopolies and property, were also forthcoming; and the occasional fee in response to a flowery dedication.

In time the social stigma of print evaporated, partly through the popularity of the theatre which knew no class distinctions and made good money, and partly because certain kinds of work were never so stigmatised. For example, street ballads, broadsides, and pamphlets—the forerunners of modern journalism—found a ready market and earned a writer £2 or £3 per title. Again, books of instruction and improvement were well received: encouraged alike by the Court and by the powerful ascendant body of Puritans, who frowned upon the immorality and trumpery inherent in poetry and fiction. Books as such however were rarely profitable for the author.

An edition of any book was limited by law, except by special dispensation, to an impression of 500 copies, and 250 was the usual size. There was no law of copyright protecting authors, and it was the custom of the writer to sell his work outright for a standard fee, usually about £6 10s, but occasionally rather more, up to about £20. Even if the writer produced a best-seller, he received no further reward unless, at the publisher's discretion, he received a fee for any revisions required for a later edition.[3]

As the 17th century advanced, the Puritans exerted increasing influence on literature—to the detriment of the humanities, except the theatre. Drama, popular with audiences of all tastes, was defended by the Court; and players, organised in troupes and wearing the livery of their aristocratic or royal employers, were regarded as respectable citizens.

It was a lucrative profession. Quite apart from earnings in the playhouses and on tour, the players were occasionally called upon to give special performances before the Queen and the nobility; when they did they boosted their takings from a single performance from about £6, the average day's 'house' at the Globe in 1600, to £35. And sometimes plays or masques were specially commissioned by the Court, earning the playwright anything between £5 and £30 ... Writing plays (worth in the normal run about £6 apiece) would not have provided a comfortable living in itself; it was better to be an actor, too, for even hired actors earned 6s a week, and by 1635 leading players commanded as much as £180 a year.[4]

Shakespeare would not have profited financially from publication—except indirectly from his patron, Southampton, to whom he dedicated his two narrative poems, *Venus and Adonis* and *Lucrece,* issued by Richard Field in 1593 and 1594. As to his plays—*Titus Andronicus* and *Romeo and Juliet*, the first two to appear in print, were pirated by John Danter in 1594 and 1597; but the rights belonged to the company, and so

Shakespeare's plays were published after his death by two fellow actors, Heminge and Condell.[5] In the absence of copyright, authors were helpless, and it was particularly galling to see their work incorrectly printed. With plays this often happened, type being set from an ill-written manuscript copy or from a reconstructed version put together by actors.

In 1642 all public playhouses were closed, and no plays—other than by private performance—were staged until the Restoration 18 years later. The Puritans were however hoist with their own petard for, while zealous in repressing 'worthless' works, whether published or performed, they had earlier resisted similar efforts by the Star Chamber, in particular the Decree of 1637, to impose a strict censorship on the book trade. In 1641 the Star Chamber was abolished, with the result that the Stationers' Company, which had hitherto controlled publishing and bookselling (other than works licensed direct by the Crown), lost its absolute authority. A flood of unlicensed publications now followed, so that in 1643—in response to a Remonstrance by the Company and in fright at the liberty it had unleashed—Parliament tried to re-impose the former *status quo*. In vain. Not only was the new Ordinance ineffective, but it roused the wrath of the great John Milton who had already flouted the Star Chamber on the very same issue. Without a moment's hesitation, therefore, he published his contentious *Doctrine and Discipline of Divorce*, and followed it up in 1644 with a trumpet blast, *Areopagitica*, 'A Speech for the Liberty of Unlicensed Printing', an historic document addressed to Parliament itself. Nobody lifted a finger against him.

Milton is of prime interest for another reason. In youth and early middle age he had conformed to the current fashion of concealing his identity as an author, neither had he thought of making money out of his work. True, he was of independent means, but that did not account for his attitude which derived from the diffidence considered appropriate to authorship of his kind. Politics however changed all that. From the early 1640s he wished to be, and was, publicly identified with his own work. His sympathy with Cromwell was no less open, and for several years he was employed as 'Latin Secretary' by the Commonwealth. His attitude to earning money by writing however remained unchanged, and he always insisted on making liberal distribution of complimentary copies. Nonetheless, after the Restoration, when deprived of his pension and other resources, he was compelled to make the historic deal with Samuel Symons for the publication of *Paradise Lost*. The agreement was dated 27 April 1667, and provided that Milton receive £5 for the first edition or impression of 1300 copies, £5 for the second, and the same again for the third. In fact he was paid £10 during his lifetime, while his widow sold the copyright (or right of publication) to Symons for a final consideration of £8. Thus the work earned a total of £18 (the equivalent of £300 or more today) for the author and his estate, not quite such a miserable sum as might first appear. But that was not the end of the tale, for the copyright was re-sold twice, passing finally into the hands of Jacob Tonson I, a highly successful publisher, of whom more anon.

*   *   *   *

It is clear from this episode that, by the latter half of the 17th century, the concept of copyright was undergoing a change. Hitherto it had been regarded almost solely as the property of the publisher, the author's interest not being recognised. As recorded in the Register of the Stationers' Company, publishers had been buying copyrights from each other ever since the mid-1500s. Such disputes as arose derived mainly from the duplication of titles, due either to deliberate piracy or to genuine mistakes in checking the Register. In either case fines for infringement were nominal.

Paradoxically the situation deteriorated with the passage of the Licensing Act 1662, which re-established the Royal Prerogative and reimposed censorship. So far from having its authority and powers of control restored, the Stationers' Company was subject to harassment at the hands of the newly appointed 'Surveyor of the Imprimery and Printing Presses', Roger L'Estrange. L'Estrange bullied publishers and printers alike, and for a short time exercised what amounted to police powers over the entire trade. Further afflictions followed with the Great Plague in 1665 and the Great Fire in 1666, which thinned out the stationers and their stocks respectively, and practically cleared St. Paul's Churchyard as the centre of the book business. However not every disaster was total. The Licensing Act was allowed to lapse during the Great Fire and was not renewed—and then only half-heartedly—until after the accession of James II in 1685. Subsequently, under William and

Mary, L'Estrange was disgraced, and in 1694 the Act lapsed altogether.

There now followed a period of anarchy for, apart from ill-defined protection of property afforded by Common Law, there was nothing to prevent anyone from printing anything. All attempts by the Stationers' Company to re-establish the authority of the Register failed—annual entries averaged less than four between 1701 and 1708—and piracy was rampant. Accordingly the London publishers applied for fresh legislation in 1703, 1706, and ultimately with success in 1709—the Bill, it is said, being drafted in its early stages by Dean Swift. However, instead of confirming the publisher's assumed right to retain a literary property in perpetuity, the new Act[6] (effective as from April 1710) made copyright the personal possession of the author, though only for a limited period. In regard to works already published, it provided that all owners of copyrights (authors or publishers or their assigns) should retain their rights for 21 years, i.e. until 1731. In regard to unpublished works, the rule was that the author retained sole rights for 14 years as from the date of first publication, the period being extended by a further 14 years if the author was still alive at the end of the first 14. New works had to be entered in the Stationers' Register as before.

The Act of Anne, as it is often called, was thus the foundation of copyright as we know it. It established the author's right to his own property, and thereby gave him the power to bargain for better terms. Whereas previously he had almost always sold his copyright outright—if it had not already been purloined without his knowledge—he could now license publication without parting with the copyright at all. In fact, as we shall see, most authors found the publishers too strong for them; so that the old practice of outright sale continued in most cases[7]—though qualified in certain important instances shortly to be described.

It was not long before a number of publishers began looking for loopholes in the new Act: specifically after 1731 when the 21-year period of protection for works published before 1710 ran out. Those in possession, e.g. Jacob Tonson II, who published the works of Shakespeare[8], Milton and Dryden, all of them valuable properties, claimed that the Common Law overrode the Act of Anne, so that in effect these copyrights were perpetual. The same argument was advanced in different guises (e.g. for the 'greater protection' of authors) in regard to copyright on the 14 years basis. Parliament rejected both pleas. Nonetheless, when in 1763 a rival publisher[9] issued James Thomson's *The Seasons*, he was sued successfully for infringement by Andrew Millar, who had bought the copyright from the author in 1729. Ultimately the issue was settled (over the same work) in 1774 when—in the historic case of Donaldson v. Becket (who had purchased from Millar)—the House of Lords decided against Common Law copyright by one vote. This meant that, thereafter, the provisions of the 1709 Act held good.

Throughout the century the struggle over copyright was complicated by genuine grievances suffered by publishers, which tended to obscure the main issue. In the first place piracy was never stamped out, only kept at bay; and there were some notorious evaders of the law—Edmund Currll being a prime example. Apart from illegal editions slipped out overnight, there was a regular trade in adaptations and abridgements, appearing mostly in magazines. Pope, Johnson, Goldsmith, and others, were all victims of such practices. Secondly, Ireland lay outside statutory jurisdiction—a matter not corrected until the Act of Union in 1801—and Irish publishers virtually depended for their living by battening upon English works. The only remedy was to publish simultaneously in both countries, or even in Ireland first. This was precisely what Samuel Richardson tried to do in 1753 with his *The History of Sir Charles Grandison*. Yet, despite the most stringent and secret precautions, a printer's workman was bribed to smuggle a set of sheets out of the country (or so it was presumed), with the result that three pirated editions appeared in Dublin before either the official Irish or English ones. A similar, though less serious, situation arose out of the importation of English language texts and translations from the Continent, likewise of scholarly editions of Greek and Latin classics: although in time this trade was partially controlled by Parliamentary action.

*   *   *   *

Copyright apart, conditions for authorship were improving for social reasons. By 1700 memories of the Civil War were growing faint, and even the troubles of the Restoration and its aftermath were diminishing. The Glorious Revolution of 1688 had put an end to serious hopes of a Catholic revival, while the Dissenters—despite repression—had no wish to renew violence.

With the accession of George I in 1714 and the domination of Government by Robert Walpole, the country entered a long period of apathy in politics. Whatever their persuasions, people wanted peace and confined disputes to verbal argument and print.

This then was the spring time of journalism. Although plenty of publications of a most varied nature were in circulation by the end of the 17th century, the periodicals launched by Richard Steele and Joseph Addison—the *Tatler* in 1709, the *Spectator* in 1711, and the *Guardian* in 1713—struck a new note, for they were immediately and immensely successful in popularising miscellanies of fact and comment.

> The 'essay', an omnibus term which might be used to refer to any of the articles in these periodicals, was in origin a serious dissertation upon topics of national interest; but its limits were so vague that writers could indulge themselves, as in a potpourri, with whatever ingredients pleased the taste of the cook and the guests. What the audience wanted, it seems, was a survey of contemporary life, written from a moral viewpoint, combining erudition and criticism with wit and humour, and the great eighteenth century essayists, mixing imagination with their reporting, gave them just that.[10]

Soon periodicals were supplemented by magazines, digests, reviews, and encyclopedias. Publications of this kind, designed to satisfy the thirst for knowledge, were not cheap and by modern standards were limited in circulation. For a 'daily' or 'weekly', 4,000 copies per issue were accounted a good total. After 1712 newspapers bore stamp duty, which further restricted their sale. Readership did not however depend on individual buyers, but on the fact that every coffee house carried a stock of papers, journals, and other ephemeral literature: so that each publication reached a public perhaps half-a-dozen times larger than the number of its subscribers.

The growth of journalism promoted interest in other *genres*. Histories, biographies, and even critical editions of admired writers of the past (e.g. Shakespeare) were a natural extension of the same impulse. But the passion for fiction, bursting into flame like a bonfire in the middle years of the century, was a more complex phenomenon. A precursor was the kind of spoof reporting at which Daniel Defoe excelled, e.g. *Robinson Crusoe* (1719) and *Moll Flanders* (1722). Political journalist and jack-of-all-trades with his pen, Defoe was a professional writer by any standard. Although his income from authorship is not known, he was in and out of the money all his life. His successors in the *genre* were those satirists and novelists, who portrayed contemporary life and manners, especially the seamy side, in the guise of a good story. A number of them achieved European reputation and have since become household names in the evolution of English literature.

As it happened, only a minority depended wholly on writing for a livelihood. For example, in his youth Jonathan Swift served for several years as secretary to Sir William Temple of Moor Park in Surrey, took Orders and received a small stipend as a parson, and enjoyed a vigorous spell as a journalist (though he refused payment). He spent the last 32 years of his life (1713–45) as Dean of St. Patrick's, Dublin, living on a salary of £700 a year, and left a sizeable fortune at his death. A best-seller for his publishers, he persisted in concealing his identity and refused to bother about business as an author. It was Pope (who bothered very much about business), who saw to the publication of *Gulliver's Travels* (1726) and secured him a fee of £200.

Another example was Samuel Richardson, who had few literary pretensions and started late as an author; but out of a simple project for a manual on manners, aimed at country-folk coming to town, sprang *Pamela; or, Virtue Rewarded,* published in 1740: with which Richardson achieved instant and volcanic success. Written in the form of letters around the love affair of a country girl employed in an upper class household, it was a tale of chastity and decency defended; and, being concerned with the everyday rather than the extraordinary, it struck a new note of realism and sincerity.

Pamela took England and Europe by storm, and is generally acknowledged as the first 'modern' novel. Success was so unexpected that the copyright had only realised 30 guineas. However Richardson's next novel, *Clarissa Harlowe*, issued in seven volumes 1747–8, sold 3,000 sets in two and a half years; while his *Sir Charles Grandison,* already mentioned, was reprinted three times within four months: which brought the author a healthy addition to his already comfortable income as a printer.[11]

A third example was Henry Fielding who began his career as a playwright (specialising in burlesque), then studied law and became a barrister in 1740. Seven years later he was appointed

London's first stipendiary magistrate; and together with his blind half-brother, Sir John, organised the Bow Street 'runners', predecessors of the Metropolitan police. In the meantime he continued to write, turning his professional knowledge and talent for satire to fresh account. His first novel, *Joseph Andrews* (1742), designed as a parody of Richardson's *Pamela* but converted, as it went along, into a creative work in its own right, sold well but earned him less than £200. With his next novel he made a better deal. *Jonathan Wild* (1743),[12] based on the life and death of a notorious criminal, was published by subscription and handsomely supported by influential friends. With *Tom Jones* (1749), a richly comic satire of low life, again written with inside knowledge, he did even better. He sold the copyright for £600 (to which the publisher added £100 *ex gratia* later), ensured a big subscription list by arranging private readings of the manuscript, and so promoted the work before publication that it became an immediate best-seller. For the copyright of his last novel, *Amelia* (1752)—whose success was assured in advance—he obtained 1,000 guineas.

In their different ways Richardson and Fielding created the *genre* and thus made the market for two other writers of European reputation—Laurence Sterne and Tobias Smollett.

Sterne was a clergyman, married to a lady of means and living a comfortable life in Yorkshire, who took to writing for the sheer pleasure of it. In 1759 he published *Tristram Shandy* as a private venture. David Garrick, the actor, was sent a copy and liked it so well—singing its praises to all his fashionable friends—that the publisher, Robert Dodsley, having first refused the book, was persuaded to take it on as a commercial proposition. It proved so successful that Sterne produced a series of sequels until shortly before his death in 1768. There was really no other reason why the book should stop: for it was a collection of anecdotes, dialogues, sketches, and comments upon life, compounded equally of humour and sentiment, entirely subjective, that succeeded more by a mastery of atmosphere than by any command of narrative. For the copyright of the first three volumes, and of two volumes of *Sermons*, the author received over £700: to which were added further substantial sums by Dodsley's successors for the copyright of *A Sentimental Journey through France and Italy* (1768), the balance of *Tristram Shandy*, and yet more volumes of *Sermons*. From these payments and from subscription editions, Sterne derived sufficient income to travel abroad and live the life of a most unclerical dilettante.

Tobias Smollett, though married to a wife with money and starting his career in medicine, differed fundamentally from Sterne in that he soon became a fully professional man of letters, turning his hand to practically every kind of writing. His industry was immense. He failed as a dramatist, but was a successful translator and editor of Le Sage, Voltaire and Cervantes. He was a competent reviewer and periodical publisher, wrote travel and other essays on a time schedule for payment by the sheet, and earned £2,000 for writing most of a *Complete History of England*, issued in instalments 1755–8 and promoted by an ingenious sales technique whereby parish clerks were bribed to place prospectuses in church pews. The enterprise was said to have made a profit of £10,000. Smollett resembled Sterne in that both were entertainers, but whereas Sterne wrote 'out of himself', Smollett cultivated the growing novel market. His *Roderick Random* (1748)—the story of a poor boy who made good despite a cataclysm of disasters—sold 6,500 copies in two years; while further novels, e.g. *Peregrine Pickle* (1751), *Sir Lancelot Greaves* (1760–1)—the first novel to be serialised in a magazine—and his last, *Humphry Clinker* (1771) all demonstrated his power of narrative and incident, above all his ability to give the public what it wanted, and to operate all the means available of earning a living by his pen.

*   *   *   *

Smollett was not the first to dedicate himself to letters without the aid of patronage or other sorts of subsidy. Support by individual patrons continued throughout the 18th century, but as a practice it was on the decline. For one thing the early Hanoverian monarchs showed scant interest in the arts, and the Court lost its primacy in this field. It was replaced to some extent by political patronage—as Defoe found to his advantage—but the most striking effect was seen in the changed conditions of drama. After the Restoration the theatre enjoyed a period of brilliant revival, thanks initially to the personal interest of Charles II. Playwrights however remained amateurs in that most of them depended upon sinecures and other royal favours for their livelihood, while performance of legitimate drama was restricted to two 'patent' theatres[13] or to aristocratic entertainments. As royal patronage declined, so did the standard of public taste with inevitable results in the quality of dramatic writing. Authors gave ground to star actors who literally took the stage, demanding pieces that allowed full scope for histrionics, backed by spectacular effects and other 'business'. At the same time a move to make the theatre more moral encouraged and exaggerated sheer sentimentality in playwriting and, by means of the Licensing Act 1737, induced the Government to introduce censorship at the hands of the Lord Chamberlain. The outcome was inevitable. Although a dramatist might make good money from both performance and publication of his work, playwriting soon became the preserve of hacks; while—with very few exceptions—men of letters, such as Fielding, lost interest in writing for the theatre.[14]

Professionalism in authorship did not therefore develop out of drama, although one of the earliest examples of a writer who knew how to drive a good bargain was a Restoration figure, John Dryden (1631–1700), who wrote a series of pieces for, and owned a share in, the King's Company of players. Dryden however was primarily a poet; and it was this, perhaps unexpected, medium that yielded the first notable practitioners who made a living out of literature. Dryden had the best of all worlds. He enjoyed a small private income, married a rich well-born wife, was appointed Poet Laureate in 1668 and Histiographer Royal in 1670. He poured out a quantity of verse and, aside from other income, he did well out of the market. His relations with the publisher, Jacob Tonson I, were generally abrasive and his remarks often ill-natured. Yet the two men were a good match, and Dryden obtained excellent terms—£1,200 for his edition of Virgil, and 250 guineas for his *Fables* with a promise of more at second edition.[15]

Dryden's death in 1700 is a convenient landmark, for the 18th—not the 17th—century was the watershed of professional writing from the business point of view. In short the 1700s witnessed the progressive replacement of personal by public patronage, i.e. by earnings from commercial publications—a change partly due to the Copyright Act of 1709 which, as we have seen, gave the author limited legal protection—but due also to the initiative of certain authors who followed Dryden's example and set a vital precedent for the future: among them, Richardson, Fielding, and others already considered.

Chronologically however, and as a pioneer in the business of authorship, Dryden's true successor was another poet, Alexander Pope (1688–1744). Bowed at an early age by curvature of the spine, afflicted with tuberculosis, and suspect as a Roman Catholic, Pope was hypersensitive in mind and body, seeking compensation in satire and spite. Although not without private means, he devoted his entire life to writing and regarded it as his sole profession. He began modestly enough, selling copyrights for small sums, e.g. £7 for *The Rape of the Lock*, £32 5s for *Windsor Forest*; but in 1715, in association with the publisher, Bernard Lintot (Tonson's chief rival), he saw to the publication by subscription of his translation of the *Iliad*, issued in six volumes (selling at six guineas each) over a period of ten years. The enterprise was well organised. Pope received £200 'copy money' (i.e. copyright in the sense of payment for the right to publish) for each volume, plus a liberal supply of free copies in addition to those supplied to the subscribers who—with the help of Swift and other friends—had been recruited in advance. In all he was said to have made at least £4,000 (possibly more than £5,000) from the work. Lintot's share was less rewarding since, for the next work—a translation of the *Odyssey* published in 1725–6—he offered Pope less copy money, and refused to supply free copies for the subsidiary group of subscribers furnished by one of Pope's two collaborators. This caused a break in their business relationship; nonetheless Pope grossed £4,500, and before this he had already earned enough to rent a villa at Twickenham and enjoy complete financial independence. His industry never flagged, and he continued to make money in every literary undertaking—an edition of Shakespeare in 1725; *The Dunciad*, a mock-heroic poem ridiculing the pedantry of his critics, in 1728–9; followed by a series of *Moral Essays* and *Imitations of Horace*, in which he used satire to castigate the manners and malpractices of contemporary society; and much other work besides. As a man of letters, Pope was respected and feared; as an entrepreneur, no less.

Another name, inseparable from the mark of professionalism, was that of Samuel Johnson (1709–84), though in contrast to Pope he always had to struggle. Johnson was an indifferent man of business and only attained financial security in 1762, when he was awarded a state pension of £300—an ironical turn, since he despised patronage, and his rejoinder to Lord Chesterfield has passed into history.[16] Even so he was totally dedicated to writing, turned his hand to almost every kind of literary task, and only escaped the epithet of 'hack' because he wrote so well.

As a prolific novelist, biographer, editor, dramatist, he played all the parts, sustained by talent and goaded by necessity. His cataloguing of the Harleian Library in 1743–5 was, in a sense, a trial run for the great *Dictionary* issued in 1755, the work by which he is best remembered, and financed by a 'conger' or group of publishers, headed by Robert Dodsley. This eight-year stint earned Johnson £1,675, not a great sum in view of the labour and cost of copying (which the author had to bear), but a great undertaking which, without Dodsley and his colleagues, would never have appeared at all. Cynics have said that while Pope disliked publishers but made money out of them, Johnson was poor because he spoke in their favour. In fact he was befriended not only by Dodsley but at an early and critical stage of his life—when he first came to London in 1737—by Edward Cave, proprietor of the *Gentleman's Magazine,* who commissioned regular contributions and employed him as a reporter of Parliamentary debates 1740–3.

As a dramatist Johnson was a failure. His play, *Irene*, was staged at Drury Lane in 1749 by his friend, David Garrick. It ran only nine nights, but Johnson received the profit on three of them (£195 17s), and afterwards sold the book to Dodsley for £100. His edition of Shakespeare, published in 1765 by Jacob Tonson III, did him small credit as an entrepreneur. The project was first advertised on a subscription basis in 1757, but by the time it appeared eight years later, Johnson admitted to having lost the subscribers' names and spent their money, some £1,300. Another instance of mishandling concerned *Lives of the Poets*, 1779–81, one of his last works, composed of 52 biographies. For this he asked only 200 guineas, received 400 but, it was said, could have bargained for three or four times that amount. Authors, according to Johnson, never wrote but 'for want of money, which is the only motive of writing I know of'—a quip partly discounted by his own selfless dedication to letters. He might have added that no motive is sufficient without a better head for business than he ever had.

Among the poets, Thomas Gray, remembered before all else for his *Elegy in a Country Churchyard* (1751), affected indifference to success, characteristic more of the 16th than of the 18th century. He refused the Laureateship in 1757 and wrote relatively little. Despite the pleading of influential friends, he refused for a long time to allow the *Elegy* even to be printed, and ultimately only agreed to anonymous publication. It was an immediate success, but Gray remained uninterested in literary earnings—he was, after all, a Cambridge don paid a salary—to the great profit of his publisher, Robert Dodsley.

Robert Burns, no stranger to misfortune, received over £500 for the subscription edition of his poems published in 1787, parting with the copyright. On the other hand William Cowper, other-wordly and often mad, earned £1,000 for his translation of Homer (1791), but kept the copyright in his own hands.

Oliver Goldsmith, a highly professional writer in a variety of *genres*, received only 60 guineas for the copyright of his novel, *The Vicar of Wakefield* (1766), and £450 for the performance and publication of his play, *The Good-Natured Man* (1768). In his best year he earned £2,000; but he was improvident, and seemed unwilling, as well as incapable, of turning his talents to good financial account.[17]

William Blake, whose life and work overlapped the next century, made his living as an artist and engraver. Apart from a small group of friends, who believed in his poetic powers, nobody wanted to buy what he wrote. Most of his poems he printed and illustrated himself. In contrast was the Scottish philosopher, David Hume. Although philosophy hardly proved profitable, he made an outstanding success of his *History of England* (1754–61), earning over £3,000: thanks largely to the friendship and acumen of his publisher, William Strahan.[18]

*   *   *   *

Most of the authors mentioned so far are of interest because they were breaking into the commercial market and dispensing with the traditional forms of patronage. Their value, in this context, is assessed not in literary terms, but by income. What did they earn, from what kind of work, and how? It is therefore time to look more closely into the mechanics of the market.

By the end of the 18th century an author had four main alternatives for publication, some of them capable of combination: sale of copyright, profit sharing, commission publication, and subscription.

The point has already been made that, even after the 1709 Act, the practice of selling copyright outright remained the general rule. Even so variations often occurred, and confusion often arises from what was meant by 'sale of copyright' or the payment of 'copy money'. In the case of Cowper's *Homer* there was no difficulty, for the author granted what was in effect a licence to publish, without parting with the copyright at all. This is often what copy money amounted to—the right to publish, an initial down-payment being tied to a specific edition or term of years; or, as sometimes happened, until the publisher gratuitously returned the copyright to the author.

Hume's friend, Strahan, was responsible for several variations. For instance he arranged with Adam Smith to 'buy the copyright' of the first edition of *The Wealth of Nations* (1776), and to divide the profits with him on subsequent editions. To Edward Gibbon he allotted two-thirds of the profits of the first volume of *Decline and Fall* (1776). Profit sharing was quite common, though suspect, as it allowed a dishonest publisher to recover more than his own outlay by inflating overheads and excluding trade discounts received from paper-makers and binders during the course of production, before arriving at any profit figure. The system fell into such disrepute that it became Walter Besant's chief complaint against publishers—what he called 'secret profits'—when he founded the Society of Authors in 1884.

For their part publishers maintained that, without full possession of copyright, or a specific licence to publish, or a profits arrangement, the venture was too risky, especially at a time when piracy was proving impossible to eliminate. We shall see in the next chapter how, in the 19th century, the new generation of publishers—notably Archibald Constable, Thomas Longman III, John Murray II, and William Blackwood—offset some of these difficulties by extending the 18th century practice of taking shares in a new book, while offering the author a large payment and a variety of rights; but this was only made possible by the great growth of reading and the book trade.

Although it has survived to this day, commission—or at worst 'vanity'—publishing, whereby the author himself or a benefactor pays for the cost of production, was never popular with the trade: if only because it offered small incentive to sales, simply yielding the publisher a discount or handling charge per copy sold. Taken too far, it undermined the concept of the author's retention of copyright.

That some works having a poor sale while the author had the copyright, had a rapid one when sold, was asserted by Lackington to be indisputable; they were purposely kept back, he said, that the booksellers [publishers] might obtain the copyright for a trifle from the disappointed author.[19]

The fourth alternative open to the author was that of subscription which, in a sense, was a variant of the old custom of dedication. Instead of applying to a single patron to underwrite the cost of a book, the author addressed himself to a large number of potential patrons. He (or his agent) would announce the title and content of the project—by advertisement in the press, by circular, or (in important instances) by private letter—and invite subscriptions: half to be paid in advance, half on delivery of the published work, to enable him to live while engaged in writing, pay the printer, and make a profit at the end of the day.

In some cases the author virtually conducted the business single-handed. In others, while playing the part of salesman to the subscribers, he co-operated with a publisher who met all costs out of the subscription income, supplied 'free' copies to the subscribers, and either remitted all or a share of the balance (less commission) to the author, or paid him a flat fee for the copyright, or even did both. That was how Pope, Fielding, and others made such large sums. The publisher found the system attractive for two reasons. While subscription offered him at worst a break-even deal, plus commission, he also made money by selling non-subscribed copies to the public. Sometimes he promoted a subscription edition from first to last himself or, as with Johnson's *Dictionary*, combined with others to find the finance.[20] Yet, although capable of yielding large profits, subscription was highly speculative: hence the relatively small sums paid for copyright when the author controlled the enterprise, since he often stood to gain more than the publisher in the final result. When the publisher bore the sole risk, however, the author had to bargain for as much 'copy money' as possible, as that might be all the income he could expect. The 'subscription' author, who acted as his own salesman, made no bones about importuning men of position as well as his own friends. He remained therefore—as in the past—a suppliant, often a nuisance, sometimes worse than that, no book ever reaching the subscribers. As noted, even Samuel Johnson fell into that trap, but there must have been many other such cases.

A fifth alternative—the modern royalty system—which, in its essentials, yields the author an agreed percentage of the retail price of each copy of his book sold in the home market, was not yet in existence. Introduced hesitantly in the middle of the 19th century, it did not—and could not—gain general acceptance until the book trade at large had come to terms on prices and discounts; and this did not happen until the Net Book Agreement of 1899.

*   *   *   *

For every successful author there were a host of failures. This has been so in every age, but particularly in the 18th century when journalism and the book trade were still far too small to support the many aspirants to professionalism in writing. One consequence was the phenomenon known as 'Grub Street', a term that has long entered the language as betokening hack writing and hack writers. Once it was a real street in the neighbourhood of Moorfields in London, accommodating many such miserable people who—sweating or shivering in their proverbial garrets—lived from hand to mouth on the proceeds of their (often considerable) talents. Sheer poverty compelled many of them to sell their souls to whomever would give them work—were it political pamphlets, scandal sheets, pornography, the grind of ghosting and devilling, or any of the other chores associated with starvation scribbling. And it was poverty that gained them a reputation for minor crookery and evil living, cheating tradesmen, haunting whorehouses and drink shops, and dodging bailiffs and landlords. But they were not alone. Grub Street had its rogues on both sides of the fence: authors such as Tom Brown and the brilliant Richard Savage (Samuel Johnson's friend); and publishers like Abel Roper and Edmund Currll (who was said to lodge his hacks three in a bed), who became a byword for piracy and scurrility.[21]

Grub Street was the product of a highly competitive cut-throat society, dominated by a handful of entrepreneurs in a trade always limited by the relatively small size of the reading and buying public. That fundamental fact showed little change until the latter part of the 18th century, when the population began to grow at a great pace under the stimulus of the Industrial Revolution. Before then authors as a body had made one formal, unsuccessful, attempt to take matters into their own hands by means of collective organisation. In 1736 was founded The Society for the Encouragement of Learning, under the presidency of the Duke of Richmond, attracting a membership of over a hundred.[22] It was a co-operative enterprise, designed to enable authors to issue works independently of publishers. The idea was an admirable one, for the Society was to bear the cost of production and share the profits with the authors, who were permitted to retain their copyrights. Although the object was to by-pass the publishers, in fact affairs were so ill managed that, quite soon, the Society had to turn to some of them for help. The reasons for failure are familiar enough. Only a handful of titles were issued, all of them of limited appeal, and the trade had small incentive to push their sales. Besides that, some of the most prominent authors—notably the great classical scholar, Dr. Bentley of Cambridge—would have nothing to do with the business, which was tamely wound up in 1748, after twelve years life. No successor, worthy of the name or function, was attempted until the next century.

This pitiful experiment was killed more by the incompetence of its promoters than by any hostility on the part of the publishers, who soon saw that they had nothing to fear. By this time however the structure of the book trade was showing signs of change. We have seen how at first printing, publishing, and bookselling were all conducted as one business, and how quite early printing became detached from the other two operations. Publishing and bookselling however remained in combination, and were commonly referred to as 'bookselling'.

As Marjorie Plant explains in her book, *The English Book Trade*, the time came when the individual bookseller felt the limitations of merely marketing his own titles, and so arranged to exchange stock with other traders—'hence the familiar form of the seventeenth century title-page: "printed by A, and may be had of B, C, and D".' She cites the example of John Dunton, one of the earliest to act in this dual capacity.

In the first instance he has had personal dealings with the author, has helped to plan the final form of the book, and has arranged for and taken the financial risks involved in its printing and circulation; in the other he is merely offering for sale various works produced quite independently of him. Here we have the essential difference between publishing and bookselling; but for a long period no such difference was recognised in common speech.

By the eighteenth century the term 'publisher' had come into use. Even so, the old idea lingered, and the new word served merely as an alternative for the old.[23]

Here we have an early indication of the tripartite pattern of the book trade, essentially as we know it now. One of the best descriptions is provided by John Britton, the antiquary and topographer, who—with his friend Dr. Thomas Rees—enjoyed a close connection with Longmans, the publishers. In their combined reminiscences,[24] they recorded that Paternoster Row and its environs (where the trade was concentrated) contained, towards the end of the 18th century, two printers, two whole-sale stationers, a depot of the Oxford University Press for the supply of bibles and prayer books to the London trade, and a large number of bookseller-publishers of different sorts. Among these, some issued periodicals and 'number' or 'part' publications, others specialised in reprints, others offered works of general literature and science, while others again were ordinary bookshops selling to the public across the counter.

Except for pirated works, and reprints—a trade that sprang to life after the House of Lords' decision on copyright in 1774—book prices were high.

If a man in the lower bracket of the white-neckcloth class—an usher at a school, for instance, or a merchant's clerk—had a taste for owning books, he would have had to choose between buying a newly published quarto volume and a good pair of breeches (each cost from 10s to 12s), or between a volume of essays and a month's supply of tea and sugar for his family of six (2s 6d). If a man bought a shilling pamphlet he sacrificed a month's supply of candles. A woman in one of the London trades during the 1770s could have bought a three-volume novel in paper covers only with the proceeds of a week's work. To purchase the *Spectator* in a dozen little 12mo volumes (15s) would have cost an Oxfordshire carpenter eight days' toil; to acquire the 1743 version of the *Dunciad* at 7s 6d would have taken almost a full week's salary of a ten-pound-a-year usher.

If the prices of new books were high before 1780, they were prohibitive afterward to all but the rich. Quartos jumped from 10s or 12s to a guinea; Boswell's *Life of Johnson*, for instance, cost £2 2s, the two-volume set. Octavos likewise doubled in price, and 12mos rose from 3s to 4s. Publishers generally preferred to issue sumptuous books in small editions, at high prices, rather than to produce more modest volumes in larger quantity.[25]

The demand for reading could not however be denied, and it was met in a variety of ways, mainly—as authors of the era of Public Lending Right will hardly be surprised to hear—by libraries. The earliest libraries had been the preserve of scholars, the property of monasteries, and largely composed of manuscripts, many dispersed or destroyed after the Dissolution in 1538. Colleges and cathedrals likewise assembled stocks of books by means of legacy or purchase. Private libraries were rare. In 1597 Sir Thomas Bodley offered his famous collection to Oxford University, while a century or so later Magdalene College, Cambridge became the repository of Samuel Pepys's lifelong interest in books, maps, music and prints. Private collecting only became popular among the well-to-do during the 18th century, but sales—as of the Harleian Library catalogued by Samuel Johnson in 1743–5—tended to show that many of the items were incunabula or rare editions above the head and beyond the pocket of the ordinary reader.

Borrowing on any scale by the public began in the coffee houses and clubs, which stocked periodicals and books for the benefit of customers. A similar service was rendered to members of the numerous literary and philosophical societies that characterised provincial life in the 18th century. In a more homely vein were the local book clubs, whereby neighbours—especially in the country—combined to buy the latest books and periodicals, lend them round to each other, and then sell them off secondhand, using the proceeds to buy afresh. For mass reading, however, the main medium was the commercial circulating library that proliferated in London, Edinburgh, the spas, and other fashionable resorts. The special attraction of this kind of library was its stock of fiction, the *genre* that swept into popularity in the 1740s with the works of Richardson and Fielding. For an annual subscription of one guinea or less, or by borrowing for a few pence a time, you could have your pick of a large range of sentimental literature or—as taste changed towards the end of the century—Gothick tales of the most horrendous sort. It was an innovation that captured a large new reading public: not merely the educated and well-to-do, but the rising class of domestics, artisans and small tradesmen, lightly educated and barely literate, whose interests the publishing trade was not slow to cultivate.

One publisher, William Lane, who operated his Minerva Press from Leadenhall Street, London, specialised in the business of library supply.

Those who were desirous of engaging 'in an employ both respectable and lucrative' were informed that a library containing from a hundred to five thousand volumes could be had at a few days' notice, along with a catalogue for the subscribers, and full instructions 'how to plan, systemize, and conduct' the library.[26]

Lane and the majority of publishers traded with retailers of all kinds, not only bookshops and libraries. Indeed shops that dealt in books and nothing else were relatively rare, and in any event stocked the traditional stationers' lines. Books, whether sold or lent, were often to be had along with medicines, millinery, jewellery, groceries, insurance, and tickets for the theatre. By the end of the 18th century the market was wide open, and books had become important merchandise: so much so that one man, James Lackington—who had first opened a bookshop in London in 1774—succeeded in breaking down the barriers of bookselling and made a fortune thereby. In short he became a remainder merchant, buying up quantities of unsold stock from publishers and selling off his purchases at cut prices. His success brought him few friends in the trade, while his next step—undercutting the price of *new* books—earned him outright hostility, although no publisher could afford to refuse his business. On the other hand he was immensely popular with the buying public and, like many before and since, success cloaked him with respectability in the end.

It might have been thought that by, say 1800, the growth of reading would have improved the lot of the average author. Not so. William Lane paid £5 to £30 outright for copyright work, and there were plenty of novelists glad to accept. Grub Street had not disappeared. In any event the period of copyright, unchanged since 1709, was so short that no author in his maturity could expect to benefit from work done in his youth. As Isaac d'Israeli, father of the statesman and friend of the literati, wrote in his *Calamities of Authors*: 'Authors continue poor, and Booksellers become opulent; an extraordinary result.'[27]

CHAPTER TWO

Radicals, Didactics and Romantics, 1800–1830

BY THE YEAR 1800 high pressures were steaming open the joints of English Society.

In the towns the process was well advanced whereby craftsmen and women engaged in workshops and cottage employments were being transformed into teams of machine minders, toiling in the factories of the midlands and the north. At the same time opportunities for work were attracting a stream of country people, excluded by the Enclosure Acts from the open fields and commons. Between 1760 and 1820 over $5\frac{1}{2}$ million acres were taken out of peasant holdings in this way, so that those who remained on the land were forced down to the level of labourers, without rights or property and working for starvation wages. The new towns expanded fast. By 1801 the population of England and Wales stood at 9 millions, a figure that would double in the next fifty years. The general impulse was one of fiercely competitive enterprise, tainted by resentment at inequality and injustice, and all of it dangerously vulnerable to violence.

The situation was sharpened by events in France, where the ideals of 1789, ably expressed in Thomas Paine's *Rights of Man* (1791–2), had at first found favour with English liberals. However as Edmund Burke foresaw, the mood changed as the Jacobin reign of terror ran its course and made way for Napoleon to dictate terms to the continent of Europe. The French bogey made reaction inevitable at home, though it did little to discourage the growth of business. Only reform suffered and, for a whole generation, the reins of power were being dragged—not by the new proletariat—but by the merchants and manufacturers out of the hands of the Establishment.

The political tension that gripped Britain in the early 19th century was relaxed, temporarily at any rate, by the Reform Act of 1832. Tension however was not confined to Parliament, but was evident in almost every aspect of daily life, not least in literature. With ideas in ferment, words were weapons, and journalism found ready readers among the new masses. Political comment made most impact in the radical press, notably in William Cobbett's *Political Register*, which was selling 50,000 copies by 1816 as a pamphlet fiercely critical of the established order. And there were others, e.g. the *Black Dwarf*, less popular but similar in tone, that acted as outlets for unrest. At the same time other forces were making inroads upon opinion.

One such force was religion. The Evangelical movement, essentially an Anglican extension of the Wesleyan revival, laid great stress upon the printed word. Its aim was to rescue the poor from brutish ignorance and dangerous thoughts, not by forbidding them to read but by encouraging them to do so—that is, literature of the 'right sort'. The process had begun earlier with education: first with the charity schools founded in the early 18th century by the Society for Promoting Christian Knowledge (SPCK), the object being 'to inculcate upon such . . . as can be prevailed on to learn, the knowledge and practice, the principles and duties of the Christian religion; and to make them good people, useful members of society, faithful servants of God and men and heirs of eternal life'.[1] Similar aims were promoted by the endowed elementary schools set up in the same era, and towards the end of the century by the Sunday schools associated with the name of Robert Raikes. The purpose of all these schools was basically the same—to teach literacy for the sake of morality: which meant reading the Scriptures and works of piety and very little else. The Dissenters followed a similar course, although their literature was slightly more attractive in that it carried a note of social protest, and their curriculum did permit the inclusion of a few harmless, non-pietistic, titles. Incidentally in the higher levels of education the Dissenting Academies— relatively liberal in their range of studies—were markedly superior to the grammar and other old-established secondary schools, where lessons were confined to the classics and beaten into the pupils with the birch.

None of these efforts kept pace with the growth of the population and the burden of illiteracy. Moreover in some quarters they encountered active hostility: from those who feared what might happen if the poor did learn to read; and from many working parents, who grudged spending their hard-earned pence on schooling, when their children were old enough to contribute to the family income. Nonetheless knowledge could not be concealed indefinitely. News spread and social unrest was a fact.

The Evangelicals therefore grasped the nettle, set up organisations for the dissemination of religious propaganda, and achieved astounding success. The movement was given initial impetus by the extraordinary career of Hannah More who, having made an entry into London literary society and achieved some small success as a playwright, fell under the spell of the Clapham Sect:[2] a group of Evangelical laymen determined to rouse the Established Church out of its torpor. Having removed to Somerset, Hannah and her sisters opened their first Sunday school in Cheddar in October 1789; and this was the start of a highly successful campaign in a number of villages in and around the Mendips, designed to educate and improve the lot of agricultural labourers, craftsmen and miners, and their families. No less remarkable was Hannah's venture into publishing. Backed by her Clapham friends, and writing nearly half the titles herself, she issued in 1795–8 over a hundred *Cheap Repository Tracts*, 'a series of readable moral tales, jolly, edifying ballads, and special Sunday readings of sermons, prayers and Bible stories, aimed at offsetting the influence of vicious broadsides and chapbooks, hawked about the countryside by peddlers, and popular with uneducated folk who had recently learned to read'.[3]

The *Tracts* sold by the million and pioneered the organisation of large scale religious publishing, e.g. by the Religious Tract Society (1799), the British and Foreign Bible Society (1804), the revitalised SPCK, the Wesleyan Book Room, and many others. It was the beginning of a revival that gathered momentum as the 19th century advanced and characterised Victorian life as we commonly regard it: ranging from extreme Sabbatarianism, to family prayers, mission work, the neo-Gothic movement in ecclesiastical architecture, and practical Christianity in all its forms. In print it became evident, not only in the publication of pamphlets, but in the distribution of millions of bibles and prayer books, and in the popularity of denominational periodicals. In 1807 the *Methodist Magazine* and the *Evangelical Magazine* were both selling around 18,000 copies each week, but these figures were far exceeded later in the century, especially by Sunday reading.

Another force that moulded men's minds was Utilitarianism, 'the philosophy . . . associated most immediately with the coterie dominated by Jeremy Bentham and James Mill'.[4] Its chief publicist was Henry Brougham, founder in 1826 of The Society for the Diffusion of Useful Knowledge, a title that described in its most arid form what Utilitarianism was all about. Briefly, it argued that knowledge was synonymous with information, especially in the field of applied science, mechanics, and the growth of manufacture and communications: with the corollary that economic forces should be allowed free play in a capitalist society—in other words, the doctrine of *laissez-faire*.

Here then was another attitude as characteristic of the 19th century as Evangelicalism and—although secular in theory—in practice perfectly compatible with it. Most Victorians subscribed simultaneously to both philosophies without being aware of their inherent incongruity, due perhaps to the Puritan origin and flavour of their message. Both set great store by the printed word. Brougham's Society issued a Library of Useful Knowledge in fortnightly parts at 6d each, soon followed by the *Penny Magazine* and the *Penny Cyclopaedia*, published by Charles Knight with the Society's backing. A related movement was the Mechanics' Institutes, the brainchild of Dr. George Birkbeck, who had started classes in practical science for artisans in Glasgow in the early 1800s. His purpose was, by means of lectures and libraries, to educate and equip working men to become better workers and more useful citizens. The Institutes grew and flourished for at least fifty years, then lost their identity by merging into the general movement for adult education and the development of public libraries, whose character was more middle than working class.

The watchword of the era was 'self-help', an expression epitomised in 1859 by Samuel Smiles's book, first conceived as 'a series of talks to young men who needed encouragement'. Smiles practised what he preached. His granddaughter relates that after the MS had been refused, first by George Routledge and then by John Murray, he decided to publish *Self-Help* 'at his own expense and risk, keeping the copyright and paying the publisher ten per cent commission', to the great profit of himself and his heirs. Later, at a public dinner, Routledge said to him:

'And when, Dr. Smiles, are we to have the honour of publishing one of your books?' To which Dr. Smiles was able to reply that Mr. Routledge had had the honour of refusing *Self-Help*. It was one of those moments dreamed of by despised authors.[5]

It might be thought from the foregoing that, between c.1800 and c.1850, the reading public was only interested in, and provided with, works of a useful or improving nature. Such indeed was the creed of the Evangelicals and Utilitarians, for in their eyes imaginative writing—poetry and novels particularly—were either useless luxuries, mere ornamentation upon the façade of life, if not actual symptoms of immorality. That was one reason why the disciples of Hannah More and the followers of Jeremy Bentham—whom I shall refer to collectively as 'the Didactics'—could never achieve their entire aim. What the Didactics left out of account was human nature—a craving for entertainment or, in terms of reading, novels, verses, plays, essays, and tales of fantasy and adventure. Lip service, it was true, was paid to some of the great writers of the past; but great care was taken to sift and select their work, and Shakespeare in particular was mercilessly bowdlerised.[6]

Richard Altick quotes Thomas Love Peacock, one of the sharpest satirists, in this connection.

In his *Crotchet Castle* (1831) Thomas Love Peacock managed a diverting scene in which Dr. Folliott's cook, a greasy and highly inflammable subject, took to bed with her the 'Steam Intellect Society's' sixpenny pamphlet on hydro-statics, written by a 'learned friend'—obviously Brougham—'who is for doing all the world's business as well as his own, and is equally well qualified to handle every branch of human knowledge.' The cook fell asleep, the candle overturned and set the curtains ablaze, and tragedy was averted only by the opportune arrival of the footman, who, Dr. Folliott supposed, had come to the cook's bedroom to help her study hydrostatics.[7]

The didactic attitude was likewise partly responsible for the unceasing popularity of pornography and penny dreadfuls and, on a slightly higher plane, for anodyne fiction of the kind minced out by the Minerva Press. More important, in terms of true literature, aided by the conditions created by the Industrial Revolution and the social turmoil of the early 1800s, it roused a reaction of a very different sort: namely a flowering of the human spirit, offspring of the revolt against rigid reasoning and repression of the previous century, that produced some of the greatest works in the English language.

*　　　*　　　*　　　*

Nearly all the Romantics—at least when they were young—rebelled as fiercely against industrialism and political censorship as against didacticism, whether for reasons of humanity or merely to twist the tails of the rich new middle class. Their rebellion moreover coincided with the emergence of a new generation of publishers, who knew how to canalise this force in the market and anticipate its future trends, both in books and periodicals. It was against this background that the *Edinburgh Review*, a quarterly, appeared in 1802.

The idea had sprung out of the sharp and salty mind of the Reverend Sydney Smith,[8] when on a visit to Edinburgh, the 'Athens of the North', so-called as the focus of Scottish learning and enlightenment, and so recognised for the previous half-century. The first editor, Francis Jeffrey, a barrister, set his mark upon the magazine from the start and kept control for nearly thirty years. He attracted contributors of the keenest intellect and eminence—Brougham, Hazlitt, Malthus, Scott and Smith, among them—and insisted on paying the handsome rate of 10 (soon raised to 20–25) guineas per printer's sheet of 16 pages. He himself swallowed his scruples sufficiently to accept an editorial fee of £200 a year—all this on the wise advice of Sydney Smith as bestowed on the publisher, Archibald Constable, who had promised Jeffrey full support and a free hand. The policy paid off. The first number was published on 10 October 1802 at the then high price of 5s, and had to be reprinted at once, the circulation shooting up from the original 750 to 13,000 by 1809.

> What mainly attracted the attention of the public was the sharp contrast between the old critical reviews, usually monthlies under the control of booksellers containing little more than abstracts of current publications, and the new quarterly which asked to be distinguished rather for the selection than for the number of its articles. The articles themselves, anonymous from the start, were not so much book reviews as disquisitions on subjects suggested by the books under review. And they were written with an irresistible combination of verve, learning, and acidity.[9]

The *Edinburgh Review* was concerned with society, politics and literature. It was Whig insofar as it pressed for the abolition of abuses and the introduction of reforms, but it cast its net wide and was respected for its integrity, whatever the issue. In the course of its long career (1802–1929), it recruited a succession of good editors and reviewers, and it never stinted space. The next generation of contributors included Thomas Carlyle, Thomas Babington Macaulay, John Stuart Mill (whose father, James Mill, had attacked it), and other giants, few of them noted for brevity. 'Macaulay's essay on Bacon ran to a hundred printed pages, that on Hastings to ninety-six.' At first the magazine was a joint enterprise between Constable and Longman, who handled the London sales; but a move by Constable to transfer the agency to Murray enabled the former to buy back Longman's interest in 1807 for £1,000. Seven years later Longman bought himself in again at a much higher figure, and after Constable failed in 1826 he took over the *Edinburgh* completely. Its success encouraged competitors of comparable quality, e.g. the Tory *Quarterly Review* (to which Scott transferred his allegiance) launched by Murray in 1809, and Blackwood's *Maga* started in 1817; but it was the *Edinburgh* that had begun the new phase in serious journalism and periodical publishing.[10]

Constable was one of the new generation of publishers. Like Longman, Murray, and Blackwood, he was an innovator. By doing business on a grand scale in an era of literary magnitude—for the quantity as well as the quality of prominent writers was astonishingly high—these men not only made their own names, but helped detach publishing from bookselling and raise the social standing of the profession. Their mutual arrangements and the dealings they had with some of their authors throw light on the state of authorship in the first half of the 19th century.

Although Constable was a man of vision and substance, and contributed much to the reputation enjoyed by Edinburgh for cultural enterprise, he is usually remembered for his business association with Walter Scott, which ultimately brought them both to ruin. Scott was a complex character, whose greatest mistake was to be, and to pretend to be, other than a writer. He was proud of his descent from Scottish borderers and longed to become a laird in his own right: for which purpose he bought an estate at Abbotsford and built a pretentious mansion, keeping open house. Had Abbotsford been all, he might never have got into trouble, for he enjoyed private means and earned a substantial income as an advocate and legal officer. It was writing, adopted as a sideline, that gave rein to his true talents, tapping the vein of historical romance that flowed through all his work. Romance was the key to his career. In literary terms it gained him a world-wide reputation and a huge income, but it also encouraged the gambler in him, so that in business he engaged in limitless speculations.

Success came quickly. In his youth he had collected folk tales and songs, an enthusiasm that led to the publication of his first notable work, an anthology of ballads, extended by essays and imitations by himself and his friends and issued in three volumes in 1802–3 under the title of *The Minstrelsy of the Scottish Border*. His next work, *The Lay of the Last Minstrel*, a total poetic pastiche, was published jointly by Constable and Longman, Scott having half the profits.[11] It was a runaway success, selling over 27,000 copies in eight years; and was followed in similar strain by *Marmion* (1808), *The Lady of the Lake* (1810), *Rokeby* (1813), and *The Lord of the Isles* (1815). 1805 was a fateful year, for it was then that Scott entered secretly into partnership with James Ballantyne, school friend and printer, and arranged that all his books be printed by that firm. Worse still, in 1809, Scott virtually abandoned Constable, who had advanced him 1,000 guineas on *Marmion*, and set up James's brother John as his publisher. James was not notably efficient as an accountant, but John was a disaster and crashed in 1813, after which Scott persuaded the long-suffering Constable to buy in all John's large stock of flops—works, of course, by writers other than Scott.

By this time Byron had caused a sensation with the first two cantos of *Childe Harold's Pilgrimage*, published by Murray in 1812. In consequence, Scott felt outclassed. While hitherto profits from poetry had sustained all his ventures, Abbotsford included, his way of life and business clearly needed a new line. He found it by returning to Constable and starting the series of 'Waverley' historical novels, written anonymously, 25 titles in 18 years, not to mention other books and articles—a truly prodigious output.[12] Catastrophe engulfed the whole enterprise in 1826, not due to overwork or ill-health, but because Scott, Constable and James Ballantyne had kept going on credit by continuously exchanging bills or IOUs—a common form of trading but which collapsed when cash had to be found in the slump of 1825. J. W. Saunders summarises the complicated arrangements between the three parties as follows:

The usual pattern was to sell to Archibald Constable the right to print two-thirds of an impression of between 10,000 and 12,000 copies for £2,500 to £3,000; then to give the remaining third to the printing firm, James Ballantyne, in which he [Scott] had a personal interest. If there were need, he could also sell the copyright for another £1,500–£2,000. By these means he was able, in good years when three novels appeared, to make £15,000 or even more, rewards on a scale unattained hitherto in the profession.[13]

The crash revealed two things: that Scott had written the 'Waverley' novels all along—his passion for anonymity was never adequately explained; and that his debts added up to £130,000, more than a third deriving from his association with Constable and Ballantyne. The subsequent story is well known. Scott took all the blame himself, and spent the rest of his life trying to pay off what he owed. He failed, dying in 1832, but the copyrights bought back at auction squared the account in the end.

*　　　*　　　*　　　*

Apart from brief links with Scott, Thomas Longman III was deeply involved with the Romantics from the very beginning. Shortly before his death in 1797, his father had taken into partnership Owen Rees, a Bristol bookseller. Two years later Rees and the young Longman bought up the business of Joseph Cottle (also of Bristol), who had recently published the *Lyrical Ballads* of William Wordsworth and Samuel Taylor Coleridge in an edition of 500 copies, paying 30 guineas for the copyright. It was an historic work, for it included Coleridge's *Ancient Mariner* and Wordsworth's Preface that heralded the whole Romantic movement with the sentence:

They [the poems] were written chiefly with a view to ascertain how far the language of conversation in the middle and lower classes of society is adapted to the purposes of poetic pleasure.

However the critics were so unkind and the sales so slow that, when Cottle sold out, the copyright was returned to the poets. Even so Longman decided to publish a second edition in two volumes in 1800, with additional poems by Wordsworth, but nothing more from Coleridge, while the famous Preface—now longer and less startling to contemporaries—was shunted to the end. No conflagration occurred. Longman remained

Wordsworth's publisher, but never had much profit from him. It took four years to sell out the collected edition of 500 copies issued in 1820, and in 1835 Wordsworth told Tom Moore that, up to then, his poetry had earned him barely £1,000. Shortly afterwards he received that very sum from Edward Moxon of Dover Street, who published his collected works in six volumes in 1836–7, but Moxon never recovered his investment. Wordsworth accepted public neglect with resignation, living most of his life in semi-retirement, contemplative and solitary in soul. His idea had been, through poetry, to reach the masses in words they could understand, communicating the beauty and beneficence of Nature and pointing the way to universal happiness. It was an ideal that trapped him too often in triviality, and led him as he grew older a long way from the fervour of the *Lyrical Ballads*. Materially he did not want, enjoying private means and a small sinecure, but recognition came in the end. In 1842 he accepted a Civil List pension of £300, and in 1843 was appointed to succeed Robert Southey as Poet Laureate. Only in his last years did his poems begin to become popular and profitable.

Like Wordsworth, Coleridge was a dreamer; but while Wordsworth was content to wait for recognition, Coleridge never found contentment of any kind. Ill-health drove him to take opium and exaggerated his inability to come to terms with life. He married unsuitably, had airy ideas of setting up a commune with Southey in America, tried his hand at publishing and editing, preached, took a job as a civil servant in Malta, travelled—in sum he seemed totally unable to sustain any ordinary activity. Yet his poetry soared at times to heights unattained by Wordsworth, and he proved himself a capable journalist. He secured modest, but not despicable, sums for his copyrights—£20 for *Kubla Khan*, £80 for *Christabel*, £150 and half-profits for *Biographia Literaria*, while his play *Remorse* was staged at Drury Lane and earned him £400. He wrote leaders for the *Morning Post* at 4 guineas a week, but rejected a handsome offer from the editor that might have brought him £2,000 a year. His lectures at the Royal Institution, though decently paid, were a failure. Yet he kept his friends. Time and again he was saved by gifts of money from the Wedgwoods, Byron, De Quincey, Southey (who took care of his family), Wordsworth and others. In 1823 he was elected an Associate of the Society (later Royal) of Literature,[14] one of ten 'persons of distinguished learning, authors of some creditable work of literature, and men of good moral character', and in the following year received a pension of 100 guineas out of a grant assigned to the Society by its Patron, George IV (always a friend of the arts), and paid out of the Privy Purse. The grant ceased on the king's death in 1830, but Coleridge's pension was privately made good by John Hookham Frere.[15] After his death in 1834, he was the subject of a fulsome obituary pronounced by Lord Ripon, who managed to conceal Coleridge's defects in the most oleaginous language, though tinged with traces of irony.

Robert Southey, a very different character, had also—like Wordsworth and Coleridge—been befriended by Joseph Cottle, the Bristol publisher. Less talented than the others, his poetry did not stand the test of time, although as a poet he was sufficiently admired to become Poet Laureate in 1813, after Scott had refused the appointment. He was however a capable biographer (*Lives* of Nelson, Wesley, and Cowper), and an accomplished essayist and man of letters. His most remarkable literary and financial effort was, for thirty years, to contribute articles (at £100 a time) to Murray's *Quarterly Review*; while his services to literature were recognised by a state pension of £300 awarded in 1835.

Of particular interest were his ideas on copyright. It will be recalled that the Copyright Act of 1709 had legislated for a term of 14 years from the date of publication of a new work, plus a further 14 years if the author was alive at the end of that time. In 1814 a new Act extended the first 14 to 28 years or the life of the author, whichever was the longer. This was the first positive step towards bettering the author's situation at law since the House of Lords' decision of 1774.[16] In other respects—apart from the improved terms agreed between certain authors and publishers, as related in the last chapter—no practical steps had been taken by authors to promote their interests as a body, since the unfortunate experience of the Society for the Encouragement of Learning, 1736–48. However, ideas were stirring, and Richard Cumberland, the dramatist (1732–1811), is known to have tried to form a new Society, although no date or details are available other than its failure.

Writing in the *Quarterly* in January 1819, Southey championed the claim for copyright in perpetuity.

The question is simply this: upon what principle, with what justice, or under what pretext of public good, are men of letters deprived of a perpetual property in the produce of their own labours, when all other persons enjoy it as their indefeasible right—a right beyond the power of any earthly authority to take away? Is it because their labour is so light,—the endowments which it requires so common,—the attainments so cheaply and easily acquired, and the present remuneration so adequate, so ample and so certain?

Southey made no immediate impression with his plea, though supported by Wordsworth who, with Burns in mind, wrote to a friend on 21 April:

What reason can be assigned that an Author who dies young should have the prospect before him of his Children being left to languish in Poverty and Dependence, while Booksellers are revelling in luxury upon gains from Works which are the delight of many Nations?[17]

For 'booksellers' read 'publishers'; this was a recurring complaint by authors and endemic to the author-publisher relationship. As voiced by Southey and Wordsworth it may, however, have contributed to the spate of authors' associations, proposed, formed, and extinguished between 1825 and 1843, as listed in Note 35 to Chapter Four: and culminating in The Society of British Authors that derived from Dickens's visit to America in 1842, but damned to dissolution soon after his return.

Meanwhile the fact remained that, outside Grub Street and the higher haunts of journalism, where a few men of letters such as Hazlitt, Southey, and Leigh Hunt, did manage to subsist more or less on their writing, the majority of authors had to ensure a livelihood by combining authorship with other forms of employment, or by reliance on private means, or sometimes both: as in the case of Wordsworth, who held the post of 'distributor of stamps for the county of Westmorland' 1813–42, or of John Keats—for a short time a hospital dresser and unpaid apothecary but who finally fell back on friends and family money. Saunders quotes a long list reaching right through the 19th century. Examples relevant to this chapter include George Crabbe, William Barnes, and Sydney Smith, parsons; Bentham, Brougham, Jeffrey and Scott, lawyers or barristers; Peacock and John Stuart Mill, Government servants.

Others were in business, e.g. Samuel Rogers, a banker, and Charles Lamb, a clerk in the East India Company; or in farming, e.g. Burns, John Clare, and James Hogg, 'the Ettrick Shepherd'—though they turned their talents towards escaping from the land. Of independent means were T. L. Beddoes, Byron, Walter Savage Landor, Thomas de Quincey, and Shelley; while Jane Austen was supported by her family.

The list cannot be comprehensive, but is sufficient to make the point that then, as now, it was exceptional for a writer to make a living from his craft. That was the corollary to Southey's claim for perpetual copyright, contesting the assumption that writing—by its nature—was not a recognised form of employment, entitling those who practised it to live by their talents and industry, as in other walks of life. Southey also realised that, in the public eye, the author's case was often vitiated by the fortunate exceptions: not only by the Scotts and the Byrons, but particularly by those who made a killing out of trivia. Martin Tupper, for example, who invented among other things safety horseshoes and glass screw-tops, made £10,000 (at half-profits with John Hatchard) out of his *Proverbial Philosophy*, a collection of platitudes first published in 1838.

*   *   *   *

Economic problems have often induced authors to blame all their troubles on publishers. The accusation that 'Barabbas was a publisher' was attributed (on the authority of Samuel Smiles), not to Byron, but to Thomas Campbell, minor poet, author of stirring pieces such as *Ye Mariners of England*, and one of the progenitors of the University of London. It was the sort of snide quip that Byron might well have made in a fit of spleen, but unlikely to have aimed at his own publisher, John Murray II, with whom he remained on remarkably good terms during his short stormy life. Indeed Murray treated him with consistent forbearance and generosity, and stood up firmly to his tantrums.

Byron was a combination of contrary characteristics: at the same time an arrogant aristocrat and a rebel against the hierarchical society to which he belonged. His behaviour, like that of Coleridge, poses problems for pyschologists. His championship of the cause of freedom, particularly of the national rising in Greece, where he died in 1824 trying to raise a regiment of insurgents, was the final act in a career of poetic genius and erotic scandal which—allied to his physical beauty and deformed foot—translated him into a European legend. His writing, like his character, was part-design, part-inspiration. He was capable of stinging satire, as in *English Bards and Scotch Reviewers*, his riposte in 1809 to rough handling by the *Edinburgh Review* of his first notable book of poems, *Hours of Idleness*,[18] published in 1807. This cost him a link with Longman and diverted him eventually to Murray who, in March 1812, issued Cantos I and II of his first major work, *Childe Harold's Pilgrimage*, which was an immediate and meteoric success. In this poem, born out of a recent journey through the Mediterranean, Byron's mastery of technique and power to express a passion for Nature and man in the wild, roused a response in contemporary taste and manners that caused him to write, 'I awoke one morning, and found myself famous'.

Typically he had presented the copyright of *Childe Harold* to a relative, R. C. Dallas; but Murray bought back the rights for £600, and over the next 12 years paid some £15,000 for the copyrights of Byron's works, viz. everything of importance except Cantos VI–XVI of *Don Juan*, his last great poem and unfinished at his death.[19] In one work after another, especially those with near-Eastern themes and settings—*The Giaour* (1813), *The Bride of Abydos* (1813), *The Corsair* (1814), which sold 25,000 copies in a month, *Lara* (1814), and those that followed—and in his passion for Greece and Italy and noble causes, Byron generated an unprecedented aura of melancholy and mystery about himself, coloured by his extraordinary attraction to women. He created in short a kind of idolatry that not even scandal—particularly the suspicion of incest with his half-sister, Augusta Leigh, which led to his virtual banishment abroad—or caustic outbursts against friends and associates, could disperse. In reality he was far more balanced than appeared; and he gave and received loyalty from a nucleus of friends, who stood by him to the end. Without them he would have foundered irretrievably for, although he had property and private means, he was a compulsive over-spender, and at one time contracted debts in excess of £30,000. Moreover the burden of commitments—partly due to acts of impulsive generosity—failed to eradicate an *idée fixe* against receiving money for his writing, at any rate in the form of direct payments from his publisher; so that Murray was put to extraordinary exertions at times to ensure that cash should reach him through mutual friends.

The aftermath of Byron's death in 1824 was in character with the turmoil of his life, and concerned the MS of his Memoirs which he had presented to Thomas Moore, the Irish poet. It was an episode, often described, and related at length in Doris Langley Moore's *The Late Lord Byron*.[20] When the news reached London that Byron had died of fever at Missolonghi, a group of friends, led by John Cam Hobhouse (his executor) determined to secure and destroy the MS which was rumoured to be scandalous, and likely to do irreparable harm to the poet's memory, as well as cause suffering to his wife, half-sister, and other intimates. Moore, himself in and out of debt,[21] had originally sold the copyright and handed the MS to Murray, who paid him 2,000 guineas for it. Soon afterwards Moore persuaded Murray to revise the deal, whereby the 2,000 guineas were to be regarded as a loan *if redeemed during Byron's lifetime*. However Byron died before redemption was possible, so the MS stayed with Murray and remained his property— although Moore was commonly thought to retain an interest in it. Directly they heard of Byron's death, Hobhouse and his friends set about their task in feverish haste. Money for the purchase of the MS presented no difficulty, but fears and emotions were so exacerbated, and Hobhouse handled Moore (who was touchy by nature) so clumsily, that the latter hung back. As the only man who had actually read the Memoirs, Moore was by no means convinced that they were so objectionable, and was now entertaining ideas of preserving them in part or even of giving them to Augusta Leigh. With this in mind, he got his own publisher, Thomas Longman, to promise the money needed to redeem what he mistakenly still regarded as a loan. Matters eventually came to a head at a meeting attended by seven people at Murray's offices at 50 Albemarle Street. Murray adopted a curious attitude. Although he had bought the Memoirs for a large sum, he had never read them and allowed himself quite readily to be convinced that they were unfit for publication. He therefore wrote off the investment, sided with Hobhouse and assisted—after furious exchanges between Moore and others—in tearing the MS into sections and feeding the pages to the flames in his own fireplace.

The epilogue was as surprising as the play. Although in strict terms he was under no obligation to do so, Moore repaid Murray the 2,000 guineas for the Memoirs that no longer existed, Longman providing the money as promised and anticipating that Moore would now write a Life of Byron for him to publish. In 1826 however Moore and Murray met in the street and made it up. Despite further mutual irritations the reconciliation was sustained so that, two years later, Murray made Moore a firm offer of 4,000 guineas to write the Life and edit the Letters for him. The sum was sufficient for Moore to repay his debt to Longman (the sum, with interest, now exceeded £3,000) who formally released Moore to do the work. It finally appeared in two volumes in 1830–1 as *Letters and Journals of Lord Byron with Notices of his Life*. At an auction at Hodgson's in February 1830, Murray bought in all Byron's remaining copyrights—except part of *Don Juan*[22]—for 3,700 guineas, and ultimately issued the collected edition of his works. Murray's skill and patience in dealing with a difficult man, and even more difficult heirs, was thus fully and finally rewarded.

It might be thought that Murray was continuously successful in all his transactions. He was not. He paid George Crabbe £3,000 for *Tales of the Hall* (1819) and other copyrights and lost heavily, while his investment in Jane Austen's *Emma* and her two posthumous novels, *Persuasion* and *Northanger Abbey* was so discouraging that he ultimately got rid of the property. But his biggest mistake was to take the plunge into daily journalism. Encouraged by the success of his *Quarterly Review*, and dazzled by young Benjamin Disraeli (who however abandoned his part in the project), Murray launched the *Representative* in January 1826. After losing £26,000 in six months, he was forced to cease publication.

The fourth name, bracketed with Constable, Longman and Murray, was that of William Blackwood, who began business in Edinburgh in 1804 as a bookseller proper. He developed the publishing side of his enterprise by taking shares in titles, notably in 1816 in the first series of Scott's *Tales of My Landlord* with Murray, the two men exchanging agencies for the sale of each other's stock in Edinburgh and London respectively. But Blackwood's boldest *coup* came a year later when he launched a monthly magazine which, after a change of title and editor, came familiarly to be known as *Maga* or *Blackwood's*.[23] The seventh number, which heralded the new guise, caused a sensation by its sweeping iconoclasm and virulent campaign against the literary establishment of the day, conducted in the main by 'Christopher North' (John Wilson), the 'Ettrick Shepherd' (James Hogg) and John Gibson Lockhart (Scott's future son-in-law). In due course, like its contemporaries (the

48

quarterlies), *Maga* lost its pre-eminence as a specialist in demolitions—it was succeeded in this role by *Fraser's Magazine* founded in 1830—and settled into respectability, surviving to this day as a rather curious, but readable, repository of comment, anecdote and reminiscence. William Blackwood died in 1834, and the firm maintained its equilibrium under his several sons, but it was John and William—taking charge in the late 1840s—who boosted its fortunes again by attracting a bevy of mid-Victorian giants, among them George Eliot, of whom more anon.

I will close this chapter by glancing at three authors, all integral to the period, who made little or no money in their lifetimes, yet achieved posthumous and lasting fame. Jane Austen, mentioned earlier, was unable to place her first book, *Pride and Prejudice* but sold *Northanger Abbey* for £10 to a Bath publisher who then had cold feet and had to be repaid. Later Thomas Egerton issued *Sense and Sensibility* at the author's expense which, to everyone's surprise and delight, made a profit of £150, and so encouraged Egerton that he agreed to take on *Pride and Prejudice* (1813) and *Mansfield Park* (1814) at his own risk. Jane then sent *Emma* to John Murray who, advised by William Gifford (editor of the *Quarterly*), duly published it in 1816. He followed with *Northanger Abbey* and *Persuasion* in 1818, but Jane had died the year before. The profits of the four books, in print before her death, did not exceed £700.

John Keats died from tuberculosis at the age of 25, after a brief career in minor medicine and five years on his own, writing poetry and struggling for recognition. He moved in literary circles and had good friends. Leigh Hunt published some of his poems in the *Examiner*, and Shelley helped with the publication of his first volume by the brothers Ollier. However the book was a failure, and Keats found another publisher, John Taylor, for *Endymion* (1818), which was devastated by J. W. Croker in the *Quarterly* and by John Gibson Lockhart in *Maga*. Depressed and spitting blood, Keats poured out his life in an inspired bout of work which included *Hyperion*, *The Eve of St. Agnes*, *La Belle Dame sans Merci*, *Lamia* and the *Odes*. The critics now began to warm towards him. Too late—he died in Rome on 23 February 1821.

Percy Bysshe Shelley, like his friend and contemporary, Byron, affronted society—not by his love affairs, which were irregular rather than promiscuous—but by his belief in anarchy and atheism. His tract, *The Necessity for Atheism*, caused him to be sent down from Oxford in 1811, and his admiration for William Godwin's *Enquiry concerning Political Justice* (1793) led to a long, and on the whole unfortunate, association with that author. The principal link resided in the fact that, after his first and unsuccessful marriage to Harriet Westbrook, who died by drowning in 1816, Shelley married Godwin's daughter Mary (by Mary Wollstonecraft, pioneer of women's rights) after keeping her as his mistress. Despite his belief in all the freedoms, Godwin proved a difficult and ungrateful father-in-law, for ever demanding money from Shelley who, over the years, gave him *c.* £5,000. Shelley also supported Leigh Hunt for a while.

Shelley however was not rich. Heir, by entail, to a vast fortune, he never came into his inheritance, since the life enjoyment was reserved to his father, Sir Timothy, from whom he was estranged. For a while he raised money by 'post obit bonds', or cash raised at a ruinous rate of discount against future expectations; but in 1815 he succeeded in selling the reversion of £18,000 to his father for an allowance of £1,000 a year. In any event Shelley rejected the ethics of inheritance and stuck to his radical opinions about religion and society. It got him into a great deal of trouble. All his works were published at his own expense (most by the Olliers) and circulated privately. The poem, *Queen Mab*, (1813) was pirated in 1821, ironically the only title that had a commercial sale, but he was unable to sue the publisher as the work was considered blasphemous and no copyright existed in blasphemy. Indeed he prudently dissociated himself from authorship; for, following an action by the Society for the Suppression of Vice, the pirate publisher was sentenced to four months in prison.

After 1818 Shelley lived in Italy, where he was in frequent touch with Byron, Keats, the Hunts and other exiles. Most of his best work was written there, e.g. *The Cenci* and *Prometheus Unbound* (1819) and many of his lyrics, inspired by antiquity and an idealist conception of liberty and love. In 1822 he was drowned, while sailing with a friend from Leghorn to Spezia, and his body was cremated in the presence of Byron and other friends. No authoritative edition of his works appeared until 1862.

The year 1830 is a convenient date at which to end this brief survey of authorship in its least romantic sense during the last phase of the Romantic Age. In that year died George IV, a generous patron and an understanding man, always ready to aid authors. He would have made an excellent Minister for the Arts.

CHAPTER THREE

Journalism and authorship in the mid-19th century;
Carlyle, Macaulay, Thackeray, and Dickens

THE DEATH of George IV gave notice, as nearly as any date can, that the residue of the 18th century was at last running out. By then, most of the anomalies, accumulated or merely unnoticed under the four Georges, had either disappeared or were on the point of extinction. In 1828 the Dissenters had been relieved of their political disabilities by the repeal of the Test and Corporation Acts, instituted in the reign of Charles II. In the following year Roman Catholics were similarly emancipated. The reform of the criminal law had been taken in hand by Robert Peel, Home Secretary, who had the gargantuan task of simplifying and humanising the tangled mass of medieval legislation that still imposed the death penalty for trivial offences.[1] During the 1830s Parliament passed a series of statutes that not only dropped the old century into the grave but hoisted the standard of the new—and it *was* new, brave, and often brash.

On 4 June 1832 the Reform Act redistributed the franchise among the middle classes in town and country, and in 1835 the Municipal Corporations Act swept away the scandal of 'close' boroughs, whereby rings of friends and relations voted each other in, year after year, to keep local government in their pockets.[2] In 1834 slavery was abolished throughout the British possessions; and in the same year the Poor Law Amendment Act, a ruthless and hated measure, ended outrelief, and brought back the workhouse test for paupers.[3] In 1836 two Acts transferred the registration of births, marriages, and deaths from the church to the civil authority, and so instituted a reasonably reliable system of population statistics. On the land the Tithe Commutation Act substituted a money rent for tithing in kind, but in Ireland the tithe war reflected a far deeper agitation, which ended only with the formation of the republic between the two world wars.[4]

In retrospect we can identify the 1830s as a period, not of revolution (for the structure of society was in fact being reinforced), but of social ferment and political empiricism continually agitated by the dynamics of the economy. This pattern was magnified all through the 1840s and beyond, seen particularly in the repeal of the Corn Laws (which ended protection for farming), the railway mania of 1845, and above all in the surging industrial expansion of Britain, now becoming the 'workshop of the world'. The formula was private enterprise at home and free trade abroad. Although public affairs were conducted by the politicians, it was the writers principally who interpreted the system in all its aspects, good and bad, and gave voice to public opinion. By writers I mean journalists, in the sense of all who contributed to the press, whether they were making separate reputations as authors of histories, biographies, novels, or even of poetry and belles lettres. Social comment found its way into every *genre*, but the commentators who counted were a new breed.

One thing was certain—the Romantic Age was over. Shelley and Byron were dead before 1830. Scott died in 1832, Coleridge in 1834, William Godwin in 1836. Southey and Wordsworth were past their zenith; while Lamb, Hazlitt, Leigh Hunt, and other established essayists had played out their part as midwives of the movement. Its successor was hard to identify. Freedom of spirit in an age of expansion was creating problems, with which neither science nor ordinary humanity could cope. For all its growing wealth and democratic drive, Britain was a jungle of contradictions—offering boundless opportunity, though barely changing the familiar pattern of poverty for the many and prosperity for the few: a situation that concerned writers as different as the Brontës, Thomas Carlyle, Charles Dickens, George Eliot, and Alfred Tennyson.

*　　　*　　　*　　　*

Because new books remained expensive until, gradually, technical advances in manufacture reduced costs, it was the newspapers, periodicals, and number or part publications that sold most readily and provided the main means of communication.[5]

At least three dailies stood high in status, having dispensed with political subsidies or other forms of partisan control. The *Morning Post* had been started in 1772 by John Bell and others, mainly as a vehicle for advertisements and a source of scandal. In 1795 it came into the hands of Daniel Stuart, who amalgamated it with other papers and made it into a profitable concern. Further, he gave it a literary quality by employing Charles Lamb for a time as dramatic critic, and Coleridge whose work he so admired that he offered him a partnership and an income of £2,000; but, as we have seen, Coleridge was too indolent to accept. In 1803 the paper passed to Nicholas Byrne who sustained it for thirty years until he had the misfortune to be assassinated. Later the paper came back into its own under Lord Glenesk. The *Morning Chronicle*, established in 1770, sprang into the limelight under James Perry who reported the opening events of the French Revolution and gave it a reputation for Opposition politics. It survived a variety of prosecutions for libel, and in its turn attracted a bevy of literati: among them Sheridan, Ricardo (the economist), Lamb, Coleridge, Moore, and Hazlitt. From 1817 to 1843 the editor was John Black, an able, outspoken journalist, much admired by James and John Stuart Mill. Although the paper lost ground financially and had to be sold for a mere £15,500 in 1834, it gained great popularity for a time through the employment of Charles Dickens who proved a brilliant Parliamentary reporter and a tireless correspondent. But the greatest (and the youngest) of the three was *The Times*, started by John Walter in 1785. In the early 1800s the paper was transformed by his son, John Walter II, who installed power-driven presses, increased advertising, and raised the circulation by employing first-class correspondents and contributors. Soon it outstripped all its rivals, and gained a unique position as a highly respected and truly independent newspaper. Much of its success was due to the wisdom of John Walter II who, in 1817, appointed Thomas Barnes as editor and, after the latter's death in 1841, J. T. Delane. Under these men *The Times* exerted an unprecedented influence, in part due to the force and freedom of its comment, but also the contact it made with the public through its correspondence columns.

As for the periodicals, some account was given in the last chapter of the rise of the *Edinburgh Review* under Jeffrey, the *Quarterly* under Gifford (succeeded by Lockhart 1825–53), and Blackwood's *Maga*, which Lockhart and 'Christopher North' imbued with such virulence. The fourth in line, *Fraser's Magazine*, founded in 1830, derived inspiration from *Maga* which it outdid—if that were possible—in power of invective; yet it was an original and progressive monthly whose editor, William Maginn, was always on the look-out for new talent and attracted, for example, the early work of Carlyle and Thackeray.

These periodicals, prominent and powerful, stood in the front rank of an army of publications of extraordinary variety—the forerunners of a yet greater host created by mass readership in the last half of the century. The wonder is that before then, say between 1820 and 1850, so many magazines of quality were able to keep going on circulations as low as 2,000–3,000 or even less. In such cases survival was due either to the personal influence and resources of the editor or proprietor, or to the school of thought to which the publication belonged, or sometimes to both. The brothers John and Leigh Hunt were inveterate campaigners in this field; and it was Leigh's friendship with so many of the leading authors that secured him a following whatever he did—and his ventures were numerous. The *Examiner*, a struggling Sunday paper, cost the Hunts two years' imprisonment (1813–15) for an attack on the Prince Regent, but survived to make known, *inter alia*, the works of Keats and Shelley; later, under the editorship of Albany Fonblanque, it enjoyed a rare spell of success, 1830–47. Meanwhile the Hunts had issued the *Reflector*, a quarterly that ran to only four issues, and *The Liberal*, in which Byron's *The Vision of Judgement* first appeared in 1822. In 1828 Leigh embarked on the *Comparison*, a weekly that lasted seven months. In the summer of 1830 he 'set up a little work', *Chat of the Week*, but was unable to pay stamp duty on it; yet in September he launched the *Tatler* (a revived title, of course), a daily, which he conducted single-handed until the end of March 1832. After that he edited his *London Journal* with the backing of Charles Knight 1834–5, and *The Monthly Repository* 1837–8. All this time, and almost until his death in 1859, he was an assiduous contributor to other journals, and had other work published as well. There is no doubt that, whatever the value of his own writings, he fully deserved the pension of £200 awarded him in 1847, if only for the many chances he gave to fellow writers. He too had received generous help in his time.

James Mill and his son, John Stuart Mill, were likewise life-long journalists, though of a more political, less literary, stamp. James helped Jeremy Bentham found the *Westminster Review* in 1823 as the organ of Utilitarianism, and his son contributed to it. Father and son both wrote for its successor, the *London Review*, of which John Stuart was proprietor 1837–40. Other magazines that exerted an influence disporportionate to their circulation included the *London Magazine* (1820–9), which published Charles Lamb's *Essay of Elia* and De Qunicey's *Confessions of an Opium Eater*. Lamb was pretty well paid at 20 guineas per sheet (16 pages), when the usual rate was £1 per page. Unfortunately John Scott, the editor, lost his life in an unnecessary duel over an alleged criticism of Lockhart, whose substitute, J. H. Christie, fired the fatal shot. Another literary personality, William Jerdan—founder member of the Royal Society of Literature and much concerned with the formation of an authors' co-operative—edited the *Literary Gazette* (1817), which was said to be able to sell an edition of any book. Its contemporary in kind, the *Athenaeum* (1828), a critical review that gained a high reputation during nearly a century of life, was finally absorbed in the *Nation*, in turn incorporated in the *New Statesman*. It is of interest that the *Spectator* (1828), another revived title founded by R. S. Rintoul and still in active circulation, took nearly ten years to reach a sale of 3,000 copies.

These were some of the prestige publications of the 1820s and 1830s that offered outlets to professional writers. By their nature their readership was restricted and their life-span often short; even those that survived changed their nature or lost their identity, but that is inherent in journalism of any kind, and the 1840s witnessed a continuing process of birth and death among periodicals, especially the 'heavies'. Among the newly born were three weeklies of significance today. *Punch* (1841) made such a slow start that it had to be taken over by its printers, Bradbury and Evans, despite the brilliance of its editor, Mark Lemon, and his remarkable team of contributors that included Thackeray, Henry Mayhew, Douglas Jerrold and Thomas Hood. On the other hand the *Illustrated London News* (1842) was an immediate success, reaching a sale of 60,000 copies within twelve months. In contrast the *Economist* (1843) remained in relative obscurity until the advent of Walter Bagehot, the historian, who really 'made' the paper during his editorship, 1860–79.

A parallel process was at work in the popular journalism of the period. Apart from the denominational publications—most of them subsidised for cheapness—the chief commercial ventures were those connected with the brothers Chambers of Edinburgh and with Charles Knight, publisher for the Society for the Diffusion of Useful Knowledge. In February 1832

William and Robert Chambers issued the first number of their *Chambers' Journal*, a four-page weekly selling at 1½d. Its purpose was to offer information and entertainment—from geography and history to the useful arts, plus a modicum of fiction —'improving' in character but free of sectarian strings. Success was immediate and the *Journal* was soon being published in several editions, with a combined sale in excess of 50,000 copies. Astutely the brothers added other miscellanies to their list, and later published their monumental *Encyclopaedia* in serial form.

Charles Knight launched the *Penny Magazine* in March 1832 and the *Penny Cyclopaedia* in the following year, grossing even greater sales than the Chambers; but he had his troubles. The fact that the Society for the Diffusion of Useful Knowledge acted as sponsor was a mixed blessing. Its financial resources were of course essential, although not sufficient to sustain Knight's large ideas, and soon after the completion of the *Cyclopedia* in 1844, the whole 'Penny' enterprise had to be wound up. For Knight the Society's aversion to publishing anything not strictly utilitarian was a serious handicap. Even so he managed to commission contributions on un-useful subjects, such as literature and the fine arts, from writers of the quality of G. L. Craik[6] and George Henry Lewes. More important, while working for the Society, he retained his independence as a publisher and issued several series, e.g. pictorial volumes in parts and shilling digests in paperback, that just about balanced his losses. Essentially he was a missionary, serving the cause of cheap and 'wholesome' literature for the masses, fiction included. Unlike the Chambers (and other far less reputable operators in this field)[7] he never made a fortune, but was held in high respect for his ideals and his devotion and—as often happens with pioneers—his aims were attained by others.

*   *   *   *

Such in broad outline was the newspaper and periodical market in the first half of the 19th century, and it was here—in this market—that a group of contemporaries found openings that set them on course for success in authorship.

Thomas Carlyle (1795–1881), the oldest of the group, was perhaps the least attractive, both in character and in work. Son of a Scottish mason, his youth was spartan though not poverty stricken, and he had a natural aptitude for learning. He read German, and became a specialist in translation and an authority on German life and literature. Although he disliked teaching, this proved his main support while edging his way into journalism. Between 1820 and 1834, when he finally settled in Chelsea, his average yearly income was of the order of £200–£300, derived mainly from translations, contributions to Brewster's *Encyclopaedia*, and articles for the *Edinburgh Review*, *Fraser's*, and other magazines. His marriage to Jane Baillie Welsh in 1826 must be accounted a success, intellectually at least. They had no children; and Carlyle was always prone to illness, real and imagined, hated noise, and suffered from dyspepsia, insomnia, and constipation—quite enough to explain his moodiness, irritability, and dictatorial conversation, though sexual frustration may also have contributed. Radical in outlook and impatient of all 'shams', he graduated in thought towards an admiration for effective government by strong men, a trend reflected in his studies of Oliver Cromwell and Frederick the Great. Nowadays he would have been classified as right-wing, even Fascist, in his role as philosopher-historian. But his style is arresting, his knowledge deep and electric with ideas, and his sentences laced with sardonic humour.

It was this robustness and resilience that sustained him in his early struggles, for he and Jane exercised a self-discipline in their domestic economy that compels admiration. In 1831 they visited London with assets of no more than £100, and tried to place Thomas's first book, *Sartor Resartus*. Under pressure from Jeffrey, Murray accepted it at half-profits, but withdrew when the type was actually being set. In the end it was published in instalments in *Fraser's Magazine*, for which Carlyle received £82. In 1836 it was re-issued in book form in America, and in 1838 in London by Fraser, with a further edition in 1841. The turning-point for Carlyle came in 1837 with the publication of the first volume of *The French Revolution*, again by Fraser. The story of the MS is well known. On loan to J. S. Mill, the pages were appropriated by the maid to light a fire, which caused Mill such distress the he immediately offered Carlyle £200 in compensation, and had to be comforted for what had happened. Carlyle was amazingly calm, would only accept £100, and got down to the re-writing. The second volume in 1839 fetched £110, with smaller sums from America, where his friend, Ralph Waldo Emerson, helped look after his affairs. The book established Carlyle's reputation and became a standard work, earning steady returns on a per edition basis—henceforward Carlyle's normal business arrangement with his publishers.

But the financial highlight of 1837 was Carlyle's series of six lectures on German Literature, fee £135; followed in 1838 by twelve on the History of Literature, £260; in 1839 by six on Revolutions of Modern Europe, £200; and in 1840 by six on Heroes and Hero-Worship, 200 guineas. The latter set was issued by Fraser in a joint edition with *Sartor* in 1841. By 1839 Carlyle was able to say that 'this year for the first time I am not at all poor'. Indeed from the early 1840s onwards he was making a steady, though still modest, income—from an even stream of new books and new editions of past ones, including payments from America. In 1847 new editions of *The French Revolution* and *Miscellanies* (first published by Fraser in 1840) brought him £700, and by the following year he had a balance of £1,500 in the Dumfries Bank. Careful by habit, he was a consistent saver, and invested wisely in railway stock where in due course he had holdings worth at least £10,000. In 1854 he felt able to spend £170 on sound-proofing his study at his house in Cheyne Row. Four years later Chapman & Hall paid him £2,800 for the first 5,000 copies of the first two volumes of his greatest work, *Frederick the Great*, four more volumes following 1861–5. It gave him great satisfaction to be able to refuse a state pension, offered him by Disraeli in 1874, for his had been a classic career of self-denial and self-help. For all his faults of egocentricity and bad temper, Carlyle was not at heart a mean man. Having endured poverty as an author, he supported the movement that resulted in the Copyright Act 1842 and—as will be related—he backed Dickens in his campaign for a mutual copyright agreement with America.

*   *   *   *

The second oldest in the group was another historian, Thomas Babington Macaulay (1800–59). Son of Zachary, the philanthropist and campaigner against slavery, Thomas was obliged as a young man to pay off his father's creditors and generally support the family, following Zachary's insolvency. This meant spare living, self-denial and hard work, about which Thomas never complained, for he was naturally industrious and given to literary interests from an early age; but the experience coloured his attitude to his subsequent career. With £300 a year from his Fellowship at Trinity College, Cambridge, and £400 a year from his appointment in 1829 as a Commissioner in Bankruptcy, and a small but growing income from journalism, he was just able to make ends meet. In 1825 he had begun to write for the *Edinburgh Review*, and he continued to do so for nearly twenty years, becoming the magazine's mainstay with long, learned, but highly stimulating articles and reviews: among them biographical pieces on Bacon, Machiavelli, Clive, Hastings, and others, that have entered the stream of English literature. These essays were published in three volumes by Longman in 1843. Macaulay's poverty did not last too long. After Jeffrey's retirement in 1829, he refused the editorship of the *Edinburgh Review*, entered the pre-Reform Parliament, and after the 1832 Act was appointed Commissioner, then Secretary, of the Board of Control. His chance came in 1834, when made a member of the Supreme Council of India at a salary of £10,000 a year. The services that he rendered there, notably the preparation of a criminal code, are not the concern of this book; but as a bachelor of modest tastes, addicted to work, his expenditure was small, and he was able to save money at the rate of £6,000–£7,000 a year. In 1837 he inherited £10,000 from an uncle, and returned to England with a nest egg of £30,000, on the interest of which he was then able to devote himself to politics and writing.

In 1839, thanks partly to the intervention of Adam Black, the publisher, he became Liberal MP for Edinburgh, and immediately made his presence felt in the debates on copyright reform. For eight years he remained in Parliament, holding two ministerial posts, but his chief interest was in literature—stimulated in 1842 by the resounding reception given to his *Lays of Ancient Rome*. Not thinking it had commercial possibilities, Macaulay gave the copyright to Longman, on the understanding that it would be published in a small edition and that there should be 'no puffing of any sort'. In the event the success was so great and so sustained—selling 100,000 copies over the next 25 years—that Longman returned the copyright, and paid Macaulay and his heirs substantial sums out of the profits. Macaulay then concentrated on his *magnum opus*, his *History of England*, to which he applied all his vast learning and much arduous research, visiting as many of the historic sites as possible to gain first-hand impressions and to absorb atmosphere. The work has been criticised for various inaccuracies and for its partisan Whig approach, nonetheless the *History* stands solid as a monument of information, interpretation, and fine narrative writing. Its success on publication was immediate.

The first two volumes appeared in November 1848, and by the following May the work was in its fifth edition. It was also pirated on a princely scale in the USA, as his earlier Edinburgh essays had been. The third and fourth volumes, issued in 1855, were even more successful. In the original agreement it was stipulated that Macaulay should receive £500 a year for 5 years, and two-thirds of the profits after the sale of the first 6,000 copies. Later the share was raised to three-quarters. It was 'on account' of his share that Longman paid him £20,000 in May 1856.[8]

Macaulay never finished the *History*. Although a sick man after 1852, he had returned to, and stayed in, Parliament until final retirement in 1856; and was created a peer in the following year. In 1859 he died, leaving a fragment of the fifth and final volume, edited by Lady Trevelyan, and issued in 1861.

*   *   *   *

Carlyle and Macaulay were historians; Thackeray and Dickens, the two younger members of the group I have selected, were novelists and authors of a variety of fiction. All began their writing careers as journalists, and its was through journalism that they made their reputations as leading men of letters. It was not an easy route to fame, certainly not for Thackeray.

William Makepeace Thackeray (1811–63) was by instinct a gambler, a trait soon evident when he lost £1,500 at cards while a student at Cambridge. As heir to £20,000 this did not worry him unduly, nor did he feel pressed to engage permanently in any safe or respectable occupation. On the contrary he travelled abroad, read for the bar, studied art, and in 1833 invested in an obscure publication, *The National Standard*, which he edited jointly with William Maginn. But 1833 was a fateful year. The *Standard* failed after a few months, and suddenly Thackeray lost almost all his private fortune with the collapse of an Indian agency house. In 1834 he had to face a cold hard world, virtually without means. The experience transformed him, and he developed his dormant talents in a whirlwind of activity, but the struggle was dour. During the next decade he fought his way forward as a freelance writer and artist. His knowledge of French and German stood him in good stead, and for a while he acted as Paris correspondent of the *Constitutional and Public Ledger*, also contributing as an 'authority' to the *Foreign Quarterly Review*—literary editor, John Forster. Otherwise he wrote a multitude of pieces—satirical, light-hearted, realistic, besides book and art reviews—for such differing publications as the *Globe, Examiner, Edinburgh Review, Westminster Review, The Times* (in which he reviewed Carlyle's *French Revolution*), *Morning Chronicle*, and others. His most secure connection at first was with *Fraser's*, edited by his friend, William Maginn, who published notably three of his fictional serials, *The Yellowplush Papers, Catherine*, and *A Shabby Genteel Story*. Later he transferred to *Punch* as a regular writer and illustrator, and to which he contributed—among much else—*The Book of Snobs*. Under his influence, the sharp radicalism of the paper was modified in favour of a friendlier tone—characterised, for example, by his own diverting sketches of foreigners and their odd un-English habits.

Payment for all this work varied widely. At first Thackeray was glad to receive an average rate of 10–12 guineas a sheet; but he also accepted one guinea per 'close column' from a paper called the *Corsair*, and as little as £2 for a book review in *The Times*. For his drawings, he charged extra at £2 each, signing them 'Michael Angelo Titmarsh'—he was constantly using pen names of a comic sort, and this helped create an aura of good humour around him. Although his income improved as he became better known—in 1844, for instance, a connection with the *Morning Chronicle* was worth £300 a year—he enjoyed no general recognition until the late 1840s. Earlier Carlyle had described him as 'writing for his life', and that was true. However, despite financial insecurity, Thackeray lived comfortably, kept a numerous household, was clubbable and gathered a good company of friends, especially of fellow writers. Later, when a celebrity, he was adopted by high society and he enjoyed the experience; but—although never spoiled by success—he tended to become touchy as he got older, and featured in more than one memorable quarrel.

To his great credit his demeanour was not disturbed by the tragedy of his private life. In 1836 he had married Isabella Shawe who, after bearing him three daughters (one died), lost her reason and—as it turned out—never recovered it. In the end Thackeray had to arrange a legal separation and find a home for his wife, where she lived into very old age. In 1846 he brought his daughters to live with him in London. By this time he had completed several books, including a long novel, *The Luck of Barry Lyndon*, published in *Fraser's* in 1843–4, but not noticeably successful. Shortly afterwards he set to work on *Vanity Fair* which was issued in 20 monthly parts between January 1847 and July 1848 by Bradbury and Evans: for which he received £60 per part. i.e. '2 printed Sheets with 2 etchings on steel and as many drawings on wood as may be thought necessary'. The book was a masterpiece, at the same time a well-told tale full of incident and character, and a commentary upon society. *Vanity Fair* made his name and set him on the road to fortune—he earned further substantial sums from the volume sales[9]—and, in public estimation, it placed him on a par with Charles Dickens.

Thackeray had now reached the high plateau of his career, and he stayed there until his death in December 1863. No longer dependent on journalism,[10] he concentrated henceforward on novels, Christmas books and similar slighter works, on lecturing, and at the end on a special connection with the *Cornhill Magazine*. He set himself a goal—to earn enough money to replace the £20,000 he had lost as a young man and to provide his daughters with a fair competence. He prepared two series of lectures, *The English Humourists of the Eighteenth Century*, and *The Four Georges*, and delivered them in London and the provinces, and on two trips to the USA, in the early and mid-1850s. Altogether he earned approximately £10,000 from this enterprise, including publication. Bradbury and Evans remained his principal publishers, paying him £2,000 for 24 numbers (£83 each) for *Pendennis*, a novel unmistakably autobiographical, that appeared 1848–50, with half-profits thereafter; and so the system continued but at higher rates. For *The Newcomes* he received £3,600, 1853–5, plus a further £500 for the American and German rights. For *The Virginians* he was paid £6,000, 1857–9, but in this case the publishers lost money. Meanwhile a rival, George Smith of Smith Elder & Co, was destined to play an equally important role in Thackeray's life. Smith outbid Bradbury and Evans for *The History of Henry Esmond*, a historical novel published in volume form in 1852. He also captured two of the Christmas stories, *The Kickleburys on the Rhine* (1851) and *The Rose and the Ring* (1854), and the publication rights of the first of the two sets of lectures. But Smith's main venture was to launch a new shilling monthly, the *Cornhill Magazine*, in December 1859, offering terms of extraordinary, almost reckless, dimensions. These were briefly:

i) each number to contain a substantial instalment of a major novel written by Thackeray, at £350 per month,

ii) further payments to be made on subsequent publication in volume form,

iii) Thackeray to edit the magazine for a fee of £1,000 a year, and to commission material from other writers to fill up the issues.

These were the best terms ever offered to Thackeray and he hastened to accept them, for they meant he would be earning over £400 a month from the *Cornhill* alone. As it happened he was hard put to it to fulfil his part of the bargain, as he was tired out after completing *The Virginians* and had to re-write an earlier work to cover the first six instalments. So he agreed with Smith to invite Anthony Trollope to supply *Framley Parsonage* for the next serial, and pay him £1,000 for it—the best that Trollope had had up till then. But Thackeray provided subsequent serials and he also contributed a monthly essay at 12 guineas *per page*, a very high rate, under the title of *The Roundabout Papers*. Besides this he succeeded in recruiting a star team of writers and illustrators—Matthew Arnold, Elizabeth Barrett Browning, Bulwer-Lytton, G. H. Lewes, John Ruskin, Alfred Tennyson, to name but some, and paid them liberally and promptly. It was a policy that succeeded from the start. The first number of the *Cornhill* sold 120,000 copies—easily a record for an English literary periodical, and Smith was so delighted that he doubled Thackeray's annual fee. The circulation duly dropped to around 85,000, but this was far ahead of any rival, e.g. *Macmillan's Magazine*, which had been launched two months before *Cornhill*, and attracted first-class contributors during a life of nearly 50 years. The *Cornhill* (published by Murray) still survives, though in suspension at the time of writing. Thackeray resigned from the editorship in March 1862, but remained a contributor almost till his death. His estate realised a sum little short of the £20,000 he had set himself to save.

As mentioned earlier, after the publication of *Vanity Fair*, the public came to regard Thackeray and Dickens as major novelists of equal stature, even as rivals, a comparison cultivated by certain critics and partisans who, by taking sides, engendered hostility between the two men who had been friends before. This was unnecessary and unseemly, and blame must be laid on men like Forster, Dickens's close companion and man of business, rather than on Dickens himself—although on the whole Dickens showed far less generosity of spirit towards Thackeray than did Thackeray towards him. The fact too that, as from 1847, publication of their respective works often overlapped—beginning with *Dombey and Son* and *Vanity Fair*—added fuel to the fire. Apart from this, open conflict broke out on several occasions. For instance in 1850 Forster took offence (not for the first time) at Thackeray's denigration of men of letters in *Punch* and *Pendennis*, to which Thackeray replied in an article in the *Morning Chronicle* entitled 'The Dignity of Literature'. Again Thackeray opposed the proposal by Dickens and Bulwer-Lytton in 1850–1 to form the Guild of Literature and Art, which led ultimately to Thackeray defending the Royal Literary Fund, when it was subjected to a virulent and sustained attack by Dickens and his friends in 1858.[11] In that year also occurred Thackeray's quarrel with the journalist, Edmund Yates, and the latter's dismissal from membership of the Garrick Club, despite Dickens's efforts to defend him. But these thunderstorms apart, the real difference between the two men was of deeper origin. While both mirrored society through fiction, Dickens was primarily concerned with people at the foot of the social ladder, Thackeray with those on the middle and upper rungs: in effect, complementary rather than comparative attitudes, and explicable in terms of the youthful experiences of the two men.

*   *   *   *

Charles Dickens (1812–70), like Macaulay, had the misfortune when a young man, to have to support his parents following the insolvency of his father. John Dickens, the original of Mr. Micawber, was imprisoned twice for debt, in 1824 and 1834, and found it a not uncongenial experience. Not so Charles upon whom these troubles made a deep impression. On the first occasion the boy was a mere 12 years old and was put out to work at Warren's Blacking Factory, a place and period in his life that he always remembered with horror. On the second occasion he was already in employment as a Parliamentary reporter, working successively for the *True Sun*, the *Mirror of Parliament* (a contemporary of *Hansard*) and the *Morning Chronicle*, and he had to mortgage his earnings for weeks ahead in order to overcome the crisis. He excelled at his work, and although never fond of politicians he had the good fortune to attend the final stages of the 1832 Reform Bill and other reforming legislation of the mid-1830s. These statutes aroused his intense interest and often stirred his feelings as well. As his biographer, Una Pope-Hennessy says, he was always 'emotion-alizing his experience'. Thus, through his novels, he communi-cated—to far greater effect than any factual report—the realities of poverty and injustice. Only those interested in social history are acquainted with the intricacies of the Poor Law Amendment Act 1834, but—to this day—how many millions of people all over the world have been made aware of the peculiar hell of the Victorian workhouse, as described in *Oliver Twist*?

The *Morning Chronicle* paid Dickens 5 guineas a week. He was their best reporter, able not only to write vivid copy but assiduous in delivering it more promptly than his rivals on *The Times*. By 1836 however he was fast building up an alternative source of income. It had all started three years earlier when *The Monthly Magazine*, a minor periodical that had recently changed hands, began publishing some freelance sketches he had written as a reporter. These early efforts were unpaid, but soon Dickens was placing them in the *Morning Chronicle* and its offshoot the *Evening Chronicle*, signing them 'Boz'. They were well liked, and in 1836 were published by John Macrone as *Sketches by Boz* in two volumes with illustrations by Cruikshank.[12] Before this he had been approached by the recently founded firm of publishers, Chapman & Hall,[13] who asked him to write the text for some illustrations of sporting life drawn by Robert Seymour. Dickens was not a specialist in sport and managed to turn the proposition round, so that his text—about characters and incidents he felt better able to contrive—was to be supported by the pictures. Such were the preliminaries to the *Pickwick Papers*, published in 20 monthly parts from March 1836 to November 1837 in green wrappers at 1s each. Initially Dickens received a monthly stipend of £14 3s 6d which, together with his reporter's pay and other freelance work (in hand and planned) encouraged him to marry Catherine Hogarth on 2 April 1836. Surprisingly the series got off to a slow start with an initial print of only 1,000 copies; but after Sam Weller had made his appearance in the fifth number, it began to race away and at the end was selling nearly 40,000. Seymour had committed suicide after the first number and was replaced, after unsuccessful applications by 'Michael Angelo Titmarsh' and others, by Hablot Browne, who paired 'Boz' with 'Phiz'. They were a phenomenal pair.

Sudden success is intoxicating but is apt to breed problems. What with printing next month's part and reprinting past ones to meet a galloping demand, not to mention Dickens's occasional inability to produce copy on time, Chapman & Hall had their share of difficulties. However all was soon solved, including revised terms for Dickens who, in March 1837, was presented with a bonus of £500 (and various gifts in kind). Ultimately he settled for a total of £2,000, which worked out at £100 per part, instead of the original £14. The publishers were said to have cleared £14,000. Even that was not the end. A new and complicated agreement was drawn up whereby, after the lapse of five years (i.e. in 1842), Dickens was permitted to regain a one-third share of the copyright which in the first instance had been sold outright. All this was linked to a plan for extracting Dickens from a wild muddle of commitments in which the author, by his own volition, had landed himself. Briefly it amount to this. As *Pickwick* gathered momentum, Dickens came deeply to regret the sale of the copyright of the *Sketches* to Macrone, to whom he had also promised a novel, *Gabriel Vardon*, for £200. In addition he had promised to write two novels for Richard Bentley[15] at £500 each, and edit his new magazine, *Bentley's Miscellany*, for which he had agreed to write 16 pages of each issue. With the help of friends, notably Tom Mitton and John Forster, who became (in effect) unpaid literary agents, the matter was straightened out to the extent that Chapman & Hall bought the copyright of the *Sketches* from Macrone for £2,000 and set the sum against a five-year run of *Pickwick* in the manner described. They also insisted that Dickens write another book for them, to appear in 20 monthly parts as before, but at the higher fee of £150 per month, the copyright to revert to the author after 5 years. Such was the design for *Nicholas Nickleby* which duly appeared in 1838–9. As for the contracts with Richard Bentley, nothing much—it seemed—could be altered there: although, as so often happened with Dickens, a honeymoon of friendship (albeit punctured and patched now and again) was transmuted into implacable hate, which could only have one ending. Such indeed was the pattern of events. *Oliver Twist*, the first of the two novels promised to Bentley, was serialised in the *Miscellany* and, thanks to Forster's counsel, would be followed by *Barnaby Rudge* (the new name for *Gabriel Vardon*), thus relieving Dickens of the necessity of writing a separate work additional to his contributions to the *Miscellany*. However, although higher payments had been agreed, they were far lower than those offered by

Chapman & Hall, and Dickens's resentment against Bentley gathered such force that it boiled over like lava out of a volcano. In February 1839 he resigned as editor of the *Miscellany* and, shortly afterwards—aided by Forster—he persuaded Chapman & Hall to come to the rescue again. Accordingly they bought in the rights of *Oliver Twist* and—to Dickens's intense relief—the contract for *Barnaby Rudge* was cancelled.

It is not proposed to follow Dickens's every tack with his publishers to the very end of his life. Clearly he suffered from bouts of persecution mania and, however happily a business association started, it seemed to end sooner or later in disaster. One reason—though not the only one, for his temperament was too volatile to absorb with equanimity all the pressures of his private as well as of his public life—was the fact that his market value as a writer was growing so fast that it outdistanced any contract within a year or two; and since the royalty system had not yet been adopted in Britain, whereby his remuneration would have automatically kept pace with sales, the practice of guaranteed payments plus profit-sharing (however meticulously observed) did not prove an adequate substitute. So it came about that, at recurring intervals, he became convinced that his publishers were making vast profits at his expense; and that in turn generated a deep sense of grievance.

For the moment however the situation was in balance. *Nicholas Nickleby* proved as successful as *Pickwick*, and Chapman & Hall were ready to accept Dickens's next proposal: that, as from the end of March 1840, he would edit a new weekly magazine consisting 'entirely of original matter', entitled *Master Humphrey's Clock*, for which he was to receive £50 per week plus 50% of the profits. This magazine acted as the vehicle for *The Old Curiosity Shop* (1840–1) and *Barnaby Rudge* (1841); but sales were irregular, starting well enough at 60,000, reaching a maximum of 100,000 but then dropping to a minimum of 30,000. As may be imagined, Dickens's mood reflected these returns. However he had no choice but to go on writing, for he was not yet in a position to profit substantially from the re-issue of his early successes. With his next novel, *Martin Chuzzlewit*, he returned to part publication (instead of magazine serialisation), 20 monthly numbers (1843–4), on the same financial terms as before.[16] It was the relative failure of this book that led to the next break, since Chapman & Hall suggested that Dickens remit part of his regular stipend (£200 per month) to offset the losses on publication: reasonable enough when seen in disinterested retrospect, but unwise in dealing with Dickens, who was enraged.

Meanwhile Dickens had paid an historic visit to America, January to June 1842. His popularity in the States was gratifying but the gross pirating of his works (and those of other British authors) was a disgrace, and his main purpose was to plead for a mutual agreement between the two countries on copyright. Since this incident belonged to a new phase in the development of domestic and international copyright during the 1830s and 1840s, including the passage of important legislation, the subject will be considered in the next chapter, together with an account of the foundation and failure of a Society of Authors, in which Dickens played a leading part.

On his return Dickens wrote an uncontroversial account of his visit to the USA, mainly concerned with impressions of prisons and other institutions and omitting the question of copyright. *American Notes* (1842) sold well in both countries and earned him about £1,000.[17] It was in the following year, during the disappointing run of *Martin Chuzzlewit*, that he decided to write the first of his Christmas books, *A Christmas Carol*—to make good the lack of profits on the novel, pay for his numerous household and meet the demands of his feckless parents, a continuing financial anxiety. The *Carol* was published on commission, Dickens standing the cost of production and receiving all the sales income, less a handling charge to Chapman & Hall. Unhappily the early returns were less than expected—though by the end of 1844 they had brought in £726—but this fresh disappointment, coupled with the contretemps over the suggestion that he forgo part of his stipend until *Martin Chuzzlewit* turned the corner, was the final straw. Dickens decided to look elsewhere.

He did not have to look far—to Bradbury and Evans, not publishers but printers to the trade, including Chapman & Hall. In this instance Tom Mitton was the intermediary as Forster was in the dubious position of acting as literary adviser to Chapman & Hall, and for this reason (if for no other) he felt disinclined to advise Dickens to make a fresh move. Once again however new arrangements were successfully concluded, and without apparent distress to any of the parties concerned. In brief, in their new role as publishers, Bradbury and Evans dealt satisfactorily with Chapman & Hall and advanced Dickens the sum of £2,800, sufficient to meet all his expenses, including a visit to Italy, and to free him from anxiety for some time ahead. The advance was secured by anticipated profits on the *Carol*, the possibility of a new journal, the harvesting of existing copyrights as and when they reverted to the author, and a quarter-share in the profits of future books.[18]

Dickens stayed more or less amicably with Bradbury and Evans from 1844 until 1858, when he returned to Chapman & Hall. The relationship however nearly foundered at the start. Although greatly encouraged by the success of *The Chimes*, his Christmas book for 1844, which sold at least 20,000 copies and yielded him a profit of around £1,500,[19] his venture into daily journalism was a disaster. In all arose out of a *fracas* with his old paper, the *Morning Chronicle*, where a new editor found his offer of articles too expensive. Deeply insulted, Dickens determined to launch a rival on his return from Italy. Backed by Bradbury and Evans, the first number of the *Daily News* duly appeared on 21 January 1846; but as editor Dickens over-reached himself. Awarding himself a generous salary (£2,000 p.a.), he acted high-handedly with contributors, then lost interest and resigned after a few weeks. However the situation was salved by the success of *Dombey and Son*, published in parts, October 1846–April 1848, that jumped to a circulation of over 30,000 copies and held its ground. The book confirmed his popularity and greatly strengthened his finances.

By the end of the accounting period in June 1848 a total of 667,359 copies of the twenty numbers had been sold, an average of over 33,000 each, for gross revenues (including advertising) of £24,486 5s 1d. Dickens's share of the profits was £9,165 11s 10d; Bradbury and Evans, entitled to one-quarter of the profits plus 10% commission on gross sales, retained £5,503 16s 3d.[20]

For the next 22 years, until his death in 1870, Dickens never flagged. Although sales varied—some titles doing better in parts or in serials, others in volume editions—they stayed remarkably high; and his last book, *The Mystery of Edwin Drood* (1870), never finished, was running at 50,000 per part. Dickens made a lot of money; though he never equalled Macaulay's cheque for £20,000 'on account' of a single work.

Between 1846 and 1870, his annual earnings from his writings, exclusive of the two journals, averaged just over

£2,900, substantial receipts, but hardly entitling him to the nickname bestowed by one journal of 'a literary Croesus'.[21]

The two journals referred to were *Household Words* which he 'conducted' or edited on salary 1850–9 and *All the Year Round* 1859–70. These were weeklies containing *inter alia* instalments of *Hard Times* (1854) and of *A Tale of Two Cities* (1859) and *Great Expectations* (1860–1). In addition he turned his acting talents to highly profitable account. Always fond of theatricals, he organised and took part in numerous amateur presentations, and in the early 1850s began giving public readings for charitable causes. After 1858 he converted a private hobby into a commercial venture, and employed a manager for the purpose. Although the preparation of the scripts—mainly scenarios from his own works—took time and stage performances were exhausting, he loved the work which added materially to his income. In his second visit to the USA in 1867–8, for example, he earned £13,000 in two months alone, and that was not the end of the account.

By ordinary standards Dickens, therefore, was indeed 'a literary Croesus'. At a time when almost all authors were at the mercy of their publishers, he made his own terms; and, thanks to the loyalty of friends such as Mitton and Forster and to his own unpredictable, often disagreeable, temperament he generally got them.

CHAPTER FOUR

Copyright developments, domestic and international, 1830s–1860s. Dickens's visit to USA in 1842. The first Society of British Authors, 1843

IT HAS BEEN shown how, after about 1830, periodicals and part publication provided authors with the main means of communicating new works to the public *en masse*. Such means did not inhibit publication in volume form, indeed serialisation usually preceded it, by which time a work could be issued as a relatively cheap reprint. But to launch a new book in volume form tended to restrict sales owing to cost—a 'three-decker' novel being commonly priced at 31s 6d the set.

In 1823 there were only a handful of guinea-and-a-half novels, but by 1840 fifty-one out of fifty-eight new novels bore this price ... The result was that fiction-lovers flocked, not to the bookshops, but to the circulating libraries ... and the libraries became more firmly established as the publishers' best customers. Publishers could afford to be indifferent to the fact that they had priced their wares out of the individual buyer's reach: so long as the libraries took a substantial part of an edition, their profit was safe ... The average edition of a serious book was around 750 copies ... Only in very exceptional circumstances such as Scott's novels, did editions in the early nineteenth century run to 6,000 copies. Throughout the century, the ordinary circulating library novel seldom had an edition of more than a thousand or 1,250 copies.[1]

Archibald Constable had been the first publisher of substance to contemplate the possibilities of new low-priced books for mass sale. In 1825 he had talked to Scott of 'a three shilling or half-crown volume every month', but bankruptcy and death had forestalled his grandiose plans, which duly gave place to the serialisation and instalment schemes described in Chapter Three, from which Dickens and others profited. As time passed technical advances in paper making, printing and binding, and the removal of excise duties, had an effect on prices: as also the demand for reading matter by travellers on the new railways, for whom 'libraries' of cheap reprints (and a few originals) at 1s–3s each were made available by enterprising firms. Nonetheless prices of new books stayed high; and not even the dramatic collapse in 1852 of the Booksellers' Association, founded four years earlier by a cartel of London publisher-booksellers to combat price cutting, made any immediate difference. In this dispute most authors interested in the issue were persuaded to support the 'rebels' led by John Chapman, an importer of American books, who opposed all control of retail prices and wanted 'free trade', i.e. freedom for the retailer to sell a book at any price he liked. Authors took the line that the cheaper the book the larger the sale; they were not convinced by the argument that treating books as groceries or haberdashery might lead to the extinction of bookshops proper. Two authors—George Grote, the historian, and H. H. Milman, Dean of St. Paul's—sat with Lord Campbell on the court of arbitration which came down firmly on the side of 'free trade'.[2]

By c. 1850 therefore the book trade was still in the early stages of change. Likewise relations between authors and publishers were still regulated by the three or four contractual conventions—sale of copyright (often no more than a licence linked to an edition or period of time, after which the copyright reverted to the author),[3] commission publishing, or profit sharing (or 'half-profits'). Subscription in the 18th century style was now exceptional, while the royalty system was yet to come. On the other hand authors and publishers were closely involved in the question of copyright which, after 1830, experienced a series of important and complex changes.

The Copyright Act of 1814 had proved wanting on several grounds, and moves to replace it were soon being made. One glaring omission had been its failure to protect playwrights against unauthorised stage productions. So long as a play remained unpublished, there was nothing to prevent its presentation on the boards by anyone who came into possession of the script.[4] This, then, was the first step.

In 1833 ... the Dramatic Copyright Act (3 & 4 Will. 4, c.15), commonly known as Bulwer-Lytton's Act[5] ... gave to the author of 'any tragedy, comedy, play, opera, farce or other piece of dramatic entertainment' the sole liberty of representing it 'or causing it to be represented at any place or places of dramatic entertainment whatsoever' in Great Britain and the Dominions for 28 years from publication, with a reversionary period to the author for the rest of his life.[6]

The inadequacies of this Act, soon evident in all kinds of evasions, are considered in the next chapter. Meanwhile the second step towards reforming domestic copyright, followed nine years later.

In 1842 the Literary Copyright Act (5 & 6 Vict., c.45) consolidated the law relating to the protection of literary, dramatic, and musical property and brought within the terms of a single statute the two rights so far recognised, 'copyright' or the right of 'multiplying' copies and 'performing right' or the right of representation.[7]

Furthermore, the period of protection was extended from 28 to 42 years after first publication or performance, or the life of the author plus seven years, whichever the longer. As it turned out, the Act experienced a long period of gestation, the progenitor being Thomas Noon Talfourd,[8] who displayed remarkable pertinacity in introducing a Private Bill to no less than five sessions of Parliament 1837–41. However he made things unnecessarily difficult by omitting to lobby the book trade in advance, and by failing even to brief leading authors until too late a stage, and then only a handful of them. In consequence his proposals were swamped by a plethora of petitions from publishers, printers, and others—even up to his final attempt when the Bill foundered very early in the 1841 session. Talfourd was no tactician. He drew a bead on certain targets and nothing would alter his aim. For instance he wanted to extend the period of copyright to the life of the author plus 60 years, not a minute less; and added that, if an author sold his copyright, he might—after 28 years (the current term)—recover his rights and pass them on to his descendants for the full term proposed. This raised an outcry. Ordinary publishers objected strongly to paying twice for the purchase of copyright, while those who specialised in the issue of cheap reprints of out-of-copyright works were equally vociferous. Nor was the opposition confined to the trade. Macaulay, then a Cabinet Minister, as well as a leading man of letters, made an unaccountably vicious attack on the very concept of copyright:

The principle of copyright is this. It is a tax on readers for the purpose of giving a bounty to writers. The tax is an exceedingly bad one; it is a tax on one of the most innocent pleasures; and never let us forget that a tax on innocent pleasures is a premium on vicious pleasures.[9]

Talfourd lost his seat at Reading at the 1841 election, when the Tories were returned to power, but the cudgels were immediately taken up by Lord Mahon (the future Earl Stanhope and President of the Royal Literary Fund) who achieved a quick, and seemingly easy, success. In fact Mahon was a clever tactician and left nothing to chance. He secured the support of leading publishers (notably the John Murray and the Thomas Longman of the day) by streamlining Talfourd's provisions to regulate the import of cheap foreign editions, and so swung the book trade to his side. In Parliament he pacified the redoubtable Lord Brougham,[10] compromised with Macaulay, won over Sir Robert Peel, the new Prime Minister, and—at the last moment—sidestepped a proposal to hold up proceedings in favour of a Customs measure that duplicated some of the provisions of his own Bill. Royal Assent was received on 1 July 1842. Although the Act was by any criterion a great step forward, and was destined to last until 1911, flaws soon appeared: due principally to the fact that it 'presented a new code of copyright, covering the ground of previous laws, but not in terms repealing them'.[11] In other words, any earlier provisions not specifically repealed remained in force, and so—taken in conjunction with the normal continuity of change—the Act generated so many problems of interpretation that, in its Report published in 1878, the Royal Commission on Copyright was forced to condemn it in forthright terms.

*   *   *   *

The 1842 Act was not an isolated piece of legislation, but part of a pattern of law-making for the better protection of authors' rights at home and abroad. The process was lengthy, affected the entire book trade and—following the Dramatic Copyright Act 1833—involved no less than 'five copyright acts and five relevant customs acts in the eighteen years from 1838 to 1855, and four relevant acts in the eleven years between 1875 and 1886'.[12]

The first of these was the International Copyright Act 1838 which, by means of Orders in Council, extended copyright protection to authors of books published in foreign countries, provided that British authors received similar protection in the countries concerned. In contrast to Talfourd's efforts for domestic copyright, the 1838 Act passed through Parliament without difficulty, possibly because no one grasped its importance. In fact it was an historic event, although Britain was not the first in the field. A similar law had been enacted by Prussia in the previous year, and following the formation of the Customs Union (Zollverein) in 1834, there seemed a good chance of linking up with all 39 of the German states, large and small. Likewise, thanks to the indefatigable Senator Henry Clay, championed on this side of the Atlantic by Harriet Martineau[13] and others, hopes were high for concluding a mutual copyright treaty with the USA, the most formidable and unmanageable source of competition and piracy.

In the event no fresh treaty was concluded with any country, and the subject lapsed until the 1842 legislation revived interest. On 30 June a meeting of authors and publishers at the Freemasons' Tavern in London, chaired by Thomas Longman IV, deplored the absence of action, and emphasised that the best way to stop the smuggling of 'copies of Spurious Editions into Great Britain and its dependencies' was to conclude 'treaties with Foreign Powers for the mutual recognition of Literary Property'.[14]

The 1842 Copyright and Customs Acts went some way to meet this demand: preventing the publication of any copyright work without the owner's consent, and prohibiting the import of any reprint of such work for 'sale or hire' in the UK, although nothing was said about 'private use'—a concession to tourists and travellers abolished two years later. Furthermore all pirate copies were to be destroyed, and lists of copyright works supplied to the customs officers to make their task easier. By an oversight this provision was restricted to the UK, with the result that British colonies and dependencies profited vigorously from the omission, especially Canada,[15] which continued to let in a flood of pirate reprints from the USA. Fresh legislation in 1845 and 1847 tried to plug the gap: first by extending the restriction to the colonies; and when this failed, by introducing a duty to be levied at the port entry, part of the proceeds to be remitted to the copyright owners. The results were farcical. Bulwer-Lytton, a best-selling author, received in one year less than £2 from his share of the duty throughout the entire British Empire. In

Canada, where the problem was most acute, all kinds of legislative shifts were used to make the system work, but to no avail. But the fault did not lie entirely on one side. Despite a brave attempt by John Murray III to capture the overseas market with his 'Colonial and Home Library', British publishers made only feeble efforts to cater for the taste and pocket of the colonial reader. Neither were they willing to license Canadian firms to publish on their behalf. And so, thanks partly to ineptitude and partly to the refusal of the USA to recognise international copyright, pirate reprints continued to pour over the border—to the benefit of American publishers and Canadian consumers.

However some progress was made with other countries, following an Act passed in 1844 to 'amend the law relating to international copyright'. Largely the work of Gladstone, President of the Board of Trade, its main aim was to bring the 1838 international Act into line with the 1842 domestic Act and open up relations with foreign states—in which matter it had some success, starting with a treaty with Prussia in 1846. A related Act in 1852 dealt with translations.[16]

Although treaties were signed with a dozen foreign countries between 1846 and 1861, the rights of the foreign author in Britain long remained obscure: largely because, for some twenty years, the law was differently interpreted in various British courts—notably the Court of Chancery and the three Common Law courts (Queen's Bench, Common Pleas, and Exchequer). Barnes states that 'broadly speaking, up to 1835 legal decisions went against foreigners securing copyright'.[17] Nonetheless there were some publishers who voluntarily respected international copyright, both in Britain and in the USA:[18] these being the chief countries concerned with literature owing to the common heritage of the English language; while music—which played an important part in the copyright disputes of the period—was of course open to the whole world. As will be related shortly, Dickens was the chief sufferer among contemporary British authors, and his visit to the USA in 1842 raised a storm, as he hoped it would. On the other hand Harriet Beecher Stowe provided rich plunder for British publishers with *Uncle Tom's Cabin* in 1852, which quickly sold over a million copies in this country, without a penny reaching the unfortunate author.

Other American authors suffered similar treatment—among them, Washington Irving, Emerson, Hawthorne, and Melville.

76

Their works were frequently reprinted by entrepreneurs such as Henry George Bohn and George Routledge—at the expense not only of the authors themselves but, in particular, of two established British publishers, John Murray III and Richard Bentley, whose firms had bought some of the copyrights in a straightforward manner. In 1850 Murray and Bentley took their rivals to law and, after various manoeuvres, sold them the copyrights in question.[19] Ultimately the whole matter was taken to the House of Lords and decided on 1 August 1854, when it was decided that:

> only if a foreigner travelled to Britain [and British dependencies] and remained there long enough to witness the publication of his work was he entitled to copyright protection. Otherwise he could neither claim copyright himself nor sell the right to a British subject, including a publisher.[20]

As a result American authors merely had to take a trip to Canada or the West Indies and be there on the day of publication to secure protection for a new work under British law. No corresponding right of any sort was available to British authors until the first US International Copyright Act 1891, and then only if certain onerous conditions were complied with. 37 years (from 1854 to 1891) were a long time to wait, but the delay was partly due to the fact that the 1854 decision relieved American authors and publishers of any over-riding need to campaign for international copyright in their own country. Without the obligation of reciprocity, pressure dropped to near-zero.[21]

*   *   *   *

It may be thought that authors played only a small part in the copyright struggles of this period. That was not so. The long campaign for international copyright was supported from the first by a group of men and women of letters—Bulwer-Lytton and Harriet Martineau among them—who, in 1836, drew up a petition,[22] addressed to the Senate and House of Representatives 'in Congress assembled'. This petition was

> presented to the Senate by Henry Clay on 2 February 1837, signed by 56 British authors, headed by Thomas Moore, praying Congress to grant to them the exclusive benefit of

their writings within the United States. The signatories ... included Lady Blessington, Bulwer [Lytton], Campbell, Disraeli, Maria Edgeworth, Hallam, Harriet Martineau, Milman, Rogers, Southey and Talfourd. It was prepared—probably jointly—by Harriet Martineau and her publishers, Saunders and Otley, and sent to Clay (a personal friend of hers) through the American explorer, Capt. Charles Wilkes ... Harriet Martineau sent copies of it, with letters in support to influential American friends. To Everett[23] she wrote on 8 November 1836 complaining of 'the late shameless aggressions of Messrs Harper of New York on the property of Messrs Saunders and Otley'.[24] 'Every author of note is signing', she said, 'the Americans in London are confident that we shall obtain a Copyright Law, this very Session: & indeed I believe every American (not a bookseller) is willing to do us justice'.[25]

Harriet's optimism was misplaced, despite the persistence of Senator Clay who submitted Bills in favour of international copyright in 1837, 1838, 1840 and 1842, in addition to presenting numerous petitions. The atmosphere therefore was highly charged before Dickens's visit to America from January to June 1842; but that did not prevent him from speaking out almost at once—at a public dinner at Boston on 1 February and at another at Hartford on 8 February. He ended his Boston speech thus:

You have in America great writers ... who will live in all time, and are as familiar to our lips as household words ... I take leave to say, in the presence of some of these gentlemen, that I hope the time is not far distant when they, in America, will receive of right some substantial profit and return in England from their labours; and when we, in England, shall receive some substantial profit and return from ours. Pray do not misunderstand me. Securing for myself from day to day the means of an honourable subsistence, I would rather have the affectionate regard of my fellow men, than I would have heaps and mines of gold. But the two things do not seem to be incompatible ... There must be an international arrangement in this respect: England has done her part, and I am confident that the time is not far distant when America will do hers. It becomes the character of a great country; *firstly*, because it is justice; *secondly*, because without it you never can have, and keep, a literature of your own.[26]

Dickens spoke in similar terms at Hartford and declared his determination to campaign for international copyright so long as he stayed in the States. His Hartford speech provoked immediate and mostly hostile comment: to the effect that he was abusing his hosts' hospitality, and that it was due to the absence of a copyright law that he owed his popularity in America. The real reason for this outburst was of course economic, underlined by the current depression. Payments to authors, it was argued, would raise the price of books, leading to a fall in sales and profits, and so bring ruin to printers, papermakers, and everyone else involved in the trade of books.[27] In a letter to John Forster of 24 February, Dickens attacked his critics as bitterly as they had attacked him.

The notion that I, a man alone by himself, in America, should venture to suggest to the Americans that there was one point on which they were neither just to their own countrymen nor to us, actually struck the boldest dumb. Washington Irving, Prescott, Hoffman, Bryant, Halleck, Dana, Washington Allston—every man who writes in this country is devoted to the question, and not one of them *dares* to raise his voice and complain of the atrocious state of the law. It is nothing that of all men living I am the greatest loser by it. It is nothing that I have a claim to speak and be heard. The wonder is that a breathing man can be found with temerity enough to suggest to the Americans the possibility of their having done wrong. I wish you could have seen the faces that I saw, down both sides of the table at Hartford, when I began to talk about Scott.[28] I wish you could have heard how I gave it out. My blood so boiled as I thought of the monstrous injustice that I felt as if I were twelve feet high when I thrust it down their throats.[29]

Although fully justified in his campaign, Dickens was not being fair to his American friends. Many had taken up the cudgels for international copyright, though none had spoken out so forcefully as he, but none perhaps had been in such a powerful and privileged position to do so. Shortly afterwards however, at a dinner in New York, Washington Irving gave a toast to 'International Copyright', and Cornelius Matthews 'made a long and fervent plea in its support'.[30] Moreover Dickens received strong backing in the *Tribune*, edited by Horace Greeley, 'which published two editorials urging international copyright, probably written by Greeley himself. The first, 14 February, demanded it on grounds of personal justice to Dickens ... The second, 21 February ... added justice to American writers to the demand for abstract justice.'[31]

Dickens had meanwhile asked John Forster to obtain a memorial on the subject, duly drafted by Bulwer-Lytton and signed by twelve British authors, which he forwarded with a covering letter for publication, early in May, in a number of American newspapers and journals. He also attached a separate supporting letter from Thomas Carlyle, who mentioned that he had signed the 1836 petition. Editorial reaction was mixed, and the eminence of the signatories doubted.[32] Dickens concluded:

> I'll tell you what the two obstacles to the passing of an international copyright law with England are: firstly, the national love of 'doing' a man in any bargain or matter or business; secondly, national vanity.[33]

Dickens arrived back in London on 29 June, too tired to attend the meeting next day at the Freemasons' Tavern in support of international copyright. However he soon recovered and threw himself into all the business arising out of his American visit, beginning with a printed circular,[34] dated 7 July and addressed to 'British Authors and Journals' in which he described his experiences in the States, declaring

> I will never from this time enter into any negociation with any person for the transmission, across the Atlantic, of early proofs of anything I write; and that I will forego all profit derivable from such a source.

He also urged fellow authors to have no truck with 'editors and proprietors of newspapers almost exclusively devoted to the republication of popular English works'.

*   *   *   *

As we have seen, neither Dickens's exertions, nor those of other authors, publishers, and sympathisers on either side of the Atlantic produced any immediate change in the situation so far as America was concerned. They did however hasten the signing of the reciprocal agreements with the European countries, and provoke a fresh attempt among British authors to combine for their own protection, the first of any significance since the 18th century.[35] This episode formed the subject of an article, 'The First Society of British Authors', contributed by Walter Besant to the July 1889 issue of *The Contemporary Review* and reprinted in his *Essays and Historiettes*, published by Chatto & Windus in 1903.[36] Besant said that, on his return to England, Dickens 'made a startling discovery'.

This was nothing short of the fact that his publishers had been making a fortune out of his books while he had not. Nothing so stimulates a sense of injustice as a personal wrong. He raged and fumed; he talked over the subject with other men; he found them full of bitterness, though they had so much less cause of complaint, and he agreed to join with them in an attempt to effect, by combination, a remedy for the wrongs of himself and his fraternity.

The founders of this combination first met in some informal preliminary manner, of which no record has been kept. They formed themselves, also in an unknown and unremembered manner, into an association, to be called the Society of British Authors; they nominated a Provisional Committee, consisting of the original founders, and they called their first formal meeting at the British Hotel, Cockspur Street.

The date of this meeting was 25 March 1843. It appears that the 'original group included Charles Mackay, John Robertson [later editor of the *Westminster Review*], John Britton and G. L. Craik; by 19 March they had persuaded Carlyle to join them at a further informal meeting on 21 March, when resolutions were passed which were sanctioned on 25 March'.[37] Besant continued:

At this meeting Thomas Campbell took the chair. No report preserves the names of those present, but the speakers were Thomas Carlyle, Sir Edward Lytton Bulwer, John Poole, and J. Westland Marston. John Robertson ... read a draft prospectus, and a sub-committee consisting of Carlyle, Campbell, Bulwer, Robert Bell, Charles Mackay, John Britton, and John Robertson was appointed to consider and revise the prospectus.

Shortly afterwards Carlyle threw in his hand. He thought the prospectus unexceptionable but impracticable and, despite pressure by Robertson, refused to help in any way—'because nobody but a madman can expect any good out of it under the present circumstances'.[38] A second meeting was held on 8 April at which Dickens took the chair. 19 persons attended, including

Bell, Forster, Mackay, and Thackeray; and it was decided to print a revised 'Proposed Prospectus'[39] and send it round 'to the principal writers of the country, asking for suggestions, and for co-operation with the movement'.[40]

Besant poured scorn on this document, dubbing it 'the feeblest and the most futile that ever was put together by any body of oppressed and indignant mortals. They had nothing to advance by way of grievance, nothing to propose, to suggest, to offer. They had not even enough backbone to set forth their wrongs'. The substance was set out under four heads:

1) To register the names and works of all the authors in the British Empire.

2) To secure the observance of the laws for the protection of authors and their property.

3) To obtain such alterations of existing laws, and the enactment of such new laws, both national and international, as may from time to time be deemed necessary.

4) To establish correspondence with authors, both at home and abroad in reference to the objects of the Society, and the great interests of civilization involved in them.

Apart from suggestions for the formation of a library in London, lectures, means of registration, and the appointment of various subcommittees to procure legal advice and advance authors' interests in Parliament and elsewhere, that was all. Besant thundered:

On the great question of equitable publishing not a word to show that such a question could be raised; on the one point—the only point—which can unite members of any profession, their material interests, not a word of hope or even of understanding ... However, at the end of this precious document, the Committee contrived to hit upon one practical idea—the only one in the whole document, and one of which they were totally unable to perceive the importance.

'A field of industry', they say, 'vast, tangled, and important, lies before the Society. The present state of the literary trades—publishing, printing, bookbinding, paper-making, bookselling; the condition of the advertising system, of the circulating libraries, of the book clubs, of the publishing societies—these, and similar subjects, cannot fail to yield to inquiry a great tangible good not in existence at present ...'

To acquire this information should have been their first object; if they had placed this end before themselves at the outset, the Society might have lived and flourished and done good work.

They began, in fact, with an impossible theory: that authorship is a profession as distinct as law or medicine; and that it is possible to unite its members, as those called to the Bar are united, into a guild or company governed by its own laws. At the most, authorship is a collection of professions . . . There is one thing, and one thing only, for which those who write books and papers which are sold can possibly unite—viz., their material interests. The authors of 1843 were like Dickens' American friends; they whispered to each other 'Yes—yes—we are horribly treated—it is quite true, we all know it: but for Heaven's sake don't say so in public; in epigram as much as you please; but in plain English—no.'

Although he had chaired the meeting on 8 April, indeed as a result of that experience, Dickens withdrew his support almost at once. In a letter to Charles Babbage, the mathematician, of 27 April, he wrote:

You may suppose, from seeing my name in the Printed Letter[41] you have received, that I am favorable to the proposed Society. I am decidedly opposed to it. I went there on the day I was in the chair, after much solicitation; and being put into it, opened the Proceedings by telling the meeting that I approved of the Design in theory, but in practice considered it hopeless. I may tell you—I did not tell them—that the nature of the meeting, and the character and position of the men attending it, cried Failure trumpet-tongued in my ears. To quote an expression from Tennyson, I may say that if it were the best Society in the world, the grossness of some natures in it,[42] would have weight to drag it down.

In the wisdom of all you urge in the Notes you have sent me, taking them as statements of Theory, I entirely concur. But in practice I feel sure that the present Publishing system cannot be overset, until Authors are different men. The first step to be taken, is, to move as a body in the question of copyright—enforce the existing laws—and try to obtain better. For that purpose, I hold that Authors and Publishers must unite, as the wealth, business-habits, and interests of the latter class are of great importance to such an end. The

Longmans and Murray have been with me proposing such an association. That I shall support. But having seen the Cockspur Street Society, I am as well convinced of its invincible hopelessness as if I saw it written by a Celestial Penman in the book of Fate.[43]

On the same date Dickens wrote to Bulwer-Lytton:

I wish to speak with you in relation to the Brood of birds at the British Coffee House in Cockspur Street, who have certainly taken my name in vain, and I dare say have taken yours likewise. I also wish to impart to you the purport of some communications I have had from the Longmans and Murray.[44]

Although, as is abundantly clear, Dickens had no use for the collective ability of fellow authors, he was prepared to support an organisation representative of the book trade as a whole; and that was the meaning of his reference to the Longmans and Murray. On 17 May at a meeting held at Thomas Longman's office and chaired by Dickens, it was agreed to found the 'Association for the Protection of Literature':[45] its aim being to support the 1842 Act, extend international copyright, and in particular to rouse opposition to the import of pirated works from abroad—in other words to promote all the copyright and customs legislation enacted and in contemplation during the 1840s. The Association was reasonably representative of the trade, with authors, publishers, printers, a paper-maker, and an editor on the Committee. A lawyer, Alfred Turner, was appointed Secretary, and there seemed a fair prospect of getting something done. However it was not long before dissension arose between the various interests—specifically over Bernhard Tauchnitz,[46] the Leipzig publisher, who apprised the Association of his plans for issuing English copyright works for sale on the Continent and making voluntary payments for the right to do so. He was in fact anticipating international copyright as an act of good will and as a sound investment. The publisher members of the Association objected, while the authors—some of whom had already signed up with Tauchnitz—did not, and duly resigned. And so, although it struggled on until 1849, the Association—like others of its kind—collapsed.

Dickens's efforts to help authors, however, were by no means at an end, although his emotional energy seemed fated to set him at odds with his fellows. In 1839 he had been elected to the Committee of the Royal Literary Fund, which owed its origin to the initiative of the Reverend David Williams (1738–1816). Aided by a few friends, Williams had founded a society in 1790 to assist authors and their dependents who had fallen on hard times. An important benefactor was George IV who, as Prince Regent, had granted the Society a Charter in 1818, besides contributing substantially to its income. In its early days the Fund had been administered in a somewhat haphazard fashion, but after the appointment of Octavian Blewitt as Secretary in 1839 matters had much improved. Blewitt was honest and efficient and kept costs down to a minimum, but gradually Dickens became dissatisfied and headed a faction of self-styled Reformers who, for three or more years, harried those in charge. In the end Dickens, Charles W. Dilke, editor of *The Athenaeum*, and John Forster published a pamphlet, dated March 1858, which alleged *inter alia* that the cost of the administration was absorbing nearly half the annual income, that the Managing Committee had acted unconstitutionally, and that the grants given to authors were parsimonious and 'paid and received like a poor-rate'. Only the last point carried weight, for many of the Reformers' facts and figures were slanted or inaccurate, so that the Committee was able to rebut them with a well-researched reply. Further exchanges followed, but there was little doubt, when all was over, that the Committee had won the day.[47]

Long before this, however—in 1850—Dickens had helped start a rival organisation for assisting authors. This was the Guild of Literature and Art, planned at Knebworth with Bulwer-Lytton and

> in essence a scheme for persuading authors and painters to band themselves together in their own interests. It was proposed that each member should take out a life-policy at some recognized insurance office, and that those who through ill-health or age were uninsurable should be elected as associates of the Guild and share, if indigent, in the benefactions of the Fund to be accumulated by the founders. Certain land in the vicinity of Stevenage was by the generosity of Bulwer-Lytton to be made over to the Guild, and moneys to be derived from certain theatrical performances as well as the copyright in certain plays were to be ear-marked for building houses and endowing the Guild.[48]

Dickens worked very hard at this scheme, organising and acting in several plays which were staged at Devonshire House and other places in London and the provinces. £4,000 was raised in this way, and in 1854 the Guild was duly incorporated by Act of Parliament—though with the proviso that scheme could not become operative for seven years. It was not until July 1865 that three houses, 'built in the Gothic style' at Stevenage were ready for occupation—but then, alas, no one wanted to occupy them, even rent free. The houses were unsuitable on several counts, but essentially

> To authors and artists the whole scheme was tainted with the idea of patronage, and, though paved with blameless intention, the road to Stevenage appeared to them the road to extinction.[49]

It remains sadly to record that the Guild was dissolved in 1897, and its funds apportioned equally between the Royal Literary Fund and the Artists' General Benevolent Institution.

*   *   *   *

A far more drastic fate had long overtaken the Society of British Authors, also known as the 'Cockspur Street Society',[50] born and buried in 1843. During its short life, the Society had managed to attract about a hundred members: among them notables such as Bulwer-Lytton, Charles W. Dilke, William Hazlitt, Thomas Hood, Leigh Hunt, Douglas Jerrold, Harriet Martineau, Mary Russell Mitford, and W. M. Thackeray; but absentees included Browning, Carlyle, Dickens, Tennyson and Wordsworth; while some of the original pioneers, such as Hallam, Milman and Rogers dropped out at an early stage.

Besant commented:

> It is characteristic of the opinion formed at the outset concerning the Society that the *Athenaeum* and the *Literary Gazette* never accord it a single paragraph. Yet the editor of the *Athenaeum* was one of its members ... The journal ... strongly advocates an alliance between authors and publishers for the protection of —whom?—the latter ... In a word, literary property in the eyes of the literary papers of this date—and, no doubt, in the eyes of the world—belonged as a right, exclusively and naturally, to publishers. Authors—the producers of literary property—were still considered as publishers' hacks.

Before its demise, the Secretary of the Society received a shoal of letters[51] in reply to the 'Proposed Prospectus'. By far the most helpful and far-seeing came from Harriet Martineau, writing from Tynemouth on 25 April.[52] She strongly supported the whole idea and, despite ill-health, offered personal assistance.

I do think a society of authors desirable, and I do see it to be my duty to assist if possible in establishing it.
The field of beneficent operation ... seems to me almost boundless. The objects indicated in your prospectus—so various and so important—make one wonder how one can have gone on so long suffering under evils which union might ere this have obviated, and deprived of advantages which union might long ago have secured.

She then enlarged upon the 'impossibility of making our books cheap', the need for research into the state and workings of the book trade, the vast potential readership of a rapidly rising population, and the evils of malignant reviewing. She emphasised the lack of good children's books—'no one ... can for a moment compare English juvenile literature with the German'—and while acknowledging the importance of copyright, she underlined again and again the need to reduce prices.

Perfect copyright laws would aid us to a certain extent; but what we want more in relation to the price of our book, is mutual assistance to extricate us from the transition state between old patronage, and that free communication between speaker and hearers—writers and readers—which must be arrived at sooner or later.

Not many others responded in such practical terms. Robert Bell drafted a more workman-like constitution for the Society. T. N. Talfourd suggested co-operative publishing. Horace Smith[53] referred tantalisingly to 'a similar attempt being made many years ago, principally at the instigation of Mr. Cumberland, which failed from a want of accordance among its members as to the best mode of conducting it'—prophetic words destined to be heard on many future occasions in connection with authors' affairs. On the other hand a letter from George Henry Lewes[54] was typical of the spinelessness that characterised the enterprise.

I thought I had been sufficiently explicit . . . in assuring you of my good wishes and willingness to belong to the Society when organised, but also of my incapacity and unwillingness to assist in the organisation. I am not a practical man; my business is to think and not to act. No one is more earnest in desiring to elevate the profession of literature to its true position. But my hopes of reform are from *within*, and not from *without*. Opinion must first be influenced, and then the organisation of a profession will evolve itself from the opinion . . . etc.

Besant wrote tartly:

His intellect, you see, was too lofty to stoop to things practical. Later on, it is true, when that intellect got the management of George Eliot's novels, it proved extremely practical. But just then it soared above things mundane.

Finally, a letter from Anna Maria Hall, wife of Samuel Carter Hall, revealed that even the Secretary had lost heart and that the Society was still-born.[55]

I am sure you will believe me, when I tell you that Mr. Hall and myself regret most truly that any opinion we should have expressed could give you pain. I knew that Mr. Dickens did not think your plan as certain as you did yourself, and persons may change their opinions without doing a wrong thing. Your confidence of success in the first instance prevented, perhaps, persons from saying all they thought and all they feared. Of *your* integrity of purpose there could be no doubt . . . etc.[56]

Besant made two concluding comments on the whole episode. The first emphasised the extraordinary insularity of men and women of letters in England at this time. No one had bothered to study the experience of the Société des Gens de Lettres in France, founded in 1837, and which despite initial difficulties had survived and was making good progress. Secondly he placed most of the blame for failure upon the shoulders of the Secretary, John Robertson. On the face of it, that seems a biassed and unfair judgement. Robertson may well have been impatient of criticism (as Mrs. Hall hinted), and he certainly irritated Carlyle (he was not alone in this), but can any one person be saddled with responsibility for success or failure in an enterprise of this kind? The answer is 'Yes', for this is exactly what happened in 1883–4. Without Besant the second Society of [British] Authors would have failed like the first. He wrote:

> In every new society it is one man, and one man alone, who at the outset determines the success and the future of the association. It is one man who rules, infuses spirit, collects ideas, orders the line of march, lays down the policy, and thinks for the society. This is perfectly well known and understood by all who have ever worked upon committees or associated themselves with any combined effort. Therefore we must reluctantly acknowledge that the failure of this Society was due to the incompetence of the man who first started it and became its honorary secretary. Apathy on the part of those concerned, jealousy, even where personal interests are at stake, interference, hostility, and misunderstanding—these are difficulties which every association should expect. That so many good men withheld their names at first ought not to have mattered at all, so long as the projector and manager have a clear and definite programme to advocate. This the French Society had and held it steadily in sight and ultimately succeeded. This Mr. Robertson had not. Therefore he failed.

CHAPTER FIVE

Charles Reade and the theatre. The Royal Commission on Copyright 1875–7. Dramatic copyright and the Dramatic Authors Society. Two women writers—Harriet Martineau and George Eliot—and an entertainer, Anthony Trollope

FORTY YEARS, almost to a month, elapsed between the demise of the first (Cockspur Street) Society of Authors in June 1843 and the preliminaries of the second (Savile Club) Society in September 1883. All that happened in those years can be considered as part of a process that compelled authors to try again—to set up an organisation for their own protection and advancement that really worked, and to ensure its survival. The root difficulties were familiar, and the inability to combine during the 1840s and 1850s merely sharpened the need for self-help throughout the book trade. There had been one failure after another: the authors in 1843, authors and publishers in 1849, publishers and booksellers in 1852. Besides this, by the mid-1850s—despite all the legislation enacted since 1833—copyright, both domestic and international, was still in a state of disorder. Most authors were at the mercy of their publishers, while authors and publishers alike were bedevilled by American piracy. In short artistic and intellectual property was being exploited in virtually all the media available to the writer, a fact vividly illustrated in the career of Charles Reade, whose professional life spanned this intervening period of 40 years almost exactly.[1]

Charles Reade was *par excellence* an English eccentric. Even at Magdalen College, Oxford, where he matriculated in 1831 and was elected Fellow in 1835, he was considered odd—in a place and period teeming with anomalies. Dr. Routh, for example, deaf, doddering and bewigged, clung to the post of College President until he died in his hundreth year; and a crowd would assemble on Sundays merely to see him shuffle into chapel. Reade was odd in his own way. He neither drank nor smoked, he wore a bright coloured coat, played the violin and danced, and preferred reading dramatic literature and history to playing cricket (which he was said to play well). As a Fellow however he had to observe two rules. One was to remain a bachelor, which he did all his life; the other was to become a clergyman, doctor of medicine, or lawyer. He preferred the last alternative, entered Lincoln's Inn and was called to the Bar in 1842. He rarely practised as a barrister but—always litigious—he became well versed in the law, particularly in relation to authorship. For a number of years he lived mainly in London, in lodgings near Leicester Square; visited Oxford occasionally where he kept on his rooms and filled a few college offices; but otherwise led a comfortable Bohemian life, haunting his club (the Garrick) and the theatres, and travelling abroad—especially to Paris where he became an authority on French drama. He supported himself on his Oxford income, subsidies from his mother, and the profits of a small business dealing in old violins. His only literary exertions were to fill notebooks and compile scrapbooks with a mass of miscellaneous information, later to provide much useful material for his work, since his forte turned out to be fiction founded on fact, presented in every medium—plays, serials, articles, short stories, and full length books.

In 1849, at the age of 35, he started work—at an astonishing pace which he maintained almost until the day of his death in 1884. His first acted play was *The Ladies' Battle*, an unauthorised adaptation of a contemporary French piece, *La Bataille des Dames*, and performed in London in May 1851. Pirating French drama was a common and lucrative practice and, notwithstanding the copyright treaty with France signed that year, and the international copyright Act of 1852 protecting translations, the old free-for-all continued: mainly because the law imposed certain restrictions on the foreign playwright and also permitted 'fair imitations', a contradiction in terms. Reade made no money out of *The Ladies' Battle* and nothing out of his next two adaptations; but his fourth work for the stage, *Masks and Faces*, written in collaboration with Tom Taylor[2] and produced late in 1852, yielded £150 for the two of them. This was an outright payment according to the custom of the day, for the idea of collecting a percentage of the receipts from performances had to wait upon the initiative of Dion Boucicault,[3] then a rising actor and dramatist.

Reade did not however confine his attention to the theatre, for in 1853 he had two novels published by Richard Bentley—*Peg*

Woffington (the 'book' of *Masks and Faces*) and *Christie Johnstone*. The contract for *Peg*, signed on 3 November 1852, was illuminating: a half-profits arrangement, whereby Bentley bore the cost of publication, receiving 10% commission on the gross income, the net profit to be divided equally between author and publisher. However the disposal of any copies by way of remainder or by special sale at a lower figure than the normal trade price was left 'to the judgement and discretion of the said Richard Bentley'. In Reade's words, trumpeted later fortissimo by Besant, it gave the publisher a free hand to adulterate the accounts with 'secret and disloyal profits on the paper, the printing, and the advertisements'. The book was published at half-a-guinea and all Reade got out of the first edition was £10. He did not forget the experience.

1853 was another busy year. Reade was contributing stories to *Bentley's Magazine* and collecting facts for a novel about prison life for which he had already written a stage version, *Gold*—dual use of material which he frequently favoured as economic employment of his powers. The novel became *It is Never Too Late to Mend*, eventually published in 1856 and which made his name. Meanwhile he had returned to the theatre. A further collaboration with Tom Taylor made only a small impression, but his adaptation of *The Courier of Lyons*, played by C. J. Kean,[4] was a resounding success and proved a steady stand-by in revival as *The Lyons Mail*. Late in 1854 Reade entered theatre management by taking a lease of the St. James's Theatre in the name of a Mrs. Seymour, an actress of only moderate abilities, married to an elderly husband, and châtelaine of a respectable lodging house where, it seems, the two lodgers as well as the Seymours all joined Reade in the speculation. The plays performed included *The King's Rival*, a piece about Nell Gwynne contrived by Reade and Taylor, and several hitherto unacted works by Reade himself. They all failed, and with the production of the opera *Alcestis*, the venture came to an end.

Reade was not discouraged, although he had lost the most money, for he was busy with another ploy. With the help of Nicholas Trübner,[5] London agent of the Boston publishers, Ticknor and Fields, he got a footing in the (legitimate) American market by selling the latter the rights of several works already published, and promised them the US rights of his forthcoming *It is Never Too Late to Mend*, about which Bentley was holding fire in the UK. The contract with Ticknor and Fields was interesting for two reasons: first, it provided for a *royalty* of 10% on each copy 'sold and paid' in the USA—a very early example of this practice;[6] secondly he insisted that Ticknor and Fields take their chance with American pirates, deleting a clause in the draft contract which offered terms 'provided we are not printed upon by any other publisher'. Reade wrote:

> Now, it is not in my power to prevent a New York or Boston publisher from issuing an edition after yours. To this your exertions, not mine, must and will be addressed. All I can do is to give you a long start, and so the cream of the business. If Messrs. A or B, publishing from your sheets, as you from mine, should rob us of the milk, or some of it, this would be our joint misfortune. I should share it with you in the proportion of ten per cent. (since my profit depends on your sales), and I think you ought to share it with me.[7]

When Bentley came to hear of Reade's initiative, he took umbrage. He insisted that he was entitled to a commission on American sales, having some standing arrangement with Appleton of New York for the sale of sheets. On this occasion Reade personally paid Bentley what he would have received from Appleton, and so cleared the way for Bentley's publication of the work in the UK; but it was a foretaste of the breach to come. *It is Never Too Late to Mend* came out on 1 August 1856 and went well, gathering momentum month by month, indulging a ghoulish public by exposing the horrors of the treadmill and other prison practices. His notes and scrapbooks stood him in good stead as they enabled him to silence any critic who doubted his veracity, and to write numerous letters to the press quoting facts and figures—all good publicity.

About this time he took up residence at Mrs. Seymour's in Jermyn Street.

Reade had a room to himself at the top of the house and, except at meal-times, the four men foregathered only at the whist-table.[8]

It should be added that when, in due course, Mr. Seymour died and the other two lodgers went their various ways, Reade stuck to Mrs. Seymour and in 1869 set up house with her in Knightsbridge where they were accepted by all but the starchiest echelons of society. It seems almost certain that their relationship was platonic; she was his housekeeper and dear companion, and Reade was deeply distressed when she died in 1879.

Soon after the publication of *It is Never Too Late to Mend*, he slipped over to Paris to look for a new subject for a play. From now on however he determined to abide by the law, and came to an agreement with the authors[9] of *Les Pauvres de Paris* for the rights of translation and performance in England in return for half the proceeds. To protect his interest he had his adaptation privately printed and registered the copyright at the Stationers' Hall.[10] Then he did a rash thing, and announced in the press that he would injunct any other version of the play. This merely provoked the pirates; but worse still when a plagiaristic piece was duly staged at the Strand Theatre, Reade hesitated and proceeded only half-heartedly against the manager, Thomas Payne, because he knew him to be poor. Payne however counter-attacked on the grounds that his production was a 'fair imitation' and, together with the authors concerned, took Reade to court. Reade then woke up and, backed by Auguste Maquet, President of the French Society of Dramatic Authors, won the day, though at some cost for—as was feared—the defendants had empty pockets.

Nonetheless there were consolations. One was his introduction to Maquet, from whom he purchased the rights of a play that provided the basis of a novel, *White Lies*, published in 1857. Astonishingly this landed him in trouble, for the idea of paying for foreign dramatic rights was treated with incredulity—worse, it was unpatriotic—and even Bulwer-Lytton, an old victim of stage piracy, saw no sense in defending the copyright of a *French* playwright. But Reade was not deterred. Once convinced of the justice of a cause, he revelled in the role of crusader. However a wave of denigration now broke over him. Critics accused him of plagiarism in some of his own works published in the past—a grain a truth there, not dispersed by his inclination to reply in heat and haste. Further, by refuelling his quarrel with Bentley, he so alienated the publishing trade that he was compelled to publish his next five works on commission. What happened was this.

Bentley—slow at first in assessing Reade's popularity—now wanted to make the most out of his properties; and thanks to the imprecision of half-profits agreements about the reversion of copyright to the author, proceeded to issue a cheap edition of *Christie Johnstone* without Reade's permission. Reade went to law but lost the case on the strange grounds that he had acted too late. Because the contract had not been terminated before the cheap edition went to press, the publisher was entitled to proceed and recover his outlay, even though the author was unaware of what was afoot. Reade was not to be caught out again, and brought a successful action preventing Bentley from issuing any further editions of his works. It was a victory dearly won for Reade was now regarded by publishers as a dangerous animal. Ironically a further blow, that might have done him permanent harm, changed the climate in his favour. C. E. Mudie, owner of the largest circulating library, refused to purchase copies of his next collection of stories, *Cream*, for patently insincere reasons. The trade expressed its disapproval.

Reade was undismayed. In any event he was now making a reputation that the trade could not disregard, and in his next book he felt strong enough to make known his grievances at large. *The Eighth Commandment*,[11] published in 1860, was an autobiographical account of his experiences and a commentary upon authors' rights and publishers' practices. In the words of his biographer, Malcolm Elwin:

> This book—a lawyer's brief with a scriptural title—is a masterpiece of pungent prose. Foredoomed to failure, it was written with a spirit of defiant aggression which infused its prosaic subject with a virility and power. The narrative of his dealings with publishers and pirates, collaborators and opponents, is full of dramatic verve, his conclusions are swiftly and convincingly drawn, his comments apt and caustic.[12]

Shortly afterwards Reade was in the courts again, and to good effect. In *Reade v. Lacy* it was established that the author acquired the sole right of representation on the stage if he had made a dramatised version of a non-dramatic work *before* publication. *Reade v. Conquest* was a corollary in that the defendants had dramatised *It is Never Too Late to Mend* but forgotten that Reade had earlier written a dramatic version himself, entitled *Gold*: in other words he had reversed the usual sequence, writing the play before the novel, and so covered himself under the new ruling.[13]

This was a climacteric, though not the summit, of Reade's literary crusade; and it coincided with the publication of his second best-selling novel, *The Cloister and the Hearth*, the last of his commission titles with Nicholas Trübner, issued in four volumes in 1861, after a serial run in England and America. A carefully documented mediaeval romance, it pleased the critics and enjoyed a lasting success with the public. Moreover it brought him into touch with Dickens, who promptly engaged him to write his next subject in serial form for *All the Year Round*. Reade was now in a position to command big money, and he refused an offer of £2,000 from George Smith (of Smith Elder & Co) for a 4-year 'copyright' (or licence) of this work, ultimately published in 1863 under the title of *Hard Cash*.[14] Reade was becoming as shrewd in business as Dickens himself. He reckoned on making at least £5,000 out of the book—£800 from the serial in *All the Year Round* and £300 from *Harper's Weekly* in the USA, the balance to come from volume sales in England and America. In the event it took longer to earn the £5,000 than he expected, but as a 'revelation' of conditions in private asylums it could hardly fail; and it contributed to his reputation for clothing fact with fiction with an ability and skill approaching that of Dickens. It was an ability, furthermore, that appealed greatly to theatre audiences of the day. When *It is Never Too Late to Mend* was staged in London in 1865, the 'brutal realism' of one scene induced a respected critic to walk out of the house in protest, an event happily reflected however in the box office, from which Reade—following Boucicault's example—was drawing a percentage of receipts instead of an outright fee.

Reade's career continued on its headlong course until his death on Good Friday, 11 April 1884. During the last 20 years of his life he published half-a-dozen three-volume novels, and a torrent of stories, serials, plays and miscellaneous journalism. Much of this work was published or performed on both sides of the Atlantic and—the plays apart—most of it was highly profitable on terms arranged by himself. A few examples will suffice to finish the tale.

In 1869 he came to terms with George Smith for *Put Yourself in His Place*, a work critical of trade unions. For the serial in *Cornhill* (13 numbers, March 1869–July 1870) he was paid £2,000, plus £2,000 for a limited licence of the volume rights, exclusive of America. The book duly appeared in 1870 in three volumes, and was dramatised by Reade in the usual way as *Free Labour*. He put the play on himself at the Adelphi and elsewhere, but it was far too long to succeed, runing from 7.30 pm till past midnight, and probably absorbed all the profits from publication. But Reade could never resist the theatre. Next year he caused a social storm with *A Terrible Temptation*, a novel based on a trial involving baby-farming. Surprisingly it was first serialised in *Cassell's Family Magazine*, and then issued in the customary three volumes by Chapman & Hall in the UK and by Harper Brothers in the USA. The subject was so explosive that George Smith had been afraid to publish it, while his rival, Frederick Chapman, consulted his conscience a very long time before making a low offer for a short run—£600 for a first edition of only 1,500 copies. Reade was depressed, but accepted, and awaited the worst. The book was duly denounced as immoral by all the critics, but it produced gratifying results in America, where the sales were stupendous. Reade's nose for topicality was infallible. In 1872 he contributed a story, *The Wandering Heir*, to the Christmas number of the *Graphic* and put it on the stage a few months later. Its coincidence with the 'run' of the Tichborne trial was a master-stroke; and the play made a lot of money, as well as bringing back Ellen Terry to the theatre after an absence of six years. However its popularity expired soon after Arthur Orton, the Tichborne impostor, was sentenced to 14 years imprisonment in 1874.[15]

Reade's dramatic ventures were, like his character, an odd mixture of profit and loss; and no one—least of all Reade himself—could say what he would do, or what would happen to him, next. He courted fate and thrived on risk, above all in the theatre. Fortunately his successes were sufficient to keep him in credit, largely because they lasted so well in revival. Moreover his last adaptation from the French, a play called *Drink*, based by arrangement on Zola's *L'Assommoir*, was not only a hit but a fortune-maker. By backing the play he made a profit of £20,000; and even the young critic, William Archer—who usually found his work preposterous—thought it was well done. In all he did, Reade wrote best when driven by a moral theme, but that did not save him from occasional inconsistency. For example, he adapted two works—one by Trollope and one by Frances Hodgson Burnett—without specific permission; and although he made excuses, no one accepted them. Quite simply these two actions were inexcusable—lapses in an otherwise single-minded struggle for reform communicated through entertainment.

Nonetheless fellow authors owed Reade a heavy debt, for he fought as hard and long for the profession as for himself. To this end he never shirked adverse publicity or spending money on lawsuits or risking relations with publishers by insisting on fair terms, to the extent that he was quite ready to go into publishing himself. In all this activity principle and private interest were equally at stake—justice under the law and a just return for the writer at large. In 1873, in company with Tom Taylor and others,[16] he helped found 'The Association to Protect the Rights of Authors'[17] in order to renew battle on familiar but unresolved issues: notably the protection of the rights of playwrights, native or foreign, wherever their works were first produced, and to penalise *by statute* unauthorised dramatisations of non-dramatic works—instead of relying, as in his own experience, on a court decision in each specific case. Two years later he contributed a series of thirteen forceful letters, entitled *The Rights and Wrongs of Authors*, to the *Pall Mall Gazette* and the *New York Tribune*,[18] arguing for copyright reform, domestic and international, above all urging the Americans to recognise the rights of foreign authors.

* * * *

One positive outcome of this activity was the appointment in 1875 of a Royal Commission on Copyright, chairman, Lord Manners, with Anthony Trollope as one of the members. Its report, published in 1878, reviewed the state of the law in outspoken terms.

> The first observation which a study of the existing law suggests is that its form, as distinguished from its substance, seems to us bad. The law is wholly destitute of any sort of arrangement, incomplete, often obscure, and even when it is intelligible upon long study, it is in many parts so ill-expressed that no one who does not give such study to it can expect to understand it . . .

A digest of the report, prepared by Sir James Stephen,[19] was praised for its lucidity and described by Bowker[20] as 'one of the most valuable contributions to the literature of copyright'. One part of the report referred to the fact that, while in books there was only one copyright, in drama (and music) there were two—publication and performance; and that this caused a great deal of confusion. The point is considered at length by Gavin McFarlane in his *Copyright: The Development and Exercise of the Performing Right*, to which I am indebted for the following information.

It has already been stated that, to safeguard their rights, playwrights felt obliged to organise 'copyright performances' or public readings of their plays before publication, and that book authors would do the same to prevent unauthorised stage versions of their works being written and performed. The Commission proposed that the publication of a work should automatically confer performing right, and performance publication right. Besides this, since the 1833 and 1842 Acts, there had been a quantity of test cases on matters of definition, e.g. what exactly constituted a piece or a place of 'dramatic entertainment', and other such questions, some of which confronted Charles Reade in his theatrical career.

An important witness before the Commission was John Palgrave Simpson, Secretary of the Dramatic Authors Society, founded in 1832 in anticipation of the Dramatic Copyright Act, and three years after the formation in France of the Société des Auteurs et Compositeurs Dramatiques, with antecedents dating back to the 18th century. The objects of the DAS were to collect performance fees, pursue evaders, and generally guard the interests of its members who, by 1875, amounted to 99 and included most of the leading dramatists of the day. By then the Society was drawing an annual income of £4,000–£5,000, deriving from fees, the blanket licensing of provincial theatres, and the collection of penalties for unauthorised performances, fixed at £2 per performance by the 1833 Act. This was a remarkable record in view of the constant attempts at evasion by country and colonial managements, and of the need to pay field officers and similar agents. There were other difficulties too. For example the Society had to act on behalf of each individual, and was unable to operate as a corporate body, e.g. as a Friendly Society, since its objects were deemed to be 'in restraint of trade'. The odd thing is that, although it was said to have been amalgamated with the Society of Authors in 1884, no trace of the amalgamation appears in the latter's records, and nothing further was heard of the DAS or its functions after that date. Clearly however it set highly important precedents for the collection of performance fees, both in drama and music—with great benefit to the Performing Right Society founded in 1914 (see Chapter Ten).

One further hazard was encountered thanks to a certain Thomas Wall, who ran a highly dubious collecting agency, more to entrap unsuspecting users of dramatic and musical works than to operate as a genuine agent. It was his practice to buy up and exploit deceased authors' and composers' copyrights, either to enforce the statutory penalty of £2 per unauthorised performance, or to charge enormous 'clearance fees' (of the order of 21 guineas) merely to settle bona fide enquiries. It took two Acts of Parliament, in 1882 and 1888, to curb him and the activities of his organisation, the so-called 'Authors', Composers' and Artists' Copyright and Performing Right Protective Office', which for a time brought the whole concept of performing right into disrepute.

As to the Royal Commission on Copyright, its Report and the reforms it recommended failed to produce the required legislation; and the next series of moves constituted some of the most important work of the Society of Authors between 1884 and the Copyright Act of 1911.

*   *   *   *

Meanwhile the climate of authorship was constantly shifting in response to the ebb and flow of social change, which it both influenced and reflected. Here I wish briefly to refer to women writers who, it is suggested, represented about one fifth of those engaged in letters during the 19th century. This seems a high proportion, but agrees with the fact that women had been playing an increasingly important role in public affairs since c. 1800, achieving reforms both for the improvement of the status of their sex, e.g. the Married Women's Property Act 1882, and for the general benefit of the community. Pioneers included Hannah More for her work in schools, Elizabeth Fry in prisons, Florence Nightingale and Elizabeth Garrett Anderson in medicine, Angela Burdett-Coutts, Octavia Hill and Josephine Butler in social philanthropy, Emily Davies and Barbara Bodichon in higher education. In writing there was likewise no lack of names: in prose Maria Edgeworth, Jane Austen, Mary Russell Mitford, the Brontë sisters, Elizabeth Gaskell, Dinah Craik, Margaret Oliphant, Charlotte Mary Yonge; in poetry Christina Rossetti and Elizabeth Barrett Browning.

The list is necessarily incomplete; but while resisting the temptation to re-tell the tale of the entry into publishing of Charlotte, Emily and Anne Brontë, and of Charlotte's successful business connection with George Smith,[21] I suggest that two names stand out for the purposes of this book—those of Harriet Martineau (1802–76) and Mary Ann Evans or George Eliot

(1819–80). Although very different in character and talent, they were contemporary and acquainted, and further linked in that their work and careers made a deep impression on public opinion in their situation as women and writers.

*   *   *   *

Harriet Martineau, like Mrs. Gaskell (who married a Unitarian minister) and her brother James, a noted theologian, belonged to the Unitarian sect, and was conditioned by its rational approach to dogma and the institutions of religion. It meant that she had no inhibitions about making a career for herself as a woman; moreover that, as a *single* woman, she had no need to seek employment as a governess or schoolmarm, the usual recourse for spinsters. In her opinion there was no reason why she should not concern herself with such unfeminine subjects as politics and economics, in parity with men; and her good sense in these matters was fortified at an early age by personal poverty and the absolute necessity to make her own way in the world.

She began life as an author by sending stories to the Unitarian *Monthly Repository*, at first for nothing, then for an annual payment of £15. She also wrote penny tracts for Houlston, an old Calvinistic publisher who paid her a pound apiece. Next she entered for an essay competition promoted by the Central Unitarian Association to present its philosophy to Roman Catholics, Jews, and Mohammedans. She won all three prizes, and earned herself 10 guineas for the first, 15 for the second, and 20 for the third. She was then drawn into the controversy over reform, and between 1832 and 1834 produced three remarkable works that made her name and gave her entry to political and literary society—*Illustrations of Political Economy, Poor Law and Paupers Illustrated,* and *Illustrations of Taxation.* She described how, by sheer will power and persistence, she succeeded in finding a publisher. One after another showed interest in her plan for the first of these titles, but always withdrew at the last moment, pleading that the market was dead owing to 'public excitement' over the Reform Bill and the epidemic of cholera then raging. One firm even got as far as engaging a stitcher for the monthly numbers in which her work was to appear. Eventually, after daily trudging the London streets and knocking on door after door, and collapsing with exhaustion at night, she was forced to accept an offer from

Charles Fox, brother of the publisher of the *Monthly Repository*. Terms were ludicrously harsh, and she never forgot them. Fox insisted on prior subscription (at least 500 subscribers at 2 guineas each), and the right to withdraw after the second number if 1,000 copies had not been sold to the general public in the first fortnight; otherwise publication was to be at her risk, he to receive bookseller's commission at 30%, plus half-profits. In the event she did all the work of promotion herself, circulating a prospectus to members of both Houses of Parliament and inserting an advertisement in the daily papers. Although subscriptions fell far short of 500 and proved a hindrance in the end, her energy and courage, backed by the generosity of relations and encouragement from the Gurney family, bankers of Norwich where she had been born, yielded results. Publication day was 1 February 1832, an edition of 1,500 copies had been printed—and then she waited ten days for news. It came in the form of an urgent message from Mr. Fox. Would she please make all necessary corrections at once, as demand was twice what had been expected? 3,000 of each number was needed, a postscript proposed 4,000, a second 5,000. 'From that hour' she wrote in her autobiography, 'I have never had any other anxiety about employment than what to choose, nor any real care about money.' She was overwhelmed with letters of congratulation, requests for advice, and offers from other publishers. Critics lavished praise, except Lockhart in the *Quarterly*, whose hostile notice served to stimulate sales rather than the reverse. Harriet kept her head.

> I did not receive any thing like what I ought for the Series, owing to the hard terms under which it was published. I had found much to do with my first gains from it; and I was bound in conscience to lay by for a time of sickness or adversity, and for means of recreation, when my task was done ... It was necessary to preserve my independence of thought and speech, and my power of resting, if necessary;—to have in short the world under my feet instead of hanging round my neck.[22]

In November 1832 she settled in London and continued steadily with her work. In 1834 she decided to complete the series with some numbers on taxation. Friends advised her to seek fresh terms with the publisher who had profited greatly from the original agreement, which still applied, although it was dissoluble at the end of every five numbers. To her astonishment Fox told her he required the same terms as before—commission plus half-profits—and that these should hold good however long the series lasted. Since Fox had never secured a single subscriber himself Harriet stopped him with a lawyer's letter and gave him his commission and no more.

I did not take the work out of his hands, from considerations of convenience to all parties: but I made no secret of his having lost me for a client thenceforth.

The series went on selling steadily and earned her about £2,000 altogether. She never regretted the venture as it got her a hearing, so that she soon became the confidant of the Whig government, whose ministers consulted her on current social and financial legislation, notably the Poor Law Amendment and the Tithe Commutation Bills. In August 1834 she sailed for a long visit to the United States. Before her departure she had a conversation with James Mill who freely admitted his error in believing that 'political economy could not be conveyed in fiction, and that the public would not receive it in any but the didactic form'. In fact story-telling had been the clue to her success with the series and remained the keynote of most of her writing: as it was with Dickens who became the supreme genius at turning fact into fiction. The journey to the States cost £500, part of which she earned from journalism during her stay, the rest came from savings. Her purpose was to study American politics and problems, especially slavery, and to urge the adoption of an international copyright law. Before leaving England, and after her return in 1836, she was besieged with offers for books about her experiences. Even in America she was approached by 'Mr. Harper, the head of the redoubtable piratical publishing house in New York'. Back in London, she interviewed three publishers in one day, seeing Richard Bentley first.

He offered the most extravagant terms for a book on America, and threw in, as a bribe, an offer of a thousand pounds for the first novel I should write. Though my refusals were as positive as I could make them, I had great difficulty in getting rid of him: and I doubt whether I was so rude to Mr. Harper himself as to the London speculator.

Next came Frederick Saunders (of Saunders and Otley), who

made a favourable impression. Harriet told him she proposed to write a three-volume book—*Society in America*, published in 1837—whereupon he asked her terms. She refused to be drawn, and after a pregnant silence was offered £900 for the first edition of 3,000 copies, 25 copies for herself, and 'all proceeds of the sale in America, over and above expenses'. Harriet suggested they should think the matter over, but she was pleased with the offer and later accepted it. But the day was not over, and the last visitor proved the greatest trial, Henry Colburn.

> The interview was remarkably disagreeable, from his refusing to be refused, and pretending to believe that what I wanted was more and more money. At last, on my giving him a broad hint to go away, he said that, having no intention of giving up his object, he should spend the day at a coffee-house in the neighbourhood, whence he should shortly send in terms for my consideration . . . The moment he was gone, I slipped out into the Park to refresh my mind and body; for I was heated and wearied with the conferences of the morning . . . On my return, I found that Mr. Colburn had called again: and while we were at dinner, he sent in a letter containing his fresh terms . . . £2,000 for the present work, and £1,000 for the first novel I should write.

At 10.0 pm Colburn called yet again, but Harriet turned him down flat. To her mind the proposition was unsound, and she suspected options.

> . . . it was impossible that my work should yield what he had offered, and leave anything over for himself; and that I therefore felt that these proposals were intended to bind me to his house,—an obligation which I did not choose to incur.

The business with Saunders and Otley went well. *Society in America* duly appeared, though Harriet never received a cent from sales in the USA for the usual reasons of piracy. She then agreed to write a second book, *Retrospect of Western Travel*, for which she received £600 on the same conditions as before. It came out in 1838. Only one incident ruffled their relations, when Frederick Saunders asked her 'to write the notes'.

'What notes?'
'The notes for the Reviews, you know, Ma'am.'

Harriet showed surprise and Saunders affected amazement

that she did not know how authors commonly wrote to friends connected with periodicals 'to request favourable notices'. Harriet was shocked and refused the chore outright.

Her one full-length novel, *Deerbrook*, was published by Edward Moxon in 1838, and ran through two large editions. The heroine came from Birmingham and the hero was a surgeon: characters and setting with which Harriet was well acquainted. It therefore piqued her to hear criticisms from 'the daughters of dissenting ministers and manufacturers', for this was their background as well as hers. 'Youths and maidens in those days looked for lords and ladies in every page of a new novel.'

Despite her resilience, Harriet was sensitive in mind and body. She was near-deaf, used an ear-trumpet, and suffered recurrent spells of nervous exhaustion. In 1839 she collapsed and retired to Tynemouth, near a sister and brother-in-law, who happened to be a doctor. There she spent nearly five years in retreat. She continued to write at a more leisurely pace for a time and sent all her work to Moxon, but eventually she had to stop work altogether. Money was now a problem. Most of her savings were invested in a deferred annuity, and she steadfastly refused a state pension in case it should hamper her freedom of expression. In the end a testimonial and other gifts from friends saved the situation, the money being invested so as to bring her the largest possible income during the remainder of what promised to be a short life: for, like Florence Nightingale, she felt sure that her days were numbered. As is well known, Florence was not expected to live after her return from the Crimean war and took to her bed, where she conducted a torrent of business for the reform of nursing for nearly fifty years. With Harriet, the case was different. Thanks to mesmerism, and in spite of the determined opposition of her medical brother-in-law, she made a speedy and miraculous recovery in the summer of 1844.

The affair had a curious aftermath. She offered to write an account of her treatment, without payment, for the *Athenaeum*, which she regarded as a respectable periodical and because she wanted to 'lift up the subject out of the dirt into which it had been plunged'. The editor accepted with alacrity and her articles duly appeared as six 'Letters', which markedly increased the sale of the magazine. Then came the surprise.

Appended to the last Letter was a string of comments by the editor, insulting and slanderous to the last degree. For a course of weeks and months from that time, the periodical assailed the characters of my mesmeriser and of my fellow-patient.... It held out inducements to two medical men to terrify some of the witnesses, and traduce the others, till the controversy expired in the sheer inability of the honest party to compete with rogues who stuck at no falsehoods: and finally, the *Athenaeum* gave public notice that it would receive communications from our adversaries, and not from us.

The trial was not yet over. When Harriet gave Moxon permission to reprint the 'Letters' as a pamphlet, the editor threatened proceedings for infringement of copyright. He was silenced and Moxon re-published.

It will be recollected that shortly before this, in 1843, the first serious attempt to form a Society of Authors had ignominiously collapsed; and that Harriet was one of the few authors who sent the acting secretary, John Robertson, helpful advice—a typical gesture made when she was still ill at Tynemouth. The fact that Robertson's prospectus about the Society was a half-hearted affair and justified most of the critisms levelled at it by Besant and others, did not blind her to the real issues. This combination of perspicacity and generosity conditioned her general attitude to causes and events, especially in the world of letters, where numerous friendships never dulled her powers of observation.

To her, for example, Coleridge

... looked very old, with his rounded shoulders and drooping head, and excessively thin limbs. His eyes were as wonderful as they were ever represented to be:—light grey, extremely prominent, and actually glittering: an appearance I am told common among opium eaters.

She had no high opinion of Mary Wollstonecraft's work for the rights of women, and she regarded William Godwin as 'a curious monument of a bygone state of society', but one evening in 1834 he afforded her a memorable experience.

Before it grew too dusk (it was in July) Godwin took us through the passages of the old Parliament House, and showed us the Star Chamber, and brought the old tallies for us to examine, that we might finger the notches made by the tax-collectors before accounts were kept as now. Within three months those tallies burnt down that Star Chamber, and both Houses of Parliament.

She disliked Macaulay intensely, both as an author and MP, particularly because he had opposed the 1842 Copyright Act in its preliminary stages.

He changed his mind or his tactics afterwards; but he could not change people's feelings in regard to himself, or make any body believe that he was a man to be relied upon ... The evidence seems to indicate that he wants heart.

For Bulwer-Lytton,

I always felt a cordial interest, amidst any amount of vexation and pity for his weakness. He seems to me to be a woman of genius enclosed by misadventure in a man's form.

She found Leigh Hunt sympathetic and old-fashioned,

... with his cheery face, bright, acute, and full of sensibility; and his thick grizzled hair combed down smooth, and his homely figure;—black handkerchief, grey stockings and stout shoes, while he was full of gratitude to ladies who dress in winter in velvet, and in rich colours; and to old dames in the streets or the country who still wear scarlet cloaks.

The Carlyles were close friends, and she visited them regularly. It was thanks to Harriet that Thomas was commissioned to give the course of lectures, 1837–40, that brought him financial security. He suffered agonies of nerves.

From the time that his course was announced till it was finished, he scarcely slept, and he grew more dyspeptic and nervous every day; and we were at length entreated to say no more about his lecturing, as no fame and no money or other advantage could counterbalance the misery which the engagement caused him.

His excess of sympathy has been, I believe, the master-pain of his life. He does not know what to do with it, and with its bitterness, seeing that human life is full of pain to those who look out for it: and the savageness which has come to be a main characteristic of this singular man is, in my opinion, a mere expression of his intolerable sympathy with the suffering.

In 1845 Harriet built herself a house at Ambleside in the Lake District, where she lived for the rest of her life. With the recovery of health she became as active as ever, writing leaders for the *Daily News* and much miscellaneous journalism. Her last books were forays into philosophy, which showed that her Unitarianism had merged into agnosticism, a not uncommon experience among 'rational believers'. She calculated that she had earned altogether 'somewhere about £10,000' by her books, and might have doubled the amount 'if an international copyright law had secured to me the proceeds of the sale of my works in foreign countries. But such a law was non-existent in my busy time, and still is in regard to America'. However 'I have enough, and I am satisfied'.

*　　*　　*　　*

Harriet Martineau and Mary Ann Evans (George Eliot)[23] were well acquainted, personally and professionally. Although reared in the high-and-dry tradition of the Anglican church, Mary Ann was early influenced by the Evangelical revival and made common cause with other denominations, notably the Unitarians. She was a serious girl and read widely, and it was not long before her interest in philosophy and the sciences detached her altogether from belief in institutional religion—to the distress of her father, Robert Evans, respected land agent to the Newdigate family in Warwickshire. Her view of the Scriptures as 'histories of mingled truth and fiction' approximated to that of Harriet whom she first met in 1845, at a time when she was caring for her widowed father in modest comfort at home near Coventry. Her interest in European literature and her open and enquiring mind were making her many friends among the intelligentsia; and it was in these circumstances that she undertook her first paid literary job. This was the translation of Friedrich Strauss's *Leben Jesu* (*The Life of Jesus*) from the German, a matter of 1,500 pages that filled her time for two years and earned her an outright fee of only £20. The book was published in three volumes in 1846 by Chapman Brothers, without mention of her name. By now she was also writing reviews for the Coventry *Herald* and approaching the edge of a literary career.

Her father died in 1849 and left her £2,000 in trust and £100 in cash in lieu of household possessions. The investment yielded her about £90 a year, insufficient for independence; and so after a trip to Europe she settled in London with a view to finding work. Her first home was at No 142 Strand, in rooms rented from John Chapman,[24] publisher of her translation of Strauss, who lived over his office. Chapman maintained a patriarchal household, with wife, children, mistresss (Elizabeth Tilley, ostensibly the governess), and potential mistress in Mary Ann, but who never—it is firmly believed—allowed herself to be seduced by him. Nonetheless she developed a strong connection with Chapman, for whom she edited ten numbers, 1852-4, of the *Westminster Review*[25] which he had recently acquired. This periodical, founded by Jeremy Bentham in 1823 and closely associated with James and John Stuart Mill, was radical in temper and all-embracing in its choice of subjects—politics social improvement, religion, philosophy, history, science, and art. Books were given generous space: about 100 volumes were reviewed in each issue—English, American, French and German—and it was to this section that Mary Ann contributed most as a writer, though always anonymously. Otherwise she was immersed in editorial chores—commissioning work, interviewing writers, correcting copy, proof-reading, and seeing each monthly number through the press.

Among the contributors was George Henry Lewes, a prolific author and journalist, then in partnership with Thornton Leigh Hunt, publishing the weekly *Leader*: Hunt looking after current affairs, Lewes literature and the arts. Lewes was attracted to Mary Ann, who began to return his interest once she had got over the shock of his ugliness and small size. But Lewes's vivacity and cultivated mind charmed her completely, and she was soon made aware of the extraordinary ménage conducted with his partner. In short, father of ten children by his own wife, Hunt was sustaining an active liaison with Lewes's wife, Agnes, by whom he had four children. Lewis himself had had four children by Agnes and helped support the additional brood until the end of his life. Divorce was out of the question at the time, partly for reasons of cost, partly because he had condoned the first of Hunt's and Agnes's children, but—though tolerant in the extreme—by the time he met Mary Ann, his home had broken up and life had become understandably dreary.

In the autumn of 1853 Mary Ann moved house to Cambridge Street, where she probably began living with Lewes.[26] At all events in July 1854 she accompanied him on a long trip to Europe, returning to London a year later. From now on she regarded herself, as did an inner circle of friends, as Mrs. Lewes; but it was a most courageous action, and society took a long time to accept the pair as *de facto* husband and wife. At this time Lewes was in full spate as a writer. His major opus *The Life and Works of Goethe*, was published in two volumes by David Nutt in November 1855 and received wide acclaim, yielding the author £350 on the first edition which, together with subsequent home and foreign editions, earned Lewes over £1,000 in his lifetime. Mary Ann had also returned to her literary journalism, and in 1855 she earned £119 8s.

1856 was the turning-point in Mary Ann's literary career, as that was the year in which she started writing *Scenes from Clerical Life*, and with it the long business connection with John Blackwood who published all her novels except one, and who in so doing became a close friend to both her and Lewes. *Scenes* appeared in eleven instalments in 1857–8 in *Maga* over the pseudonym 'George Eliot'—a solid masculine name with no nonsense about it, and no inner meaning for Mary Ann other than to overcome male prejudice and shield her from scandal-mongers, though the consequential mystery caused her annoyance for a time. Blackwood paid her £263 for the series which did so well that he paid further sums for its re-publication as a book, and this in turn owed much to Mudie's initial order of 350 copies for library subscribers. In 1857 Mary Ann earned £443, Lewes £433. From then on, without abandoning incidental journalism, she devoted herself almost exclusively to fiction, creating a succession of works that placed her firmly in the front rank of English novelists.

John Blackwood was an astute publisher as well as a good friend, and he wisely improved his offers as each fresh manuscript reached him. With *Adam Bede*, he began by 'buying' or leasing the copyright for four years for £800, issuing the book—as was customary—in three volumes at 31s 6d early in 1859. After a relatively slow start, sales raced away so that a 2-volume edition (at 12s) became possible within a matter of months. By the end of the year 15,000 copies had been sold, and Blackwood voluntarily sent the author a second £800. In addition he agreed to return her the copyright, long before the expiry of the agreed term, and thereafter to pay solely on a royalty basis.

His action helped removed a contretemps over *The Mill on*

the Floss for which he had first offered £3,000 for a 4-year lease after publication in *Maga*. Mary Ann turned the offer down and thought round a proposal from Dickens to publish it in parts in *All the Year Round*, leaving the copyright in her hands, with complete freedom to choose any publisher for the book. This was followed by an even more tempting offer from Bradbury and Evans, with whom Dickens had recently parted company. In the end Mary Ann resisted temptation and accepted Blackwood's revised offer of £2,000 advance on a 3-volume edition of 4,000 copies, equivalent to a royalty of 30%, with lower rates for cheaper editions. Lewes completed the deal for her by selling the American rights to Harper and the Continental rights to Tauchnitz. *The Mill on the Floss* was published shortly before Easter 1860. Within four days it had sold 4,600 copies, then jumped to 6,000, Mudie taking 3,000 copies alone. For a 3-volume novel, it was said to be a feat not equalled since Scott's Waverley series, and its success enabled Mary Ann to invest £4,000 before the end of the year. However she had no thought of relaxation and flung herself into her next work, *Silas Marner*, which was set and printed inside two months and published in April 1861. Although a shorter book the pace of production was phenomenal, with sales equally swift and rewarding. For a one-volume edition priced at 12s, the author received an advance of £800 on a royalty of 33%; so that, on home sales of 8,000 copies, reprints and translation rights, Mary Ann earned £1,760 from *Silas Marner* alone in 1861.

Then came a break. Work on *Romola*, a historical romance set in 15th century Florence, necessitated an extended visit to Italy and a period of intensive research. Mary Ann did not therefore apply herself to the narrative until the first day of January 1862. Three weeks later she received a visit from George Smith, whose reputation was at its height as a publisher, underlined by his recent success in launching the *Cornhill*, to which Lewes had contributed from the first. Smith manoeuvred cleverly, hinted at a 'magnificent' offer, and soon after appointed Lewes consulting editor to the magazine at a handsome salary, following Thackeray's resignation. The ground therefore was well prepared, and it is not surprising that his astounding offer for *Romola* was accepted—originally, £10,000 for publication in 16 monthly parts in the *Cornhill*, but modified by Mary Ann for the sake of artistic integrity. As her biographer, Gordon S. Haight, points out she was business-like but not rapacious.

> Because she believed that *Romola* would be better understood in longer instalments she took £7,000 instead of £10,000 for it. What other novelist ever made such a sacrifice? She can hardly be blamed because *Romola* did not bolster the circulation of the *Cornhill* as much as Smith had hoped, or that, when it was issued in three volumes in July 1863, the sale was not large . . . She sent him [Smith] as a gift the story 'Brother Jacob', for which he had once offered her £250, and it appeared in the *Cornhill* in July 1864. This was not the gesture of a mercenary author.[27]

What of John Blackwood, saddened by the death of his brother William, and who had dealt so fairly and generously with Mary Ann, having paid her a sum well in excess of £8,000 since the start of their connection, and acted in some measure as a literary and business confidant? He had never been out of touch with her, and was now offering £3,000 for the remaining copyrights in the four books he had published. In the event the offer was declined and another arrangement substituted, though Blackwood had no inkling of what was afoot with *Romola*. On 19 May Mary Ann broke the news in a cool and tactful letter, to which he replied without trace of reproach. His restraint can only be regarded as admirable, and happily it brought its own reward in due time. On the other hand Mary Ann was not acting solely in her own interest. Technically Blackwood had no options on her future work, and she was free to get the best terms she could. Her overriding concern was for Lewes who, though now earning a fair income as editor and author, was in precarious health and under obligation to find money for his own sons, for Agnes, and yet more dependents.

Romola was Smith's sole venture as the publisher of Mary Ann's novels, and he refused her next, *Felix Holt*, offered him for £5,000 outright. Before this Lewes had severed his connection as consultant editor of the *Cornhill*, though he continued as adviser and contributor to Smith's new evening paper, the *Pall Mall Gazette*. Soon afterwards he agreed additionally to edit the *Fortnightly Review*, launched in 1865 by Anthony Trollope and others. This paper was to carry signed articles from 'George

Eliot', in observance of the new and revolutionary rule forbidding anonymous contributions. *Felix Holt* was recaptured by John Blackwood, who gave the £5,000 asked for and published 5,250 copies of a 3-volume edition in June 1866. Since he had bought the copyright outright, Blackwood—and not the author—stood to gain all the proceeds of subsequent editions; and from that moment on he remained sole publisher of her books. His bread had been cast upon the waters to good effect.

It was now eleven years since Mary Ann had begun living with Lewes, and it was evident that society at large—not only *literati*—was willing to accept them. They were seen constantly at 'At Home's', and few refused invitations to their house. Although Mary Ann's brothers and sister remained aloof, the younger members of the family, especially her nephew Robert, demonstrated friendship; while Lewes did everything in his power to break down barriers. Her fame, already assured, was a strong solvent of resistance, and it was to grow even stronger with the output of her remaining years.

In 1868 Blackwood published her poem, *The Spanish Gypsy*, originally conceived as a play. It was well received by the critics, sold over 4,000 copies in the first five years on the home market, and 8,000 in the USA. By 1878 royalties exceeded £1,000. Besides this relatively minor work, Mary Ann was receiving substantial fees for signed contributions to a variety of periodicals; and it would have caused no surprise if, by 1870, at the age of 50, she had decided against embarking on any further large-scale enterprise. As it happened her masterpiece, *Middlemarch*, was yet to come. Written in eight 'Books', it epitomised her power to evoke the essence and atmosphere of English provincial life as she knew it, and the effect of that environment upon individual character. Lewes handled the business. Between 1871 and 1873 *Middlemarch* was published in Britain in 5s parts, at around 5,000 copies per issue, yielding a royalty of 40%. In the USA Osgood, Ticknor & Co bought the rights for £1,200 and transferred the copyright to *Harper's Weekly*, which published the work in weekly instalments. In 1873 as a 4-volume edition it sold another 3,000 copies, while a one-volume reprint ran away with 13,000 copies in six months. Meanwhile Lewes had outwitted Tauchnitz and concluded a deal with Asher for the Continental rights; and there were further deals for colonial editions and translations. By 1879 Mary Ann had received about £9,000 from a global sale of some 30,000 copies.

Middlemarch ensured Mary Ann's complete financial independence. In 1873 her income approached £5,000, over half from investments, now being handled by a young man, John Walter Cross, whom she eventually married after Lewes's death in November 1878 and shortly before her own in December 1880. Meanwhile Lewes settled terms for her last book, *Daniel Deronda*, written around a Jewish theme and expressing her own sympathy for Jewish life and character. In literary values it fell far below the standard of *Middlemarch*, though its contemporary success was a foregone conclusion. Blackwood published it in eight parts in 1876 on the same terms as before, namely a royalty of 40%, while Harper secured the American rights for £1,700. Ancillary rights followed, Tauchnitz replacing Asher with a much improved offer of £250. Finally, instead of a lump sum for a renewed lease of copyright, Blackwood agreed to pay royalties on the sale of all the earlier novels, whose rights had now reverted to the author.

Clearly the royalty system had come to stay, although—as will become evident in the next chapter—it was not yet common practice.

*   *   *   *

George Eliot died in 1880, four years after Harriet Martineau and four before Charles Reade, all of whose careers have been considered in relation to authorship as a profession. In 1882 there died another contemporary, Anthony Trollope, whose autobiography (written in 1875–6 and published in 1883) contained a detailed record of his writing methods and business arrangements. On that score alone it justifies reference here, but additionally in that Trollope—unlike the other three authors—had no social or moral axe to grind, but was impelled simply by the desire to entertain and to do as well as he could out of his talent.

As Michael Sadleir points out in the Introduction to the World's Classics edition of the *Autobiography*,[28] Trollope suffered a long eclipse after his death. This was due, not so much to the common but often temporary reaction that sets in after a successful author's death, but to the fact that Trollope exploded a myth. Victorians and Edwardians liked to think of writers, indeed of all artists, as out-of-the-ordinary people, odd in dress, eccentric in habits, enjoying or disliking life more than most, and probably immoral. Trollope insisted in behaving in the opposite fashion and saying so. He was not a man of letters so much as a 'gentleman who wrote books'. He worked for the Post Office, starting at the bottom in 1834 and retired—having attained high seniority—in 1867 at the age of 52. He enjoyed his employment and made full use of his experiences. He married happily and had a family. He loved hunting. He got on well with people and belonged to several London clubs, liking the Garrick the best. And he described exactly how he did his writing—not in feverish bursts of inspiration late at night, but according to a strict routine.

Few men, I think, ever lived a fuller life. And I attribute the power of doing this altogether to the virtue of early hours. It was my practice to be at my table every morning at 5.30 am; and it was also my practice to allow myself no mercy. An old groom, whose business it was to call me, and to whom I paid £5 a year extra for the duty, allowed himself no mercy. During all those years at Waltham Cross [where Trollope lived 1859–72] he never was once late with the coffee which it was his duty to bring me . . .

All those I think who have lived as literary men—working daily as literary labourers—will agree with me that three hours a day will produce as much as man ought to write . . . It had at this time become my custom . . . to write with my watch before me, and to require from myself 250 words every quarter of an hour. I have found that the 250 words have been forthcoming as regularly as my watch went. But my three hours were not devoted entirely to writing. I always began my task by reading the work of the day before, an operation which would take me half an hour, and which consisted chiefly in weighing with my ear the sound of the words and phrases. . . . This division of time allowed me to produce over ten pages of an ordinary novel volume a day, and if kept up through ten months, would have given as its results three novels of three volumes each in the year . . .

When away from home and travelling by train, Trollope wrote on a tablet on his knee, oblivious of stares. His wife did a fair copy afterwards.

Thanks to this routine he completed 43 titles—one- and

3-volume novels, short stories, and other work—between 1847 and 1879, which brought him exactly £68,939 17s 5d: to which must be added the income from a further dozen or more books published before and after his death in 1882; so his total earnings must have been in the region of £80,000. What irked people was not that an author should make money—the common impression being that he either made a fortune or starved in a garret—but that he should do it 'like a clerk in a counting house' and live so ordinarily; further, that he should assess his own abilities so modestly and tell the kind of truth that others did not want to hear.

Trollope did all his business himself. The early novels he sold outright for small sums to minor publishers, and had to struggle hard to get published at all. Longman took *The Warden* in 1855 and *Barchester Towers* in 1857, both at half-profits, and although they sold slowly at first, they proved useful earners in the end. Trollope however did not care for the system.

> While there is a pecuniary risk, the whole of which must be borne by the publisher, such division is fair enough; but such a demand on the part of the publisher is monstrous as soon as the article produced is known to be a marketable commodity. I thought I had now reached that point, but Mr. Longman did not agree with me. And he endeavoured to convince me that I might lose more than I gained, even though I should get more money by going elsewhere. 'It is for you', said he, 'to think whether our names on your title-page are not worth more to you than the increased payment.' This seemed to me to savour of that high-flown doctrine of the contempt of money which I have never admired. I did think much of Messrs Longman's name, but I liked it best at the bottom of a cheque.

So he sold his next novel, *The Three Clerks*, to Richard Bentley for £250 and never regretted the deal; moreover he continued to sell outright—*Doctor Thorne* and *The Bertrams* for £400 each, and *Castle Richmond* for £600, all to Chapman & Hall. On 23 October 1859 he offered some stories to Thackeray, editor of the *Cornhill*, of which the first number was to appear on 1 January 1860. Thackeray accepted and George Smith, the publisher, offered Trollope £1,000 for the copyright of a 3-volume novel for serial publication in the magazine. That was the origin of *Framley Parsonage*. By this time Trollope and his family had moved to a house at Waltham Cross in

Hertfordshire, where they were to live for the next twelve years. This move and the connection with the *Cornhill* marked the turn in his fortunes and the beginning of assured success. His new home and the territory for which he was responsible for the Post Office—in round terms, East Anglia—enabled him to keep in close touch with London publishers and to enter the literary life of the capital, so that he made friends with a number of writers and artists, some of whom became intimates: for instance John Everett Millais, who illustrated several of his books, Thomas Hughes, G. H. Lewes, Monckton Milnes, William Howard Russell of *The Times*, Tom Taylor and W. M. Thackeray.

In 1861 he sold another novel to the *Cornhill*, and this set the rate for future payments, viz., £600 for a single volume, and £3,000 for one published in twenty parts, or the equivalent of five volumes. Quite soon he was averaging an income of £4,500 p.a. from writing, about one third of which he saved. 1862 was a very prolific year. *Orley Farm* was appearing in shilling numbers, two other stories were being serialised in the *Cornhill*, and yet another work was published about a flying visit to the northern states in the American Civil War. And so the river rushed on, two or three new titles a year, all sold outright. About the same time he ventured, with others, into publishing on his own account, investing £1,250 in a new periodical, *The Fortnightly*, all articles to be signed—a significant step dictated by his hatred of 'anonymous assassins'—with G. H. Lewes as editor. It failed and eventually had to be sold for a nominal sum to Chapman & Hall. *The Claverings* was the last story he wrote for the *Cornhill* (for which he received £2,800), but the connection with George Smith continued through the *Pall Mall Gazette*, started in 1865 under the editorship of Frederick Greenwood. Trollope also wrote for *Blackwood's* and other magazines, and had *The Last Chronicle of Barset* issued in sixpenny numbers, for which Smith paid him £3,000, not however the highest price he ever received for a single work.[29] It was à propos of this novel that he overheard a conversation between two clergymen in the Athenaeum. They were criticising Trollope's habit of re-introducing the same characters into different books, and they particularly objected to Mrs. Proudie, to whom he was much attached. Trollope however took the hint.

I got up, and standing between them, I acknowledged myself to be the culprit. 'As to Mrs. Proudie', I said, 'I will go home and kill her before the week is over.' And so I did.

In 1867 Trollope resigned from the Post Office, after failing to secure the appointment of Under-Secretary, and thereby lost his pension, but he did not really mind. Staying on would have meant giving up hunting and cutting down on much of his writing. However it amused him to publish (in the *Autobiography*) the parting letter of regret written to him by the Secretary, who happened to be his own brother-in-law, who referred to him as having been an 'ornament' to the department. He snorted slightly.

I do not at all imagine that I was an ornament to the Post Office ... but the letter may be taken as evidence that I did not allow my literary enterprises to interfere with my official work.

His resignation coincided with a second venture into publishing, though not at his own risk. On this occasion he agreed to edit a new magazine, *St. Paul's* (after refusing to let it be called *Anthony Trollope's*), for a salary of £1,000 p.a. and promise of a free hand. The publisher, James Virtue, was also a printer of substance; and so financial failure—despite first-class contributors and a circulation of 10,000—was disappointing but not a catastrophe.

The rest of Trollope's life passed unremarkably, with a sobering interlude when he stood unsuccessfully for Beverley in Yorkshire in the Liberal interest, and a visit in 1871–2 to Australia, which yielded *The Eustace Diamonds*, a best-seller. On his return he sold up at Waltham Cross and took a house in London in Montagu Square, where he died full of work and contentment nearly ten years later, in December 1882.

CHAPTER SIX

The foundation in 1884 and early years of The Society of Authors. The paramount role of Walter Besant. The International Copyright Convention at Berne, 1886. *Grievances between Authors and Publishers*, 1887

THE 1880s were a crucial decade for the profession of authorship.

On Friday 28 September 1883 twelve men held a meeting at No. 3d Sheffield Terrace, Kensington. All were concerned with the business of writing, either as established authors or as people whose work in other professions necessitated publication. All belonged to the Savile Club where, no doubt, the meeting had previously been arranged and its purpose long discussed. Their names were Walter Besant, author, who took the chair; Ulick Ralph Burke, barrister and Spanish scholar; A. Egmont Hake, author; Professor H. C. Fleming Jenkin, scientist; The Reverend W. J. Loftie, theologian and antiquary, at whose house the meeting was taking place; Wilfrid Meynell, author; S. G. C. Middlemore, journalist; J. Henry Middleton, archaeologist and architect; Walter Herries Pollock, barrister and editor; W. R. S. Ralston, barrister and Russian scholar; W. Baptiste Scoones, barrister; and J. Tristram Valentine, solicitor.

The meeting decided that a society be formed under the title of 'The Company of Authors'; and that a sub-committee or working party of five (Besant, Loftie, Meynell, Middlemore, and Pollock) should 'do all things necessary for the foundation of the society'; and that Valentine 'be appointed Honorary Secretary *pro tem.*'

This was the third serious attempt to induce authors to combine for their own advantage, and the second organisation to bear the title of The Society of Authors. The first—a co-operative publishing enterprise, called The Society for the Encouragement of Learning, described in Chapter One—lasted from 1736 to 1748. Nothing further happened until the early 19th century when there was a spate of projects and enterprises of a very mixed sort, as listed in Note 35 of Chapter Four. Some were simply dinner clubs. Others, more ambitious, incorporated in several instances incompatible aims—charitable, commercial, professional, social—culminating in 1843 in the second serious attempt to establish an effective pressure group, The Society of British Authors. As related in Chapter Four, it died after a very short life. This left only two organisations to serve the interests of authors—The Royal Literary Fund and The Royal Society of Literature. The RLF, founded in 1790, functioned exclusively as a charity for the assistance of authors in distress. Although in its early days it had arranged a variety of social events, all these and its annual dinners (which were to continue until 1939), at which speeches were made by eminent people about the state of literature, had one sole purpose—that of raising money. The Fund is an active and effective organisation to this day, but its aims have not altered. The RSL received its Charter in 1825. Its objects were primarily literary, including that of preserving 'the purity of the English language'; but at present they are summarised as 'to sustain all that is best, whether traditional or experimental, in English Letters, and to encourage a catholic appreciation of literature'. Neither organisation was designed to define, defend and promote the interests of authorship in terms of law and business; hence the time was bound to come when a separate independent body would have to be set up for such purposes. And that was the motive for the meeting at Sheffield Terrace in September 1883.

*   *   *   *

The working party of five met twelve times in the next four months, so that on 18 February 1884 it was possible to hold a General Meeting at 1 Adam Street, Adelphi, the offices of the Society for the Promotion of Social Science, with Sir William Frederick Pollock[1] in the chair. The working party had accomplished much. It had persuaded 14 prominent people to become Vice-Presidents, and had enrolled 68 members 'representing all branches of Literature, Science, and Art'. It had also drafted a 'Preliminary Prospectus', which was laid on the table and formally adopted. The original committee of twelve then formally resigned to make way for a Council,

> to be elected from the present body of Fellows, who shall carry on the Society's operations in accordance with the wishes of the Members, draw up Rules and Regulations for

the constitution of the Society, and take such steps as may seem desirable in accordance with the spirit of the Prospectus, and in furtherance of the Interests of Authors.[2]

The new Council met at Baptiste Scoone's chambers, 19 Garrick Street, and consisted of 18 names, among them a majority of those who had attended the historic occasion at Sheffield Terrace, with the notable addition of Charles Reade and George Augustus Sala, the journalist. It met eight times between 18 February and 26 May 1884 when—for constitutional and practical reasons—it was agreed to set up a separate and smaller Committee of Management, composed of eight Council members, with Walter Besant as permanent chairman. Meanwhile the Council remained in being, more as a source of prestige than of action; likewise the phalanx of Vice-Presidents, most of whom were honorary. The purpose of course was to persuade prominent people in the arts and professions to give standing to the new organisation; and in that it succeeded very well. Among those listed as representatives of various aspects of authorship were: for poetry, Matthew Arnold and Edward Lytton (son of Bulwer-Lytton); for science, John Tyndall and Thomas Huxley; for history, Edward Dicey and James Anthony Froude; for theology, James Martineau (the Unitarian Divine) and Henry Manning (the Roman Catholic Cardinal); for fiction, R. D. Blackmore, Wilkie Collins, Charles Reade and Charlotte M. Yonge; for drama, Reade, Herman Merivale and W. S. Gilbert; for journalism, George Augustus Sala. And there were others who, under various heads, added lustre, e.g. Richard Burton, the explorer; Alma Tadema, the painter; Walter Copinger, the expert on copyright; and John Ruskin and William Michael Rossetti, art critics and men of letters.

Only one post at first remained vacant—in the public eye perhaps the most important of all—the Presidency. After initial refusal it was finally accepted—thanks to the persistence of Besant—by the Poet Laureate, Alfred Tennyson, and announced on 26 May. This was a great triumph which, as Besant wrote later, 'won for us at the outset respectful consideration . . . Had we elected or been compelled to accept any lesser man than the Laureate, our progress would have been far more difficult. With him at our head we were from the first accepted seriously'.

By this time the press had had time to consider the purpose and prospects of the Society ('Company' was soon dropped).

The general tone was encouraging. Comment was concentrated on the three main objects listed in the Prospectus—regarded as laudable almost without exception, though their practicability was another matter.

i) the need for an international copyright convention with the USA.

ii) the introduction of a Bill for the registration of titles.

iii) the maintenance of friendly relations between authors and publishers, by means of properly drawn agreements.

The sharpest criticism was confined to 'the maintenance of friendly relations' etc, which most regarded as an euphemism. For example, on 23 February *The Saturday Review* warned the Society against trying to be a Trade Union and encourage strikes, for 'most political and social economists are ready to lay it down as an invariable rule that no strike has ever prospered'. On 24 February *The Observer* remarked:

> The authors have, of course, as good a right to combine for their own advantage as any other class of men, and in many respects no public servants so much require to act in unison as those who supply the literature of the nation. The only question is their ability to do so. The lawyers and the doctors may form their 'trades union' with ease because the State protects them in their rights and immunities ... In like manner, the masons or the carpenters can easily combine, and even limit the circle of their trades, by refusing to teach more than a specified number of apprentices, and declining to work with any one who is not in the bonds of their brotherhood. It is not so with authors. Unhappily, book making is about the only business which men take up without having been trained for it by a sufficient pupillage; and, indeed, it is too often, like cab-driving and the small coal trade, adopted after all other avenues to a livelihood have closed. Hence a union of authors, capable of exerting a gentle pressure on publishers, could only be successful if everyone capable of doing the work publishers require to be done were enrolled in the guild.

On 12 March *The World* published a long facetious poem which began:

A LITTLE ROW IN THE ROW[3]

Some Literary Gents the other day did meet
All in a private chamber, which looks on Garrick Street;
There they did meet together, and solemnly they swore
That as they had been done enough they would be done no
    more;

On 5 June *The Bookseller* reported the formation of a
SOCIETY FOR THE PREVENTION OF CRUELTY TO
AUTHORS, whose aims included compelling publishers to
publish all manuscripts sent to them; establishing perpetual
copyright; introducing the custom of daily payments to authors
and furnishing them with daily accounts of sales; providing that
copyrights should revert to authors when publishers seemed to
be making too much profit out of their books; doubling all
royalties payable under existing agreements; etc, etc.

On 30 May *The Times* clearly approved, though it wondered
why the job was not being done by the Royal Society of
Literature. 'Its object is declared to be the advancement of
literature. The protection of literature ought to fall within its
province.' However,

The promoters of the Incorporated Society of Authors would
probably have been as little inclined to try to mould the
venerable Royal Society of Literature in St. Martin's-place to
their ends as the leaders of the Social Science Congress to
leave the amendment of civilization to the quarterly meetings
of the Middlesex magistrates. Their aims are intensely
practical, and they care nothing for the compilation of
transactions. They do not disguise that their motives are
selfish, and that they are organised for class objects. . . .
Literary selfishness, provided it be sagacious and of a nature
to accomplish its work, cannot be too resolute and direct. If
authors can agree and teach one another to do what is best
for themselves, they will be doing what is best for the
community at large.

No difficulty—certainly no press criticism—deterred Besant
and his friends from putting the Society on its feet, and thereafter pursuing its aims with the utmost vigour. The first task had
been to settle the constitution: the business of drafting the
Memorandum and Articles of Association being given to a sub-

committee consisting of J. Comyns Carr, Walter Herries Pollock, and E. M. Underdown QC (Hon. Counsel). The work was soon done. Application was made to the Board of Trade to register the Society as a Company limited by shares, with a licence to omit the word 'Limited' in the title; and on 30 June the Certificate of Incorporation was duly received. The capital was fixed at £1,000 divided into 1,000 shares of £1 each. All members of the Council (limited to 60) had to be shareholders, but responsibility for the administration of the Society rested with the Committee of Management, consisting of 12 members elected from the Council, three such members retiring each year. Subsequently election to the Committee was thrown open to the entire membership. The annual subscription was fixed at one guinea, life subscription at ten guineas. Some confusion was caused by terminology, since you could apply to join as a Fellow, a Member, or an Associate. Some Fellows it seemed paid subscriptions, others not, whereas all Members and Associates paid without question. After a few years Fellows were abolished, while Members remained as before, i.e. authors of at least one full-length work, published or performed. Associates were aspirants. Apart from this and other alterations necessitated by changes in Company law, by Special Resolutions in 1893 and 1908, and by inevitable rises in subscription rates, the 1884 constitution has survived in many of its essentials to the present day.[4]

While the Council continued to use 19 Garrick Street, as occasion demanded, the Committee of Management met weekly—after the summer break—at 6 Queen Anne's Gate, Westminster, the offices of J. Tristram Valentine. Valentine had already been appointed 'Secretary and Solicitor to the Company', an honorary post that was soon to cause trouble. For the time being he was willing to look after legal business and advise members, making no charge 'until the annual income of the Society should reach Two Hundred pounds'—all this apart from day-to-day clerical work allotted to a member of his staff, J. Venner Gray, who was to be paid £25 per annum, plus postages and other out-of-pocket expenses.

The Society was now equipped, more or less, to begin business; and no one was more aware than Besant of the need to show results. However the euphoria generated by the pre-liminaries of foundation was sustained by one further event in the autumn of 1884. This occurred on 18 October when Sir

Robert Fowler, Lord Mayor of London, invited members of the Society, *as a Society*, to a banquet at the Mansion House. Although Tennyson was prevented from attending by a 'severe domestic calamity', the occasion went off well and challenging speeches were made. In Besant's words: 'We were suddenly and unexpectedly dragged out in the light and exhibited to the world'. Sala and W. S. Gilbert amused the company with witticisms. Responding for drama, Gilbert said that critics, managers, and the public were indiposed or unable to distinguish adequately between original works which cost the author seven or eight months' careful intellectual preparation and French three-act indecencies which did not cost a week's mental labour. On the serious side several speakers pleaded for international copyright, notably F. O. Adams CB, British Minister to Switzerland, who referred to moves that were to lead to the Berne Convention of 1886. As usual it was Besant who made the most of the occasion. He was at pains to remove any impression that the sole intention of the founders of the Society was hostility to publishers. The interests of publishers and authors were identical, he said, with the one exception that the publishers could not do without the authors, whereas the authors might possibly do without the publishers. (Laughter.) One cause of difficulty was the absence of agreements, which should be carefully drawn up and, if necessary, submitted to the solicitors of the Society. Authors ought in cases where they were entitled to part-profits or royalties to have, as in all other partnerships, free access to documents and the production of vouchers. (Hear! Hear!)

The reference to agreements between authors and publishers, and a concluding remark about the right of novelists to control the dramatising of their own works, would—together with the reform of copyright—constitute the main business of the Society in its early years.

*   *   *   *

By this time, little more than a year after the first exploratory meeting, it was obvious that the Society would not have been born, or survived birth, without Besant. Squire Sprigge, a future Secretary and Chairman, wrote later:

I am not belittling the part which the first Council and Committee . . . played when I say that they almost all gave their original adherence to 'oblige Besant' ... He was loved as well as respected. He had gone to the top of the literary profession with a few quick strides, and success made no difference to him. The absolutely simple, genial, unassuming man was unaltered ... All Besant's friends followed him because they knew the man rather than his cause ... Men of repute in the literary and business world belonged from the beginning of the movement. Admirable volunteer service was done by counsel, solicitors and auditors, a strong Committee of Management was backed by an influential array of vice-presidents, and the first president was Tennyson. Most of these were recruited ... by half-a-dozen men who knew them intimately and were related to them, and these half-a-dozen men were Besant's friends.

Who then was Besant? As an author his name means little except to students of Victorian fiction, admirers of Richard Jefferies (of whom Besant was characteristically a champion), and students of the history of London, for Besant's mammoth single-handed *Survey* occupied the last years of his life. Successful as he was in his day as journalist and author, he is not so remembered now. His reputation rests on other foundations.

Born at Portsea in 1836, he had a peripatetic education at the hands of tutors and in private schools, in the course of which he became a boarder at Stockwell Grammar School, then in a superior neighbourhood south of the Thames, before entering King's College, London and ultimately Christ's College, Cambridge in 1855. He was thoroughly grounded in the classics and in mathematics but, with a natural love of reading and a gifted inquisitive mind, he also acquired a wide knowledge of English, French and German literature. Short-sight prevented him from enjoying sport; so he went walking and exploring, prying particularly into churches and old buildings, and in this way made himself an authority on the City of London at a time when many of its historic slums were being pulled down. He was gregarious and made many friends, and although at heart a deeply serious and moral man, he reacted with such distaste against the narrow Evangelicalism of the Anglican Church, that any ideas once entertained of becoming a clergyman vanished soon after leaving Cambridge. With a respectable degree in classics and mathematics, he turned to teaching—at Leamington College, 1859–61: followed by an exotic, but highly formative experience, as senior professor of the Royal College, Mauritius, 1861–7. The Rector was an Austrian, totally unfitted for the task, at odds with the staff and the pupils who were French in speech and thought. Besant did two things. He did much to restore harmony, so that the College could operate at least as a *lycée* (its true status, despite the grand title); and he read and talked as much French as he possibly could.

After six years he returned to England, settled in London, and began to write—specialising in French studies. His first book, *Early French Poetry* was published in 1868, followed by a series of articles in a variety of magazines. On the outbreak of the Franco-Prussian war in 1870, he wrote up the history of the Marseillaise (recently restored as the national anthem) and sent it to the *Daily News*. The editor—and other editors—asked for more, not only on French subjects. In 1873 appeared a collection of essays, *The French Humorists*, which was well received. By this time Besant was in a position to place as much as he could write; but this was not all. Since 1868 he had been Secretary of the Palestine Exploration Fund, a post he was to hold for 18 years, with more than mere competence. Indeed as fund raiser, administrator, editor of transactions, and scholarly colleague of the experts involved, he not only made the Fund a resounding success, but gained a separate reputation for practical and academic ability himself. In his autobiography he revealed how opportune the job was. 'The salary was sufficient for bread and cheese, the hours were not excessive, leaving plenty of time for my own work, and the associations were eminently respectable.' It was this background of congenial and paid employment (the salary was £200 p.a., rising to £300) that encouraged him to experiment with own writing, beyond the boundaries of French studies and periodic journalism.

In 1868 he had made the acquaintance of James Rice, editor and proprietor of *Once a Week*, to which he became a regular contributor. In 1871 they decided to collaborate in writing a novel on the theme of the Prodigal Son, to appear first in serial form, and then as a 'three-decker'.[5] *Ready Money Mortiboy* was an immediate success, as were *The Golden Butterfly* and *The Chaplain of the Fleet*, while seven other titles made respectable showing. The collaboration only ceased with Rice's death in 1881; but Besant continued to write romances—and other works—at the rate of about one a year for most of the rest of his life.

By the 1880s therefore Besant was an established man of letters, and in several fields—novelist, historian, critic, and scholar. Besides this, he was widely respected as an administrator, and much liked as a man. Such was the reputation he brought to bear on his labours for the Society of Authors.

*   *   *   *

It so happened that 1884, the year of the Society's birth, coincided with historic developments in copyright, for in that year the first of the three International Conferences on Copyright took place at Berne, preparatory to the signing of the Convention in 1886, an historic event duly ratified by the nine participating countries. Although not a plenary member of the first Conference, Britain had sent an official observer to Berne; and on his recommendation—supported by a deputation of authors, artists, and publishers that called on the Board of Trade on 15 March 1886—the Government finally agreed to make common cause with the other countries. And so, by means of an Order in Council under the International Copyright Act 1886 Britain became a party to the Convention.[6]

This was one of the first occasions when the newly formed Society of Authors made itself felt as a body, since it was responsible for organising the March deputation and all the authors on it were members of the Society. Its main aim was to urge the Government to reform the law of copyright as a whole, for which purpose its honorary counsel, E. M. Underdown QC, had drafted a Bill founded on the report of the Royal Commission. Both A. J. Mundella, President of the Board of Trade, and James Bryce, under-secretary of state at the Foreign Office, who spoke on behalf of the recently elected Liberal Government, expressed sympathy, but like all politicians knew the limitations of their position.

> BRYCE. Am I right in understanding that you conceive it would be easier and better to have a complete Copyright Amendment and Consolidation Act, than an Act which simply empowers Her Majesty's Government to sign the Berne Convention and make such amendments in the law as are necessary for the purpose?
> DEPUTATION. Clearly.
> BRYCE. Am I right in understanding that, if it is found impossible to carry through a Bill which would amend and

consolidate the whole law, you would rather have a Bill enabling us to sign the Berne Convention than no Bill at all?
DEPUTATION. Certainly.[7]

And with that, the deputation had to be content. They were not to know that Bryce's first question would not be answered for another 25 years.

*   *   *   *

In the two years preceding this interview, the Society had struggled through a series of domestic crises of a kind that threatened to extinguish it at any time, had it not been for Besant. The first crisis was exploded by the Secretary, Valentine, who resigned his post on 29 January 1885, shortly after presenting the first year's accounts (to 31 December 1884), which included a substantial item for legal advice. With a total income of £285 0s 6d, this would not only have emptied the Society's treasury but have made it impossible to sustain any worthwhile activities, without a miraculous intake of new members.[8] It was clear that Valentine had small belief in the Society's future, and so the Committee of Management at once set about searching for a new office[9] and a new secretary, solving both problems within a matter of weeks. By early March the Society was installed at 24 Salisbury Street, Strand, later described as a 'small street removed to make way for the Savoy Hotel', and a new honorary secretary appointed in the person of Alexander Galt Ross, brother of 'Robbie' Ross, Oscar Wilde's friend. Ross, lately down from Caius College, Cambridge, was recruited by Besant who brought him into the Society's circle at the Savile Club. As a young man of means he could afford to do the work for an honorarium of £10 p.a. and, it was said, to provide a good deal of the office furniture himself. Indeed it is likely that many other out-of-pocket expenses were met by him and Besant, then working close by in the Adelphi as Secretary of the Palestine Exploration Fund.

Ross acted as honorary secretary until his resignation at the end of 1888, when he was elected to the Committee of Management. By June 1887 the office had been moved again, this time to 4 Portugal Street, Lincoln's Inn Fields, and Ross was being assisted by James Stanley Little, who was paid £100 p.a. as 'executive secretary'.[10] Little had earlier been supported by the Society in a case against the publishers, Swan

Sonnenschein & Co, with whom, he wrote later, 'I had three years—and they made an old man of me when I had only just become a man at all'. In January 1889 S. Squire Sprigge[11] took over from Ross (and Little) as Secretary, and by the time he resigned three years later the Society had so grown in membership and influence that it required a full-time professional administrator who, as Besant informed a candidate, 'will make our Society his life's work'. Such a man was appointed in January 1892—George Herbert Thring, a qualified solicitor and son of Edward Thring, headmaster of Uppingham,[12] who was to serve the Society from 1892 until 1930.

So much for the bare facts about the beginnings of the Society. As to the character of the work and the magnitude of some of the problems, Besant provided a glimpse in his address[13] to the Annual General Meeting 1892, shortly after Thring's appointment.

We were an army of officers without any rank or file. We had to enlist recruits. The slow growth of the Society . . . shows the difficulties we had in this direction. Take the figures from the annual reports. In the first year, 1884, there were only 68 paying members; in 1886 there were only 153—and that in the third year of our existence; in 1888 there were 240; in 1889, 372; in 1891, 662; and in 1892, this year, up the present day, there have been 870, which, or course, does not include twenty-five who have paid up life membership, twenty hon. members, and fifty who may or may not pay, and if they do not, will cease to be members. So slowly have we grown; so difficult has it been to persuade those who actually benefit by our labours, openly to join our company.

We met first in Mr. Scoone's chambers, Garrick-street. After a few months we met in the offices of our first secretary and solicitor, Mr. Tristram Valentine. Then we took a step in advance, and engaged a modest office of our own. It was on the second floor of a house in Cecil-street,[14] over the office of an Income Tax Collector, who never asked us for anything. We had—when we took that step—really no more than one hundred members; some of us had to become life members in order to find the preliminary expenses. How modest that office was! How simple was its furniture! Yet it is never unpleasant for a self-made man to look back at the beginnings or for a self-made society—which we certainly are—to consider the day of small things.

Now, when it became gradually known that such a society as this existed; that a secretary was in the office all day long; and that he held consultations for nothing with all comers; all those who were in trouble over their books; all those had grievances and quarrels, began to come to us for advice and assistance. In this way began that part of the society's work, which is generally understood by the world; and in this way began our early troubles. Because, you see, it was a very easy thing to hear and receive a case; the difficulty was how to find a remedy or to obtain justice where the case demanded either. We did sometimes find a remedy, and we did obtain justice in many cases. But, partly from want of funds, and partly from the unwillingness of victims to take action, several cases fell to the ground.

Besant then quoted an instance of fraudulent publishing.

There was a certain person, who advertised for MSS. He got them by hundreds; he then demanded £40 to £60, or anything he thought proper, as a price for producing the work. Some, of course, refused to pay, and wanted their MSS back. Others paid, but their MSS were never published. We had thirteen cases against the man, all clearly proved. But we could not prosecute because, out of the thirteen, only two were ready to come forward, and their cases, as we were advised, were of too long standing to be available. Therefore, for the time, the man escaped.

Besant was far too modest to talk about his own contribution to the Society, which was incalculable.[15] In addition to personal qualities of enthusiasm, generosity, and loyalty to friends and ideals, he combined largeness of vision, attention to detail, and inexhaustible energy. Whoever sat in the office in the early days could count on Besant calling in to help as often as three or four times a week. Squire Sprigge, who knew more than anyone how much the Society owed to Besant, wrote this in *The Author*[16] after Besant's death in 1901.

. . . he was able to show . . . a large proportion of the literary world, that to support the Society of Authors made for the benefit of all, but at first it was Besant's personality that kept the society together . . . There was no suspicion that he was doing the thing for his own aggrandisement. Everyone felt that it was his sense of justice and his desire to be helpful that inspired his actions, and were ready to follow where he was leading, even though the direction was, as he has said, not quite clear even to himself. This is the sense in which it may be said that Besant founded the Society of Authors.

*   *   *   *

Minute Books are generally dull documents and the Society's first Minute Book, though historically valuable, is no exception. However the correspondence threw a more genial light on early exchanges: little matters such as William Michael Rossetti receiving an empty and unstamped envelope 'due to a new office boy', and Theodore Watts (later Watts-Dunton) not being informed of his election, as the letter had been addressed to 'The Limes' instead of 'The Pines' at Putney, but 'I wish Mr. Swinburne would give us his support'.

J. S. Little, executive secretary 1887–8, was a lively correspondent with decided opinions. In an early letter he stated that the tendency of the day was towards shorter and shorter novels—'ultimately we shall come to the one-volume novel—we are gradually drifting that way. Rider Haggard's *Dawn* is 190,000 words and that is 50,000 too many'. On 15 August 1887 he wrote to Thomas Hardy:

> My colleague [Ross] and I breakfasted with Mr. Pearsall Smith and other gentlemen from America interested in Copyright the other day. Professor Pollock and Justin McCarthy and others were there, and Mr. Smith assured us it was useless to expect America to listen to English authors upon the abstract justice of their case, the great consideration with the Americans being to produce a good citizen which they consider is to be done by the robbery of English Authors.

In September 1887 he gave the following advice on periodicals.

> For light literature, short, pleasant or sensational stories, travels, etc: *Argosy, Belgravia, Gentleman's Magazine, Macmillan's Illustrated, Cassell's Saturday Magazine.*
>
> For work of a somewhat heavier kind: *Longman's, All the Year Round, Chambers' Journal, Cornhill.*
>
> For work of a religious or sober nature: *Sunday at Home, Quiver.*

For serious essays: *Contemporary Review, Nineteenth Century, Blackwood's.*

For sensational tales written for the half-educated masses (well paid I believe): *Bow Bells, Family Herald, Boys of England,* etc.

A month later he warned an enquirer:

I cannot recommend either of the Clubs you mention because in my opinion they are neither of them fitting clubs for a gentleman to belong to . . . The Arundel is the better; but it is frequented by semi-literary barristers and actors and is an uncomfortable place—chiefly used by the hangers-on to the various arts; while about the Crichton there is a cheapness and rowdyism—a kind of pot-house Bohemianism I am sure you would not like. These remarks apply in no small measure to the 'Savage' Club, an artistic club—which like the Crichton is much used by actors, second-rate literary men and artists of the grosser kind. The Press Club, if it still exists, is one degree worse—a place where coarse jokes are the staple of conversation . . . The Hogarth and the Arts Club are no better than minor literary clubs. The Burlington Fine Arts Club is in the main a gentleman's club and of course the Athenaeum and Savile are; but to both election is no easy matter, and even in the Savile there is not much comfort unless one is in the inner circle—it is chiefly composed of men of European or at all events very considerable reputation. . . . My advice to those about to join literary clubs (unless it be the Athenaeum or Savile) is don't.

Ross's letters were less amusing than Little's, but probably wiser, though it is not always possible to distinguish between the two. One member was told:

It is of little use to try the larger publishers or I would say submit your work to 1. Longmans, 2. Chatto & Windus, 3. Smith & Elder, but they so rarely accept anything. Try Spencer Blackett, successor to Maxwell & Co, Ward & Downay and Richard Bentley.

On 3 November 1887 A. P. Watt was recommended as the 'only reliable agent I know'. Watt's initial link with the Society was close and will be considered later in connection with the whole subject of literary agency.

Naturally most of the advice given related to authors' difficulties with publishers. In 1886–7 about a hundred such instances had been brought to the Society's notice. None concerned 'the best publishing houses', the most common being that of 'the inexperienced author who is persuaded to pay so much down for the publication of a book, which is too often one which ought never to have been published and had no chance of success'. Correspondents were advised *ad nauseam* to consult the Society before, rather than after, signing contracts with publishers who as 'men of business . . . naturally tried to make their own profits as large as possible'.

To ventilate the subject and publicise the activities of the Society, three public 'conferences' were arranged, taking place on 2, 9, and 16 March 1887 at Willis's Rooms. Each was well attended and given broad coverage in the press: so much so that the entire proceedings, with additional matter, were published for the Society later in the year by Field and Tuer of the Leadenhall Press, under the title, *The Grievances between Authors and Publishers*. Nearly 200 pages long it is a work of considerable interest, for it not only presented a reasoned statement of the author's case, but attracted constructive comments from publishers on both sides of the Atlantic, and thereby helped inform an ignorant public of the haphazard conditions of the book trade as a whole.

At the first meeting Besant led off with a paper entitled, *The Maintenance of Literary Property*, a characteristic phrase, for he hammered the point repeatedly, then and ever afterwards, that 'literary property', i.e. any work created by a writer, deserved as much care and expertise in its management as any other kind of property: such as real estate which—as everyone knew—was governed almost invariably by a formal agreement signed by the respective parties. Not so with works of authorship that, amazingly, were often disposed of without any written agreement at all, or at best on terms so imprecise that the author—to whom Besant apportioned equal blame in this matter—failed to grasp the implications. Perhaps he did not even try or thought business beneath him until it was too late? Besant then commented on the four[17] main methods of publishing, all of them familiar but controversial nonetheless. As he put it:

a) that where the publisher buys the book right out.

b) that of half-profits.
c) that of a royalty.
d) that of publishing by commission.

As to a) Besant was remarkably restrained, since one would have expected him to condemn outright any sale of copyright. In fact he employed this method for most of his own books, perhaps because—like Trollope—he did not believe his work would last and, as an established author, he could earn more money that way than by any other.

This method is purely a question of terms. A producer brings his wares to market and is offered so much for them. It is for him to take or leave. There will always be plenty of writers who cannot wait for the slow results of trade, and will prefer to sell their books at once for whatever they will fetch.

On the other hand b) provided him with material for a polemic, for to this system he attributed all the worst aspects of the trade. In his view 'half-profits', if honestly conducted, was all very well, but in practice it was frequently abused since the publisher made a 'secret profit' on the cost of paper, printing, binding, etc, either by overcharging on the original invoices or by concealing the discounts conceded by the suppliers. The same applied to advertising and other costs, not to mention the publisher's handling charge (usually 15%):[18] so that what the author got was, not half the true profit, but often a quarter or less. None of this would be possible, Besant thundered if the publisher submitted vouchers for the items charged in the cost of production, and allowed his accounts to be scrutinised. In any event a full and fair contract should be agreed in advance.

As to c) he made different reservations.

Everybody, at first, was taken with the idea of the royalty system. It is a system by which the author felt that he was bound to get something, however little. He would not feel that his work had been quite thrown away. He was incapable of understanding what the proffered royalty really meant, because he knew nothing whatever about the cost of production. All that he was sure of was that he should get something.

Was it really so advantageous? He quoted the example of a single-volume novel, published at 6s and sold to the booksellers at 4s, and contended that such a book, 'if really successful', cost about 1s 6d per copy to produce. A 10% royalty (i.e. 10% of the published price of 6s) added about 7d, thus the total cost of production (exclusive of overheads) was *c*.2s, leaving 2s profit for the publisher. A 20% royalty ('fabulous generosity!') yielded 1s 2d for the author and a profit of 1s 4d for the publisher. On a sale of 10,000 copies (what Besant called a 'no-risk' book) the author received £300 on a royalty, while the publisher made a profit of £1,000. On a 20% royalty they each got about £600. In France, Besant stated, thanks to the efforts of the Société des Gens de Lettres (whose jubilee was being celebrated in 1877), the royalty rate was $33\frac{1}{3}$%.

As to d), commission publishing was little better than half-profits, since this system too was open to false accounting, and it was well known that publishers did not 'push' commission books as they did other titles on their lists.

The strength of Besant's case lay in his exposure of the abuses to which any system was open that, in the absence of a water-tight publishing agreement, depended finally on straight dealing by one of the two parties, viz. the publisher. Profit sharing in particular implied partnership, and what sort of partnership was it that denied open access to accounts to *both* parties? In good hands neither half-profits nor the commission system was intrinsically objectionable, but the fact was that—in the absence of representative trade organisations—conditions were anarchic; and this was most evident in the jungle of discounts as between book manufacturers and publishers, publishers and booksellers (sometimes with a wholesaler in between), booksellers and retail customers. What *did* a book cost at any stage from printer and paper maker to the man who finally paid cash in a bookshop? As to the morality of publishers, a handful of houses—Black, Blackwood, Chapman & Hall, Chatto & Windus, Longman, Macmillan, Murray, Smith Elder, *et al.*—treated authors fairly according to the business customs of the day, but their small number made it almost impossible for the majority of authors to approach them. The only alternative was to deal with one or other of those who made up the 275 or more publishers who, Besant said, were to be found in London alone; and it was among many of them that the abuses occurred which he rightly exposed and condemned.

The weakness of Besant's case lay in his reference to the 'no-risk' book and his example of the 10,000-copy edition. Besant was not ignorant of book production costs for, as Secretary of the Palestine Exploration Fund, he had had first hand experience of printing and publication, but that was enterprise of a specialised sort. Perhaps too his own success as a novelist had over-simplified his view of the problem. On these two points he was ably answered by George Smith and by George Haven Putnam, the American publisher.[19] In a letter to *The Times* of 21 March 1887, Smith pointed out *inter alia* that to supply vouchers with accounts rendered to authors was cumbrous and often confusing, but he did publish a *pro forma* invoice setting out the details of production costs and sales income of a half-profits book. As to 'no-risk' and 10,000 copies, he wrote:

> He [Besant] supposes that 10,000 copies of a book have been printed, and every copy sold, and makes a calculation of the relative profit of the author and publisher upon that hypothesis. A publisher would indeed be a bold man who printed 10,000 copies of an ordinary book; and upon an extraordinary book, of which he could reckon with certainty upon selling that number, he would assuredly have to pay the author, in one shape of another, a much larger sum than Mr. Besant's illustration supposes.

In conclusion he defended the half-profits system as 'especially appropriate for medical, legal, and other works requiring frequent revision by the author'. However he, in his turn, laid himself open to attack by including in the invoice a cost item, 'Interest on cash advanced, 5 per cent': in other words, a charge for the use of the Publisher's capital, a point quickly spotted by the *Law Journal*.[20]

> The theory is that the publisher lends the money to the partnership, and therefore may charge interest for it; but such a proceeding is totally inconsistent with the relation of the half-partnership. The two halves of the capital supplied to the joint adventure are the author's manuscript on the one hand and the publisher's cash on the other . . .

Putnam had little time for half-profits and confirmed the *Law Journal*'s view of the nature of the partnership between author and publisher, though he did point out that while 'the author shares the profits, if any accrue, he does not agree to share the loss in the event of a deficiency'. In contrast he fully supported the royalty system, in common use in the USA, whereby the author received an average return of 10% on the published price, a higher rate being admissible after the sale of the first 5,000–10,000 copies.

> This rate has been arrived at . . . on the calculation that it represented about one-half the net profits remaining after the cost of printing, advertising, and putting the book on the market had been covered.

Perhaps Putnam's most telling comment on English practice was:

> . . . the want of explicit and comprehensive publishing contracts. The remedy for this difficulty must certainly rest with the authors themselves, as there is no reason why they should not insist upon securing as explicit a contract for the publishing of a book as for the building of a house, whether they are investing in the book cash capital or 'only brains and time'. In the States, it would certainly be a most exceptional thing for the publication of a book to be undertaken without a contract covering all the usual contingencies, the publishers considering such contract important for their own interest (to save them from unnecessary friction) as for the interest of their clients.

Besant could hardly have had a better statement of support from the most ardent member of the Society of Authors. In the end too he sided with Putnam in advocating the royalty system. He differed however about the rate—not 10% of the published price, but $33\frac{1}{3}$% of the actual retail price paid by the public in the bookshops, i.e. the published price less the discount offered by booksellers to customers before the adoption of the Net Book Agreement in 1899. He ended his peroration with a bright vision—a dream—two generations hence, of a world half-filled with English speaking people, 400 millions of them, all literate and eager readers. The enormous demand so created would entail 'a great army of men and women constantly engaged in writing' and all belonging to 'a great society called the Society of Authors' with branches all over the world, each with a local secretary and in correspondence with the central office.

> I have not yet learned in my dream whether the central office is to be in Chicago or in London.

Besant then revealed his true goal and he was not speaking wholly in jest. The Society would be a colossal co-operative, publishing all the books of its members, paying them not royalties but 'all the proceeds, less the cost of production and management'.

Besant's paper was of course the main attraction and the most publicised part of the first of the three meetings at Willis's Rooms; and it induced several eminent publishers hurriedly to affirm their horror of any system contaminated by 'secret profits'. Sir Francis Adams's account of the formation of the Berne Union and the adoption of the first International Copyright Convention, which followed on the first day, must have seemed tame by comparison, though it was an invaluable contribution and is summarised in Note 6 to this chapter.

At the second meeting Edmund Gosse, the poet and critic—a witty prickly person but an ally of Besant at the start—entertained the audience with a humorous rebuttal of the charge that 'this Society is an organisation for the cultivation and preservation of the Amateur'. 'What' he asked 'is an amateur?' and went on to nail the irrelevance of the question.

Was Wordsworth an amateur because he collected stamps in Westmoreland, or was Fielding an amateur because he was a Westminster magistrate?

At the third and last meeting John Hollingshead,[21] standing in for Herman Merivale,[22] both men of the theatre, ridiculed the state of the law in respect of unauthorised dramatisations of non-dramatic works—a campaign, he reminded his listeners, prosecuted with much vigour by Charles Reade. But, although Reade had taken several cases to court and won most of them, the law remained unchanged. It was one of the most glaring defects of domestic copyright, among the many bequeathed by the 1842 Copyright Act, and referred to in the last chapter.

The novel in this country . . . seems to be fair game for anybody. . . In America, in France, and in other countries . . . the writer of a work of fiction . . . retains his property in that dramatic work, or any dramatic work that may be founded upon his novel.

Not so in Britain where the 'unauthorised adapter' had free rein in that, although no dramatisation might be published without permission of the author, its presentation of the stage was apparently legal. The only recourse was to organise a bogus performance.[23]

You want to have a play performed to secure your copyright. You take it down to 'The Theatre Royal, Stoke Pogis' (sic), and you collect a small audience of 'weary ploughmen'. You stop their 'plodding home', and you get them to go into this theatre with a substantial payment, chiefly made in the beer of the realm, and you get them to form a legal quorum or audience. A sort of performance is gone through . . . These ploughmen witness this performance. The two respectable householders, who are rarely absent from any legal document in this country, then certify that a performance has been given, and the novelist may then go away perfectly satisfied that he has secured his legal rights in his play as distinct from his publishing rights in his novel.

Hollingshead then quoted some notorious instances of 'exploitation by performance'. Dickens found that, before one of his novels had run its course in monthly numbers, an unauthorised adapter (or 'skunk' as Reade used to call him) would finish the story in his own way and present the result on the stage. Mrs. Henry Wood[24] never got a farthing from the many stage versions of *East Lynne*, while 'Ouida'[25] suffered in the same manner and was caricatured into the bargain. To test the law to the uttermost, he had himself published a play complete in dialogue form in a magazine, no adaptation being necessary, and then sold the dramatic rights to J. L. Toole,[26] the theatre manager. Before Toole could produce the piece, a skunk anticipated him. Accordingly Hollingshead and Toole went to law, but lost the case, both at first hearing and on appeal, and incurred costs of £700. Subsequently their point was fully supported in the report of the Royal Commission on Copyright, published in 1878, but the law remained unchanged.

Hollingshead then described the rigmarole necessary to protect the copyright in a foreign work. You buy, say, the English rights in a play by Sardqu on a five-year lease. Exactly three months later—'neither more nor less to the day'—you have to go 'to a mediaeval institution called the Stationers' Hall' and enter it there, supplying a host of irrelevant detail which must be correct to the last comma. Within a further three months you have to make 'an utterly worthless production called a literal translation of that play. An adaptation is simply fatal'. At that point 'your copyright may be considered water-tight, and you have got the five years' lease of it'. For an opera however the situation was even more farcical because, while the copyright in the words lasted five years, that in the music lasted 42.

So that at the end of five years you are in this curious position—you are the sole possessor of the sole right of performing the music, but the words have gone from you . . . (Laughter).

The impact of the March meetings and the publication of *Grievances* later in 1887 were out of all proportion to the importance of the Society reckoned in terms of membership and the size of the bank balance. The year was significant however for several reasons. It marked the start of a fresh campaign of militancy, shortly to be described. It heralded the return of Besant as chairman of the Committee of Management and it attracted some notable authors into membership, among them Richard le Gallienne, Richard Garnett, Rider Haggard, Andrew Lang, and Oscar Wilde; followed by

1888: Sidney Lee, Henry James, and John Strange Winter (Mrs. Stannard).
1889: Grant Allen, Alfred Austin, Augustine Birrell, Jerome K. Jerome, and George Moore.
1890: Arthur Conan Doyle, Henry Harland (of the *Yellow Book*), E. W. Hornung, Rudyard Kipling, Justin McCarthy, and John Addington Symonds.
1891: J. M. Barrie, Hall Caine, W. E. H. Lecky, Mrs. Humphry Ward, and William Watson.
1892: Samuel Butler, Marie Corelli, Anthony Hope Hawkins, E. Phillips Oppenheim, Eden Phillpotts, Morley Roberts, Brandon Thomas, Arthur Waugh and Israel Zangwill.

In 1887 too existing members were generous with donations, among them George Meredith and Thomas Hardy, both future Presidents. There also occurred the first of several events that added lustre to the Society, outside the battlefield of trade relations and the law.

In this connection it fell to Alexander Galt Ross, as one of his last tasks as Hon. Secretary, to travel to Paris to deliver a letter of congratulation to the Société des Gens de Lettres on the occasion of its jubilee, 1837–87. He returned, strongly impressed with the positive achievements of the French Society—which bore fruit later—but also with a medal destined for Tennyson as the British Society's President. Unfortunately the medal lacked 'a proper case to hold it', but one was soon made in London, and in December Ross and James Stanley Little journeyed to Tennyson's home in the Isle of Wight to present it.

Next year it fell to Little, as one of *his* last jobs as Executive Secretary, to organise a dinner for American authors in recognition of their efforts to induce the US Government to pass an International Copyright Act. The dinner duly took place at the Criterion restaurant on 25 July 1888 (tickets 10s 6d, wine at the top table only), James Bryce presiding. Among the American guests invited were James Russell Lowell (recently Minister to the UK), Frances Hodgson Burnett, Marion Crawford, Bret Harte, Henry James, C. G. Leland, Brander Matthews, Louise Chandler Moulton, and James McNeill Whistler. Among British notabilities were Wilkie Collins and Oscar Wilde, the latter giving rise to a contretemps which sharpened the mental and physical agony suffered by Little during the whole business, of which he gave an account many years later.[27] There were two sources of trouble: one, that Little was enduring a bout of colic brought on by worry and wet weather; the other was the seating arrangements decided by Edmund Gosse.

> The attack [of colic] was so acute that I was compelled to lie in my undergarments on the floor in front of a gas fire, roasting the facade of my body like a saddle of mutton, hoping that the heat would draw out the pain. While in this undignified position, a knock came at the door, which naturally I disregarded; but it was so insistent that there was nothing for it but to struggle into my clothes and obey the summons. A man and a woman of enormous proportions presented themselves, and in unmistakable American accents unfolded a long tale, the purport of which was they were fit and proper persons to be invited to the dinner. It was in vain for me to urge that the invitations had all been issued long before, and that in any case the right of bidding them to the feast did not rest with me. Not until at last I revealed to them the physical torment I was undergoing, and the absolute necessity to finish my dressing and get off to Piccadilly did I get rid of them. The had used every argument to induce me to relent.

When I arrived at the Criterion another difficulty presented itself. I was immediately confronted by Oscar Wilde who, in his inimitable manner, upbraided me for having seated him at the table next to Lady Colin Campbell [who had recently referred to Wilde as 'the great white slug']. As I turned away with the assurance I would see if I could re-shuffle the name tickets, Lady Colin approached me with bitter reproaches on her lips, she being no less dissatisfied with her neighbour. Both being Irish, it may be imagined that their descriptions one of the other did not lack picturesque vividness. I had no previous knowledge, of course, that there was an old-standing war to the knife between these two. Well I had to keep smiling, welcoming guests, introducing, etc., though I was suffering the tortures of the damned, and how I got through that dinner without collapsing is a mystery to me to this day.

The dinner otherwise seems to have gone off well, for the day after Little wrote to Besant:

We scored a brilliant success last night. The reports and leaders in this morning's papers are, I think, all that could be desired. The various American guests expressed to me their feeling of satisfaction and I believe the evening went off without a hitch ... I don't know how far the dinner was successful from a culinary standpoint, as I was only able to eat the devilled lobster which was certainly admirable.

On 1 August Wilde wrote to Little:

I can only hope that if the Society gives another banquet the arrangement of the guests will not be left to a person like Gosse.

However Wilde survived the affront sufficiently to retain his membership and propose the toast of the chairman, Professor Richard Jebb, at the Society's third annual dinner on 8 July 1890, at which he made some characteristic witticisms:

... those of us, who claim at all the distinction of being men of letters, should not get up after dinner and make serious speeches, except for the purpose, so necessary in a great religious country like England, of conveying in a certain popular manner the sense of the tediousness of eternity ... Our ordinary books have passed into uncouth realism or into what is not literature at all, and when one remembers what the Universities do for us in keeping alive the Greek and Latin languages and Greek and Latin modes of thought, and then takes up some ordinary and possibly evening newspaper, one is tempted to think that the only dead language is the English language.

Alas Wilde's name was erased from membership in April 1895, no reason given. It was of course the year he went to prison.

An annual dinner was an established event in the programme of most organisations, of whatever kind, and the Society of Authors was no exception. From 1888 onwards it provided a regular social link with members, generated useful publicity about activities and aims, while the eminence of the guests helped sustain prestige. Verbosity and an excess of speeches were a small price to pay for what was, in effect, an exercise in public relations. It was the custom of the day.

CHAPTER SEVEN

The Society's campaigns. Besant starts *The Author* as a monthly. Tennyson is succeeded by Meredith as President. G. H. Thring, first salaried Secretary of the Society, copes with common frauds practised upon authors. US Copyright Act 1891. Canadian copyright problems 1895–1900. Domestic copyright—continued efforts at reform

O NCE BACK in command, Besant was determined to reinforce progress made in 1887–8 by every means in his power. His personal industry was astonishing. As a popular author and journalist, his was a household name in the press, and the Society supplied him with an unfailing flow of controversial material of which he took full advantage. Besides this, Squire Sprigge, the Secretary, was himself a competent writer; and there were other professional men, on and off the Committee of Management, willing to devote a lot of time to Society business. It therefore became possible to offer further services to members: e.g. reading manuscripts and advising young authors on their work, syndicating, and placing books for publication —in fact many of the elements of literary agency, the work falling to William Morris Colles, a barrister and member of the Council, who had an office in the same building as the Society at 4 Portugal Street.

But the most aggressive move, springing from *Grievances*, was the issue of a series of publications designed to reveal injustices and force the public to take notice of the author's case. The first three appeared in 1889.

The History of the Société des Gens de Lettres by S. Squire Sprigge was a short account of the French Society's origins and constitution, demonstrating how effective an authors' organisation could become.

Literature and the Pension List by W. Morris Colles was an inquiry into the operation of the Civil List and its alleged misuse in granting pensions to persons not qualified to benefit. The history of this fund was obscure, but essentially it derived from the time when the sovereign had to meet most public expenditure out of his own purse. After the Restoration in 1660, while military matters passed to Parliament, the cost of other public services and that of the royal household remained mainly with the king, who had repeatedly to rely on Parliament to make up the annual deficit in exchange for the surrender of certain hereditary revenues; hence the 'Civil List'. By the early 19th century matters had been regularised to the extent that almost all public servants were being paid and pensioned out of public funds; and in 1837 a Select Committee laid down new rules whereby pensions attributable to the Civil List might be awarded to

> such persons only as have just claims on the royal beneficence, or who, by their personal services to the Crown by the performance of duties to the public, or who, by their useful discoveries in science and attainments in literature and the arts, have merited the gracious consideration of their Sovereign and the gratitude of their country.[1]

With the accession of Queen Victoria, it was decided that £1,200 of new pensions might be awarded each year for this purpose.

Colles gave himself the gargantuan task of listing all the new pensions granted between 1838 and 1888, names of beneficiaries and amounts paid, and trying to make sense of the result. He was criticised for lack of accuracy, but asked—rightly—by what criterion choice was made? Apart from a few dependents of soldiers, sailors, policemen, and others who should have been supported by different funds, he found no evidence of corruption and not much of mismanagement—only a vast blanket of mediocrity and parsimony. It was right that Wordsworth should have received a pension of £300 in 1842, and Tennyson one of £200 in 1845 (though he was soon able to do without it): but what of the majority of beneficiaries, such as Edwin Atherstone who wrote historical romances and published *The Fall of Nineveh* in instalments, receiving a pension of £75 in 1858, amplified by £25 in 1860? Or Eliza Cook, poetess, recipient of £100 in 1863, in recognition of such works as *Lays of a Wild Harp*, or *The Old Arm Chair* contributed to the *Weekly Dispatch* in 1837? Moreover, while at first distinction had been the prime test, irrespective of need, the latter had soon become the rule, much of the money going to widows and orphans.

Colles did not quarrel with that, but charity *per se* was no substitute for the recognition and reward of literary worth, and it was charity of the meanest sort. The scale had steadily dropped since Wordsworth's day. A pension of £300 or even £250 had become a rarity; £25–£100 p.a. was the norm 'in consideration of literary merit'.

In the end Colles stood out for a uniform pension rate of £150 for 'distinguished men and women of letters, art, and science ... when they have arrived at the age of fifty-five, or are incapacitated from work by ill health, mental or bodily'; alternatively for their 'widows or daughters, if they are in distressed circumstances'. He also wanted the official announcement to list the various works of each new pensioner; likewise to make public the names of those whose applications had been refused, together with lists of their works.

Colles had a particular refusal in mind.

In the year 1886, the most eminent writer on Nature that this or any other country has ever seen was sick unto death and well-nigh starving. Had it not been for the assistance of a few who learned the sad circumstances of his illness he might have starved ... Yet this great writer on Nature, this great observer, whose works will never cease to instruct and to charm, was refused. His name was RICHARD JEFFERIES.

Besant was almost certainly one of the few referred to. As related in his book, *The Eulogy of Richard Jefferies*,[2] published a year after Jefferies's death in August 1887 from 'chronic fibroid phthisis', an affliction that had been causing him intense agony for the previous five or six years, Jefferies was a difficult man to help. When it had been suggested that the Royal Literary Fund might pay for him to spend the winter in Algeria or South Africa, or some other warm climate to escape the winter, he replied violently and mistakenly in the following terms:

You have put before me a very great temptation. It is impossible for you to know how great, for there can be no doubt that it is the winter that is my enemy ... But the Royal Literary Fund is a thing to accept aid from which humiliates the recipient past all bounds; it is worse than the workhouse. If long illness ultimately drove me to the workhouse, I should feel no disgrace, having done my utmost to fight with difficulties. Everyone has a right to the last relief. If this fund were maintained by pressmen, authors, journalists, editors, publishers, newspaper proprietors, and so on, that would be quite another matter. There would be no humiliation—rather the contrary—and in time one might subscribe some day and help someone else. It is no such thing. It is kept up by dukes and marquises, lords and titled people, with a Prince at their head, and a vast quantity of trumpet-blowing, in order that these people may say they are patrons of literature. Patrons of literature! Was there ever such a disgrace in the nineteenth century? Patrons of literature! The thing is simply abominable! I dare say if I were a town-born man I should not think so, but to me it wears an aspect of standing insult.

Besant commented:

Jefferies was wrong about the supporters of the Fund which is, in fact, assisted by everybody who ever makes any success in literature, and by every writer of any distinction either in letters or in other fields. He adds, however, a paragraph in which I cordially agree, and to the carrying out of the suggestion contained in it some of us have, during the last three years, devoted a great deal of time and effort.

This paragraph ran:

We ought, of course, to have a real Literary Association, to which subscription should be almost semi-compulsory. We ought to have some organisation. Literature is young yet—scarce fifty years old. The legal and medical professions have had a start of a thousand years. Our profession is young yet, but will be the first of all in the time to come.[3]

Jefferies's reference to 'fifty years' was obscure, perhaps he was thinking of the Royal Society of Literature founded in 1823; but the theme was developed in the next two booklets published by the Society of Authors in 1889 and 1890 respectively, both of them extensions of Besant's ideas propounded in *Grievances*.

The Cost of Production: no author stated, but probably written by Besant and Sprigge in collaboration. It consisted of detailed costings, with commentary, of various types of books, poetry and prose.

The Methods of Publishing by S. Squire Sprigge was an

analysis of the five main methods (including lease of copyright for a specific period of time or size of edition), definition of literary property, notes on advertisements, proof corrections, clauses in contracts, etc. Two editions were published in 1890, subsequently revised by Sprigge's successor, G. Herbert Thring.

The next booklet, written by Besant himself and issued in 1890 was much more explosive. In its annual report for the previous year, the Publication Committee of the Society for the Propagation of Christian Knowledge (SPCK) had incautiously invited suggestions for making that 'venerable Society the most efficient literary handmaid of the Church of England'. Besant weighed in with *The Literary Handmaid of the Church*, a polemic deriving partly from a study of the report and partly from earlier correspondence in the *Guardian*,[4] seeking information about terms and conditions of publication. By these means Besant ascertained that the SPCK, which was making an annual profit in excess of £7,000, paid the majority of its authors a mere £10–£50 for their work, and took the copyright as well. 'Thou shalt not steal', he thundered. The SPCK replied in a long memorandum published in *The Author* of September 1890, protesting that it often made additional *ex gratia* payments; it paid royalties to specialists; it gave away or subsidised the sale of many books; and essentially it was not a commercial organisation. None of this impressed Besant who devoted pages of the same issue to a detailed and destructive critique—he never let a subject go by default! The tirade was consistent with his general crusade against current practices in publishing, but particularised by the link between the SPCK and the Church, with which he identified the narrow Evangelicalism dominant at Cambridge in his student days.

Noting that the SPCK's honorary officers were all clerics, from the Archbishop of Canterbury downwards, he wrote:

Not one ... had boldly declared that he will no longer preside—or vicariously preside—over a great Corporation, which, unless certain ugly allegations can be explained, seems to be little better than a Society of sweaters for the greater glory of CHRIST.

Few objected to Besant's campaign sustained all through 1890–1, and it was Andrew Lang who suggested that a new grace might be devised for the benefit of 'bishops and other pious malefactors'. The one notable exception was that remarkable character, William Robertson Nicoll, who had joined the Society as early as 1884.

Nicoll was himself a cleric. He had been ordained Free Church Minister in Kelso in 1877 and soon made his name as a preacher and freelance journalist—activities that put him in touch with Matthew Hodder and Thomas Wilberforce Stoughton, who had begun business as publishers in 1868 at 27 Paternoster Row. In 1885 Nicoll's health collapsed, so that he was forced to leave Scotland and move south to London where he became editor of *The Expositor*, a successful monthly founded by H & S in 1875 and devoted to Bible scholarship and commentary. Since H & S were strong supporters of Gladstonian Liberalism, and applied themselves to the cause of social improvement, Nicoll was clearly their man. A year later they appointed him editor of *The British Weekly*, a journal of 'Christian and social progress' designed to canalise Nonconformist opinion in politics; and then successively editor of *The Bookman*, a literary monthly, in 1891, and of *Woman at Home* in 1893. There was no doubt therefore about Nicoll's standing as an editor for, apart from exercising his own gifts as a journalist, he succeeded in attracting outside talent as well— J. M. Barrie, among other notables, contributing to *The British Weekly*. From references in the Society's Minutes, it is evident that Nicoll crossed swords with Besant and the Committee on several occasions, and as a Free Churchman of broad views he objected to Besant's jibes about the SPCK and the Church of England. Behind it all lay the individualism of two forceful personalities, expressed openly in a letter published in the December 1891 issue of *The Author* in which Nicoll taunted Besant with, 'You talk as if you had a right to be our spokesman'.[5]

There was point in this, for early in 1890 Besant had persuaded the Committee to cease issuing occasional booklets as a matter of policy, since their effect was limited and spasmodic. Instead, in order to maintain continuity of contact with members of the Society, the trade, and the public, it was decided to launch an official monthly journal, *The Author*, first number May 1890, 'conducted' or edited—it need hardly be said—by Walter Besant! Crown Quarto, 24 pages in length, it was published for the Society at an estimated cost of £6 per issue by A. P. Watt, in business as a literary handyman and intermediary since 1875, and commonly acknowledged as the first professional authors' agent. He had been acting in that capacity for Besant since 1884 and had been doing odd jobs for the Society as well, such as placing advertisements in newspapers; he even managed to fill three pages of *The Author* in that way. He did not however publish the booklets, most of which were handled by Henry Glaisher at 95 The Strand; and in 1891 all business connected the *The Author* was transferred to Eyre and Spottiswoode. The magazine has been in continuous publication ever since, changing from monthly to bi-monthly in 1917, and to quarterly in July 1919, and remains an unequalled source of information about the business of writing over the past 80-odd years.

Besant's position as editor of *The Author* and chairman of the Committee of Management, his crusading zeal and generous character, and the recognition that he was the virtual founder of the Society, gave force to Nicoll's mild taunt. Besant was indeed the authors' spokesman *par excellence* and fortunately so, since the 1890s were critical for the growth and consolidation of the organisation (over 1,000 strong by 1893) and for the cause of authorship at large. Lack of leadership at this time would have frittered away, not only the credibility of the Society, but the growing awareness of authors' rights and powers, e.g. in their relations with publishers, and in the reform of copyright and other legislation. Indeed, thanks to the Society's foundation in 1884, authors were able to act corporately before either publishers or booksellers,[6] and gain the attention of the Government.

Yet Besant was aware of the dangers of his position, and at the Annual General Meeting on 17 December 1892 he resigned as chairman; but he continued to serve on the Committee of Management and edit *The Author*, and his influence barely diminished before his death in 1901. In his resignation speech—in which he summarised the story of the Society since the start—he said that people were coming to regard it as 'his Society', and that was both wrong in fact and bad for the organisation. It was obvious that the work already far exceeded the capacity of one man. Not only were others doing their share in committee, but since March 1892—when Thring had succeeded Sprigge—the administration had become the responsibility of a full-time salaried Secretary, who was a qualified solicitor and a professional in every sense. It was not a moment too soon.

                        *   *   *   *

Meanwhile, with the death of Tennyson on 6 October, the
Society was seeking a new President.[7] During his term of $8\frac{1}{2}$
years, Tennyson had remained the prestigious figure he was
required to be—distant, honoured, romantic, as befitted his
public image. Not many remembered how different had been the
aura that surrounded his unhappy beginnings, his hard climb to
fame, or the conferment of a Civil List Pension before the
sudden flood of success and subsequent skill in business.

His father—a cultivated man, disinherited in favour of a
younger son and forced into the Church against his inclina-
tions—had been a country parson in Lincolnshire, who begat
numerous children and, towards the end of this life, took to drink
and family rows. Alfred was sensitive and hated school, but was
well educated at home and flourished at Trinity College,
Cambridge, where his poetic and intellectual gifts were quickly
appreciated. It was there that he met Arthur Hallam, whose
death in 1833 left a deep mark in his memory. After his father
died in 1831, Tennyson had returned home to help to care for
the family, continue his studies and write poetry. A volume of
verses published in 1833 received a few notices, including a
savage attack in the *Quarterly Review*, which killed sales but left
him nonetheless with the elements of a reputation, if only as a
neo-Romantic. Five years later he left Lincolnshire for a
succession of homes in the vicinity of London, where he
gradually found his way into literary circles. In 1842 a further
work, in two volumes, issued by Edward Moxon, publisher of
Wordsworth and other poets, survived critical assault and
added credit to his name. A year later he lost money in backing
'Allen's Pyroglyphs', an industrial speculation, but was saved
from disaster by the award of the Civil List Pension already
mentioned. By now his worst miseries and mistakes were nearly
over. His *Princess*, published in 1847, ran through several
editions, and in 1850 came the *annus mirabilis*: when he
married Emily Sellwood, thirteen years after their engagement
had been broken off; when he was appointed Poet Laureate; and
when he published *In Memoriam*, which sold 60,000 copies
within a few months. He had arrived at last.

The business arrangements for *In Memoriam* were interesting.
Tennyson paid for the cost of production, but gave Moxon one
third of the profits plus 5% of the gross sales. *Prima facie* this

was giving a good deal away, but Moxon had stood by Tennyson over the past eight years and so supported him in bad times that, it might well be said, he was reaping a just reward. After 1850 one success followed another, whether a new title such as *Maud* (1855) or a fresh edition of previous works: so much so that Moxon was able to advance substantial sums in anticipation of returns—over £2,000, for example, in 1856. Such was the easy relationship between the two men that no written agreement was drawn up, and no hint of difficulty threatened until after Moxon's death in 1858, when his heirs had to agree to a straight commission of 10% on sales, but no profit sharing. Even so returns were well sustained. In 1859 *The Idylls of the King* sold 10,000 copies in the first week out of an edition of 40,000 priced at 7s; a second edition following in 1860, in which year Tennyson received £4,500 from Moxon's alone.

His success was now arousing the interest of other publishers: Macmillan for instance who offered too little; but George Smith put in a bid of 5,000 guineas for a volume of the same length as *Idylls* and a three-year option. Tennyson did not accept but told his wife:

Here is Mr. Smith offering me 5,000 guineas for my next volume, and of course if Mr. Smith offers me 5,000, it must be worth ten.

Tennyson was learning not only the art of negotiation, but how to husband his reputation in other ways. Realising perhaps from Dickens's experiences that piracy fattened on popularity, he refused an offer of £20,000 for a lecture tour in the USA in 1862. On the other hand his output never flagged. In 1864 *Enoch Arden* (and other poems) pleased the critics as much as the public, so that the first edition of 60,000 was soon exhausted. His relations with Moxon's successors were however deteriorating, and in 1868 Alexander Strahan, who had paid him £700 for a single poem in the magazine *Good Words*, leased all the existing rights and agreed to publish fresh work for a commission of 10% as before. *The Holy Grail*, a continuation of his treatment of the Arthurian legends begun in the *Idylls*, sold 40,000 copies before publication late in 1869: which boosted his income from poetry in 1870 to over £10,000. He was now able to command almost any sum he liked—£1,000 for a three-stanza poem published in the USA, and £500 for *The Last Tournament* issued in the *Contemporary Review*. In 1874 he transferred his custom to Strahan's partner, H. S. King, and again when the latter sold out to C. Kegan Paul. His last publisher was Macmillan. All of them did well, and relations with Tennyson remained harmonious even when an association came to an end. Kegan Paul noted:

> He was . . . a thorough man of business, and our final parting, at the end of one of our periods of agreement was that we as publishers, and he, as author, took a different view of his pecuniary value.[8]

Tennyson's writing income declined towards the end of his life, due mainly to his devotion to poetic drama, never a source of riches. Even so Macmillan was selling nearly 20,000 copies a year of his collected works shortly before his death; and as late as 1889 he was able to refuse an offer from Sir Adolf Tuck for twelve lines for a Christmas card!

*   *   *   *

Three candidates were short-listed to succeed Tennyson for the Presidency of the Society—George Meredith, Algernon Charles Swinburne, and W. E. H. Lecky, the historian—the final choice falling on Meredith almost without debate.

Although both were poets, Meredith differed deeply from Tennyson in character and career, and he never achieved the latter's popularity and wealth.[9] At heart he was a radical—a philosopher of deep feelings at war with Victorian complacency and sentiment, who expressed himself in an ironical flinty style. A tragic first marriage to Mary, daughter of Thomas Love Peacock, intensified his natural pessimism but generated a poetic masterpiece, *Modern Love*, which in 1862 passed almost unnoticed or at best incurred abuse. Much of his poetry was published at his own cost, while his early novels repelled the critics by their obscurity—*The Shaving of Shagpat* (1856); *The Ordeal of Richard Feverel* (1859); *Evan Harrington* (1860); *Vittoria* (1867)—which earned only £40 when serialised in *The Fortnightly*, January–December 1866; *The Egoist* (1879). Not until the appearance of *Diana of the Crossways* in 1885 did he gain critical approval and public success, but his reputation for difficult though distinguished work remained. He was a writer's writer; and even late in life, as a seer secluded in his cottage on Box Hill in Surrey, recipient of the Order of Merit, whose works were already enshrined in at least one collected edition, with more to follow after his death in 1909, he would say that he had no public.

No author ever lived by acclaim alone, and Meredith supported himself more or less precariously by intermittent journalism—contributing poems to leading periodicals and a weekly letter to the *Ipswich Journal*—and by reading MSS for Chapman & Hall for over 30 years in return for a small regular salary. In this capacity he exercised discernment in encouraging works by writers of the quality of Hardy and Gissing and in rejecting Mrs. Henry Wood's *East Lynne*, though no doubt his employers—who were also his own principal publishers—would not have objected to the occasional unworthy best seller. Surprisingly however he failed to see the merits of Samuel Butler's *Erewhon* or of Bernard Shaw's *Cashel Byron's Profession*. As for his own work, he enjoyed relative success after *Diana*. For instance *One of our Conquerors* (1891) was widely serialised and secured him £1,000 for six years' lease of copyright, though it failed to please the critics. By now however Meredith had come into a modest inheritance, so that adverse notices mattered less than ever. He fulfilled his last public engagement in 1896 and, during his sixteen years as President, he played the smallest possible part in the affairs of the Society. In that respect only did he resemble Tennyson. On the other hand his radicalism appealed to some of the young writers now attracted by membership—Fabians such as Shaw, Wells, and Sidney Webb; but others too—and who, at the turn of the century were beginning to replace the old guard of pioneers, like Colles, Conway, Rider Haggard, Frederick Pollock, Edmund Gosse and Besant himself.

Gosse had worked hard for the Society. A friend of Besant, he had volunteered from the first, joined the Council, served on the Committee, contributed to *The Author*, and done his full share of chores. But he was temperamental and no one was ever quite sure what he might say or do next. Uncertainty about him, however, was not surprising in view of his parentage. His mother, Emily Bowes, was a New England Puritan, and died when Edmund was still a child. His father, Philip Gosse, was a marine zoologist and Plymouth Brother, who never resolved the conflict between Darwin's *Origin of Species* and the Book of Genesis; and Edmund's account of his upbringing in *Father and Son*—a minor classic which George Moore prompted him to write—explains much of the maverick in his character. By profession he was a civil servant—assistant librarian at the British Museum 1867–75, translator to the Board of Trade 1875–1904, and librarian to the House of Lords 1904–14. By inclination he was a man of letters, not a true scholar, but an omniverous reader and prolific author—poet, literary critic and historian, translator—specialising in English literature of the 17th century and in contemporary Scandinavian writing—he was influential, for example, in introducing Ibsen to the English theatre. By nature he was generous and convivial, helpful to young writers, imaginative, impatient, and sensitive to criticism—the latter because the excitement of a subject tended to make him careless of details.

His friendship with other writers was of great service to the Society, especially in the early days—Austin Dobson, Maurice Baring, Max Beerbohm, Thomas Hardy, Henry James, George Moore, R. L. Stevenson, A. C. Swinburne—and he lent his name time and time again to Society business. He was tireless when enthused. He contributed to *Grievances* in 1887, and for the dinner in honour of American authors in 1888, he harried every potential guest to ensure a distinguished attendance. In a letter to James Stanley Little dated 4 July, he wrote:

> Henry James has declined our invitation in a letter of twenty pages in which he vehemently attempts to dissuade us from having a dinner at all . . . I have so strong a conviction that Browning would decline that I have not the heart to ask him.[10]

In time enthusiasm dimmed, and he became disenchanted with Besant's relentless accusations of 'secret profits' and other publishing misdemeanours. At a booksellers' dinner on 26 April 1895 he was reported as saying that 'great authors by their unbridled greediness are killing the goose on which they all live'. This so alarmed the Committee of Management that, at a special meeting two days later, the Secretary was instructed to ask Gosse if he had really said such a terrible thing. Gosse was unrepentant. The report, he replied, was 'very crude and incomplete, but not (so far as it goes) inexact'. Thring was then authorised to issue a printed manifesto taking Gosse to task, and regretting that 'a prominent man of letters . . . should have brought publicly a charge in such offensive terms . . . which he is either unwilling, or unable, to support by a single fact, or a solitary example, into which the Committee could enquire in the discharge of their obvious duty'.

What may seem trivial now was treated by Besant and his colleagues as treachery, on the grounds that it undermined the sanctity of literary property which was the foundation of copyright and the *raison d'être* of the Society of Authors. Unfortunately the affair was unduly inflated and probably marked the end of Gosse's active association with the Society. For his part Besant, while saving his thunder for points of principle, rarely reacted to purely personal irritations—though occasionally he let fly. In a letter to Sprigge dated 8 September 1890, referring to some act of rudeness by Robert Buchanan, poet, novelist, critic and dramatist (described in the *DNB* as of 'combative temperament'), he wrote:

Buchanan is really a very ill conditioned beast. He hates everybody—won't go into a club—and believes that the whole lot of literary men are in league against him.

I do think that authors of all men in the world are the most difficult to deal with. Why is it? I think that is is partly the rather old belief in immortality. Oh Lord! Think of the immortality of the precious novelists of the day! Well, let us work through our programme and then let somebody else fight for them.[10]

*   *   *   *

As Secretary of the Society, G. Herbert Thring was well suited by character and training to play the part of *éminence grise* for nearly 40 years. In the manuscript account he left of his labours he explained that, as a solicitor with experience of company law, he was struck—soon after he started work in March 1892—by the inadequacies of the constitution, even though it had been drawn up by lawyers and accepted by the Board of Trade less than ten years before. Counsel's advice therefore was taken afresh and, for a fee of ten guineas, he sat down 'one holiday morning' in the early summer of 1893, 'when there were many hours before me of unbroken quiet, cleared the table and set to work on my arduous task'. The draft was completed that day, and by July the revised Articles of Association had been duly approved and adopted. In fact Thring made no startling changes, but confined himself to overhauling the existing machinery which provided that:

a) the Council was to be co-existent with the shareholders, who constituted the controlling interest.

b) the Council was to be elected by the Committee of Management, which in turn was self-electing from members of the Council. Two Committee men were to retire each year, but were immediately eligible for re-election.

In short the Society was governed by a beneficent oligarchy which, its enemies said, looked very like a close corporation —home address, the Savile Club. There was substance in this, for however fairly and efficiently the Society was run in the years following the 1893 revision, and however devoted and disinterested the administration, the framing of the constitution in such narrow terms laid the whole organisation open to attack.

At first criticism was indirect and made for the most part by members dissatisfied with the Society's services to them: e.g. those who had accepted bad contracts, or who had placed books without contracts at all, and then rushed for advice too late; or those who expected cases to be fought in the courts without any hope of success; or simply starry-eyed failures who wanted to be converted into best-selling authors. Complaints of this kind, familiar to any professional organisation, formed part of a deeper discontent and were cumulative. In 1896 the Committee made one forward move by electing women to the Council, among them, Charlotte M. Yonge, Mrs. Lynn Linton, and Mrs. Humphry Ward; but that hardly sufficed. AGMs, peaceful too long, became less so; and in 1904 an eccentric member, Hume Nisbet, launched an all-out attack in connection with an article in *The Author* on ghosting, a practice of which he had seemed unaware, and followed this up with a privately printed book,[11] circulated gratis, in which he castigated the Society and all its works. This was one of the preliminaries to a full-scale revision of the constitution, carried out in 1907–8 by Sidney Webb, which *inter alia* made Committee elections open to the entire membership.

Most of Thring's work—characteristic of the office ever since—was divided between advising individual members and conducting campaigns for authors at large. Until the first world war the Society was involved in as many as 100 legal cases a year relating to authors' rights—infringements of copyright, non-fulfilment of contracts, bankruptcies of publishers, etc. The services of the Society's solicitors, Field Roscoe and Company, were therefore continually in demand, so that Thring came to know those partners well, who dealt with Society business. Basil Field, he described, as a careful, though not brilliant, lawyer, a man of tact and pleasant to deal with, and a genial host. Frederick Emery, who took over in 1902, was dour, deliberate and slow. He always got a second opinion when in doubt (too often, Thring thought), and was inclined to miss chances through caution. Eventually Emery was eased out in favour of C. D. Medley, who was quick, determined, and good at identifying the essentials and clarifying complexities.

One of the commonest frauds arose out of vanity publishing—common because this was still a period of jungle warfare in the trade and because there were, and there are still, always authors determined to get into print at any cost. A typical example was the London Literary Society, whose practices were exposed in the June 1890 issue of *The Author*. The routine was all too familiar. Having studied an attractive prospectus, the victim paid an annual subscription of one guinea, and received in return a magnificently engraved receipt or diploma, which permitted him to add the magic letters L.L.S. after his name. On submitting a story, he was sent a reader's report, surprisingly favourable considering that this was his first effort, and advised to place the piece with a publication called *Lloyd's Magazine*. The name sounded good—Lloyd's?

> The editor was very civil, and assured me he would be pleased to print my story, adding casually that some alterations would have to be made . . . before the MS would be ready for the printer's hands, but that half-a-guinea would cover these necessary expenses.

The half-guinea was sent, and in due course the editor wrote again to the effect that the story would appear in the next issue if the author would invest in 24 copies of the magazine at 6d each. He did so, and received a rag entirely composed of contributions obviously obtained in the same way as his own. But that was not the end. Resignation from the L.L.S. brought the reminder that three months' notice was necessary, meanwhile the second year's subscription was due. It was paid. Twelve months later a renewal form arrived but was disregarded. In the following year came a claim for two years' subscription, together with a threatening letter: at which point the L.L.S. went bankrupt. The author considered he had bought his experience cheaply.

The promoters of fraudulent concerns, such as the L.L.S., often survived by starting the trick all over again under another name, or several names, repeating the process until possibly ennui intervened or the law caught up with them. There was rarely any lack of customers. But the most notorious example of vanity publishing, with which the Society of Authors was connected as defendants in a libel action, is related in the next chapter. The plaintiff was one of the founders of the Poetry Society, Galloway Kyle.

A variant of an odd kind was operated by a certain George Bainton of Coventry, said to be a clergyman, who in the summer of 1888 wrote to a large number of established authors, including Alfred Austin, R. D. Blackmore, Hall Caine, Marie Corelli, Wilkie Collins, W. S. Gilbert, George Gissing, Rider Haggard, Thomas Hardy, Henry James, George Meredith, and Charlotte M. Yonge. The message was essentially the same in each case. Mr. Bainton wanted, he said

> to address our young people, in response to their request, by way of a lecture upon the art of composition and the means essential to secure a forcible and interesting style of expression . . . To that end I have taken the very great liberty to write to you and solicit your generous help. May I be permitted to ask whether in early life you gave yourself to any special training with a view to the formation of style, and also whether you can give us any information of your own methods that would aid us to realise . . . the secrets of your own great powers in the use of a clear and forcible English . . . I write to you because your finely conceived novels etc etc . . .

The letter was so flattering and mellifluous that it should have aroused immediate suspicion, but it did not, and Mr. Bainton collected no less than 187 replies which he was further permitted to use 'in the event of my being desirous to put the lecture into printed form'. Two years later each contributor received a letter stating that the lecture had been expanded into a book,[12] 'extract enclosed'. This produced an uproar and complaints poured into the Society's office. Hall Caine expressed the general feeling:

> The man wrote to me to say that he was about to lecture on style to his young men, who were enthusiastic readers of mine, etc., etc., and would take it as an honour, etc., if I would write them a letter on my personal aims and

endeavours, early efforts, etc., with much of the same sort. Of course I was drawn by the silly subterfuge, and when, some time later, a second letter asked permission to print my answer in a pamphlet that was to contain 'the text of the lecture', I was once more made victim. It was not until the book appeared that I realised that the man had written to everybody, that his 'young men' were all fudge, that the book was the thing, and that thanks to the folly of folks like myself, he had got it cheap.[13]

George Bainton was allowed to publish an apologia in *The Author*[14] and pleaded innocence and ignorance. He had not made a penny out of the book, but his 'young men' had greatly benefited. He was hurt by the way he had been treated. 'Is this the spirit in which the Society of Authors is conducted?' Besant replied: '. . . it is one of continued hostility to all who invade or attack the rights of authors'.

*   *   *   *

Campaigning—the other side of the Society's work—was monopolised in the 1890s by the continuing struggle for the revision of copyright. The situation inherited by Thring was that, at home, the 1842 Act was still substantially in force, but so out of date that as long ago as 1878 the Royal Commission had condemned it out of hand.

One of the first moves made by the Society, shortly after its foundation in 1884, was to instruct honorary counsel, E. M. Underdown QC, to draft an amending Bill, but in view of the forthcoming Berne Conference on international copyright to delay promoting it in Parliament. It will be recalled that, in March 1886, the Society's deputation to the Board of Trade had preferred a new domestic Act; but—if that was not considered practicable—agreed to support legislation designed simply to allow the Government to sign the Berne Convention, which it duly did. The deputation left however with the clear impression that the Government would soon be introducing a copyright Bill of its own.

As nothing happened, the Society decided to delay no longer; and the Bill was introduced as a Private Member's measure by Lord Monkswell in the House of Lords on 25 November 1890, second reading on 13 May 1891. It never reached the House of Commons, but the Society kept the subject alive, publishing a booklet, *Copyright Law Reform*, by J. M. Lely, a barrister member, who had worked on the redrafting necessary during the interval after Berne.[15]

At this point came a long awaited development in America, with the passage of the Chace Act, taking effect on 1 July 1891. The USA had not signed the Berne Convention and, despite sustained efforts by a number of American authors and publishers, piracy of British works had been a running sore for over fifty years. As late as June 1890 *The Author* published a long article by Wilkie Collins (who had died the previous year), which took the form of an open letter to an American friend. In one passage he referred to his best-selling novel, *The Woman in White*:

How many unauthorised editions of this one novel of mine—published without my deriving any profit from them—made their appearance in America? I can only tell you, as a basis for calculation, *one* American publisher informed a friend of mine that he has sold one hundred and twenty thousand copies . . . He never sent me sixpence.

Goodbye for the present, Colonel. I must go back to my regular work, and make money for my American robbers, under the sanction of Congress.

The Chace Act was hailed as a victory, and in gratitude Sprigge (Thring's predecessor) had—on behalf of the Society—presented a piece of plate to the Secretary of the American Copyright League—for which incidentally he ingeniously secured exemption from import duty. Yet the Act did not conform to the principles of Berne, in that it offered only limited copyright protection, and conditional upon works by foreign authors being printed in the States. The 'manufacturing' clause had not been in the original Bill, but was inserted as a concession to the printing unions, who would otherwise have blocked the measure.[16]

Meanwhile any fresh move to promote the reform of domestic copyright in Britain was suspended: partly to await clarification of the Chace Act, partly because no one in the House of Commons thought that the subject stood any chance of success. But there was a third reason.

Hitherto Canadian copyright protection had been theoretically covered by Imperial copyright law, such as it was. As explained in Chapter Four, according to the Foreign

Reprints Act 1847 Canada was permitted to import pirated reprints of British works from the USA, provided she levied a duty and remitted part of the proceeds to the author. The results were farcical, nevertheless the law stood. In time the obvious inadequacies of the system, coupled with the sense of independence generated by the British North America Act 1867,[17] prompted the Canadian Government to pass two Copyright Acts of its own: that of 1875 protected British works, if reprinted and republished in Canada, against the importation of foreign reprints; that of 1889 made it a *condition* of copyright that an English work be manufactured in Canada *within one month* after publication elsewhere. This anticipated the provisions of the Chace Act, but whereas the USA was a foreign state, Canada still belonged to the British Empire and was subject to certain overriding legislation incumbent on all the constituent territories. Thus, although the 1875 Act had been ratified by Westminster, not so the Act of 1889, which gave the Society the opportunity to throw its whole weight into opposition.

A deputation called on Lord Ripon at the Colonial Office, a petition bearing 1,500 signatures was organised, and friends in Canada briefed. In 1895 Hall Caine visited the colony at his own expense, and conducted high-level diplomacy with both the Canadian Government and the Colonial Office, producing compromise proposals that however proved unacceptable to the Society. Then Thring took over. Thanks to an introduction by Gilbert Parker,[18] he managed to interview the Canadian Premier, Sir Wilfrid Laurier, when the latter was in London in 1898; and later in the same year he went over to Ottawa himself. While holding no brief for British copyright law, he managed to persuade the Canadians that their proposals were disastrously worse: with the result that the 1889 Act was never 'proclaimed' in Canada and remained a dead letter.[19] At best all these events added up to 'negative success'; but the respite was only temporary for the contretemps with Canada recurred soon after the passage of the Copyright Act 1911 which finally replaced the Act of 1842.

The Society had not acted alone in the negotiations. The Copyright Association, founded in 1872 and mainly supported by publishers, was also—as the name implied—intimately concerned. In general the two bodies worked reasonably well together, but co-operation was never as close as it ought to have been, possibly because the Secretary of the Association, F. R. Daldy, considered copyright as his personal preserve—a sentiment not accepted by either Besant or Thring. Moreover the formation of the Publishers Association in 1896 seemed to spell the end of the Copyright Association, but the move was welcomed by the Society as it promised possibilities of collective bargaining and of alliance in matters of common interest, copyright being one. Within a few months the two organisations agreed on a short amending Bill, limited to correcting specific anomalies in domestic copyright, and entrusted the Parliamentary business to Lord Monkswell as before. Then a new complication arose. In 1898 the Copyright Association launched a rival Bill, designed to amend and consolidate all previous copyright legislation. In theory this was admirable, but as Thring (always a realist) pointed out, it offered so many opportunities for opposition and protraction that it had even less chance than the Society's limited measure. However the Association's Bill was being piloted by Lord Herschell—a survivor of the Royal Commission—and for a time the two Bills ran side by side. They were considered concurrently by a Select Committee of the Lords, and a great deal of evidence taken. Then providentially Lord Herschell died, his place being taken by Lord Thring (Herbert Thring's uncle), who persuaded the two contenders to withdraw their separate Bills and allow him to draft a new one[20] which they could both support.

As a result a compromise measure was ordered to be printed on 24 July 1899, and in the main covered three aspects: copyright proper (the right of multiplying copies of books), performing right (the right of publicly performing dramatic and musical works), and lecturing right. The Bill also sought to extend copyright to the life of the author plus 30 years. Thring wanted 50 years, to accord with the practice in a number of other countries, but not perpetual copyright, a notion desired—among others—by Mark Twain, who argued the case in person before the Select Committee. The Bill, presented by Lord Monkswell, passed the Lords in 1899 and again in 1900, but failed—like its predecessor—to reach the Commons. However, at the opening of Parliament on 14 February 1901, the King's Speech contained the phrase, 'legislation has been prepared for amending the law of literary copyright'; and on the same day Gerald Balfour, President of the Board of Trade, said he would bring in a Bill at an early date. Time however slipped by. In desperation the Society prepared to present the Minister with a petition; but the plan fizzled out, and finally *The Author* had regretfully to report that copyright reform seemed 'to have died of senile decay'.

CHAPTER EIGHT

The first literary agents. The Society of Authors versus
Galloway Kyle. Popular journalism after *c*. 1880. Disap-
pearance of the 3-volume novel. Gissing and the 'commercialisation of literature'. Net Book Agreement as a firm
basis for the royalty system. The opportunism of Bennett
and Wells

IN HIS BOOK, *The Author's Empty Purse & The Rise of the
Literary Agent*,[1] James Hepburn speculates as to why the
Society of Authors failed to establish an effective literary agency
at the outset of its career. The point is valid and needs clarification. It may be argued that, following the example of the
Société des Gens de Lettres, any authors' organisation in Britain
ought to have included—as a prime duty—the placing of
manuscripts, the drafting of agreements, and the collection of
income, on behalf of its members. Although this activity was not
overlooked, the problems confronting the infant Society in the
1880s were such that they made the administration of an agency
almost impossible, at any rate as a regular part of its work.

Soon after its foundation the Society condensed its main aims
into three—the definition and defence of literary property, the
reform of domestic copyright, and the promotion of international copyright. The first of these influenced everything else, since
it meant having to drive home to Parliament and the public what
the fundamental rights of authorship were: that, by his work, an
author creates a piece of property which—though intangible or
incorporeal—is as real in law and fact as, say, a house or a
parcel of land, and requiring no less care and respect in any
business connected with it. In the 1880s this seemingly
incontrovertible statement was not properly understood or
accepted,[2] even by many authors, despite 175 years of copyright
legislation: which explains why the Society had to concentrate
on campaigning for first principles. This commitment absorbed
a large part of its slender resources—in terms both of money
and the crusading skill and zeal of Besant and his handful of
helpers—almost till the end of the century. As related earlier, it

involved exerting continual pressure upon Parliament, publicising and criticising the machinery of publishing (e.g. in the booklets, *The Cost of Production* and *The Methods of Publication*, and in innumerable articles in *The Author*), exposing abuses, etc: to which was added the daily task of advising members on individual problems, vetting contracts, recommending reliable publishers, and whenever necessary taking legal action.

From this it is obvious that—apart from reading manuscripts (a service eventually dropped)—agency work had to be omitted from the ordinary routine and supplied separately. This was to be the role played by William Morris Colles, barrister and journalist, an early member of the Society's Council and Committee of Management, and friend of Besant. He also stood in as Secretary during a short interregnum and was responsible for *Literature and the Pension List*, one of the Society's booklets mentioned earlier. Late in 1890 it was announced in *The Author* that Colles had been appointed Hon. Sec. of the Authors' Syndicate, operating from his own offices in the same building, and on the same floor, as the Society at 4 Portugal Street. The Syndicate was independent, except that it proposed to serve only members of the Society and to sell their serial rights in return for a small commission. Business however expanded fast, and quite soon the Syndicate was offering a full range of agency services ... 'it concludes agreements, collects royalties, examines and passes accounts, and generally relieves members of the trouble of managing business details'. This last point was underlined. 'The business of the Syndicate is not to *advise* members of the Society, but to *manage* their affairs for them.'[3]

Colles was respected personally. He was a friend of the publisher, William Heinemann, who normally disliked agents (A. P. Watt in particular) and whose biographer described Colles as 'a big, burly, bearded lawyer, with a wheezy infectious laugh—a sort of well-spoken, decent-minded, entirely reputable, nineteenth-century Falstaff'.[4] Professionally however Colles proved a disappointment. Although he acted for a time for several successful writers, including Arnold Bennett, Eden Phillpotts, A. E. W. Mason, and Somerset Maugham, he failed to keep their custom, the relationship usually ending in ill humour. The Society too became increasingly dissatisfied. Early in the 1900s it ceased to advertise the Syndicate in *The Author* and then severed the connection altogether. Late in 1909 it supported Maugham in a court case brought by Colles over a claim for commission. The jury found for the plaintiff, who was awarded half-commission (£21 10s) plus costs, a judgement of which the Committee of Management was at pains to express its public disapproval.[5]

Colles's comparative failure at a time when literary agency was a pioneer industry had a dual effect, for it lost both Colles himself and the Society a unique opportunity to establish a highly profitable business when other agents were making their names and fortunes. In fact the Society made a fresh start on a slightly different basis when, in 1912, it set up its Collection Bureau—following the adoption of the statutory licence period (of 50 years after an author's death) in the Copyright Act 1911. Since that date the Society has acted for a number of literary estates, not in open competition as a placing agent for the work of living writers, but usually in response to a request by an author nearing the end of his life, or by his executors and heirs. An early example was the estate of R. L. Stevenson, a later one, Bernard Shaw.

Colles was by no means the first of his kind. The origins of literary agency are explored by James Hepburn in an interesting section of his book, in which he refers to a variety of 'precursors', both printed and personal: e.g. the writers' guides and aids to authorship, such as *The Search for a Publisher*, first issued in 1855; the informal exertions of men like John Forster on behalf of Dickens and G. H. Lewes on behalf of George Eliot, each operating as a business consultant and intermediary, but unpaid; the often disinterested advice of publishers' readers, such as George Meredith who proved so helpful to Thomas Hardy and George Gissing; the commercial theatre and lecture agents, the latter creating a prosperous market for British writers on tour in America; and the various press agencies that sought and placed advertisements, and supplied contributions (features, stories, serials, etc) usually on a syndication basis, i.e. joint publication by national, provincial and overseas newspapers, the author receiving a fixed fee per thousand words.

It is generally accepted that the first true literary agent was A. P. Watt, and that he started on his own about the year 1875.[6] His background was typical of others operating in the middle reaches of the trade—first in bookselling, then in publishing where as brother-in-law and partner of Alexander Strahan he learned to handle every aspect of the business, including negotiations with authors, among whom he made a number of friends. When Strahan's firm faded in the early 1870s, Watt broke away and used his connections to set up as an agent offering a variety of services—advertising, publishing, representation, and valuing literary property—and continued in this collective capacity for several years. As we have seen, he published the first twelve issues of *The Author* (1890–1) and sold advertising space for it; but this must have by then become a secondary occupation, for he was already actively representing authors, Wilkie Collins and Besant among the first, and very soon he was doing nothing else. In an interview published in *The Bookman* in October 1892, he recalled:

> When I started to sell copyrights some years ago, the literary agent was an unknown factor in the world of letters. My friend, Dr. George MacDonald, asked me to sell his stories, which I did—and I think I may say with success ... At the time I was doing this for him, it occurred to me that other authors might be glad to be relieved of what Mr. Walter Besant has called 'the intolerable trouble of haggling and bargaining', and one author recommending my services to another—for I never advertise, you know—I gradually came to occupy the position I now hold.

His remark about 'not advertising' was disingenuous for, in and after 1893 he published a booklet entitled *Letters addressed to A. P. Watt*, in which one well-known writer after another paid tribute to Watt's energy and acumen, and to the way he had increased their incomes: among them, Rider Haggard, Thomas Hardy, Anthony Hope Hawkins, Rudyard Kipling, and Stanley Weyman. Praise also came from some publishers for, as Watt was careful to point out, no bargain is worth anything in the long run, if it benefits only one party.

Watt was followed by J. B. Pinker[7] in 1896, Curtis Brown[8] in 1899, and many others, good and bad, so that in the centenary year of Watt's enterprise over 80 agencies were listed in *The Writers and Artists' Yearbook*. Their individual careers are incidental to this book, but clearly Watt established literary agency as an essential element in the sequence of relationships within the book trade. It constituted a fresh division of labour that, at its simplest, benefited certain authors for the reasons he advanced: but which in succeeding years gained steadily in importance with the development of new media of communication (film, radio, television, etc.) and the consequent growth in scope, complexity, and value of subsidiary rights associated with publication.

The attitude of most publishers towards literary agency was at first ambivalent and long remained so. Some, like William Heinemann, felt it was a parasitical employment and that Watt was the chief parasite.[9] Writing in the *Athenaeum* in November 1893 and in *The Author* in October 1901, he committed himself to the view that to be an agent required no special qualifications, no capital even, but only sharp wits, a suave manner, and plenty of push; and that his intrusion between author and publisher worked to the advantage of neither. Bias of this kind is always unconvincing, and Heinemann's remarks must have seemed so even then, for they could be made to refer to almost any business intermediary who must necessarily stand or fall by his own ability—by knowing the market, estimating the potential of what is being sold, finding the right buyer, and agreeing a price acceptable to both sides without losing the confidence of either. Without these accomplishments, no agent in any trade can hope to survive.

As for the literary agent, the case was put bluntly by Curtis Brown a few years later:

Much that has been written about the literary agent has been futile, because the writers have not understood that authors can be divided into two classes: first, those whose work the publisher doesn't particularly want; and second, those whose work the publisher does want, or would want if he knew of it; and that it is only with the second class that a sound literary agent has, or should have, to do. Unless an author's work gives decided promise, he is of little interest to the publisher, or to the first-class agent. No agent, except one who takes 'retainers', can afford to spend much time over him. He can generally find a market for his work as well as a good agent, and better than a bad agent; and he can afford a more thorough canvass than either ... The only agent who really counts, either for the author, or with the publisher, or with his own banker, is the one who sells the kind of work for which publishers are in competition, and who takes advantage of that competition to get the best market price for the author.[10]

The attitude of the Society of Authors was at first as ambivalent as that of the publishers. Colles apart, it was not in open competition with agents, yet relations were never easy. Personally Besant had nothing but praise for Watt; nonetheless both he and Thring (who succeeded him as editor) filled *The Author* with dire warnings against doubtful agents, and always found space for correspondents who had suffered at their hands. The view was held that agents sat on both sides of the fence, and that they were 'not so much authors' agents as agents' agents and publishers' agents'—a view supported in *The Author* in 1911 by Bernard Shaw, then a prominent member of the Society's Council and Committee of Management, who concluded that agents ought to pay their authors a percentage of the annual profits from all the books they placed. At best successful agents were tolerated, but caution always crept in, so that the Literary Agency Agreement issued by the Society in 1912 advised members to limit any agreement with an agent to 12 months; the latter to act for all rights but to complete no contract without the author's specific permission and signature, and thereafter to collect moneys due in return for a fixed commission of 10 per cent.

Behind all these objurgations lay the fact that, in the early 1900s, authors were still being harassed by dubious characters of many kinds in the book and periodical trade; and that agency, in whatever form, was a profitable area for such people. A crooked agent, no less than an honest one, offered apparently a similar range of services—from reading a MS to placing it with a publisher. But while the crook exacted 'fees' and 'expenses', culminating possibly in vanity publication paid for by the author, the honest agent supplied advice and aid (even cash in advance, as Pinker did for Bennett and Conrad), but got nothing back before his commission due under the contract. Furthermore good agents filtered the flow of unpublishable work, enlarged the market by suggesting themes and treatments, and often preserved good relations between authors and publishers by relieving them of the awkward necessity of bargaining—all this compatible with exploiting (in the best sense) literary output to the full. However, as Curtis Brown said, the number of agents of proved worth able to invest in beginners was small. Thus, with rare exceptions, they were of use only to successful authors, serving them professionally like solicitors or stockbrokers, and allowing them time to write and earn. The result was that the great majority of authors, who had to combine writing with some other form of employment in order to make a living, preferred to handle their own affairs; and, if members of the Society, they relied upon its officers for legal and business advice, without payment other than their annual subscription. The activities of agents did not however inhibit successful authors from joining or staying with the Society, which frequently found itself advising ' both parties, besides operating as a powerful pressure group operating on behalf of authors at large. That situation is unchanged today.

To sum up. The initial suspicions of literary agency took many years to dispel. In some sense it was a problem incapable of solution for, by virtue of his situation, an agent is always open to disappoint an author, while a publisher will resent any move to transfer a profitable or promising writer from his list, or any feeling that he is being compelled to pay over the odds. The columns of *The Author* and *The Bookseller* have never been free of complaints of this kind. Moreover, despite pressure from the Society,[11] and because of their own innate competitiveness and liability to split up into new partnerships, agents were for many years reluctant to combine for their own advantage: i.e. to draw up a code of practice, enforce standards, offer common ground for consultation, and present the trade with some general guarantee of integrity. Raymond Savage tried twice to start such an organisation between the wars, but without success; and it was only in 1975 that the Association of Authors' Agents was formed under the chairmanship of Mark Hamilton of A. M. Heath, although even then the largest firm, Curtis Brown, held out.

Meanwhile any failure (such as the dramatic collapse of the Pinker agency in the 1940s), or any hint of malpractice so prevalent in the early days, served to sharpen distrust. Thring was implacable in his antagonism, and in Galloway Kyle he was presented with a classic case that took 16 years to bring to a head.

It all began in 1902 when Thring first became aware of the existence of the Authors' Association. Naturally he was suspicious of anything that seemed like a rival to the Society; but advice to authors, it transpired, was only one of several services offered by this organisation. The prospectus was ambiguous. It denied that the Association was a literary agency, yet charged a commission for placing MSS. It also undertook typing and duplicating, and read work for a fee. Above all its existed 'to assist and advise the beginner in literature'. Thring suspected the worst. He detected that the President, the Countess of Aberdeen, had already resigned; and that her resignation had left the Council of the Association without a quorum. He felt sure that Galloway Kyle, advertised as General Secretary and Editor, was the sole operator and that his office at 62 Paternoster Row was a 'front'. However little further was heard of the Association which ceased trading in 1906.

Kyle was then associated with the founding of the Poetry Society in 1909, and later became editor of the Society's journal, *The Poetry Review*; and there is no doubt that he gave good service over many years both to the Society and the cause of poetry at large. But he courted trouble by simultaneously carrying on a publishing business under the name of Erskine MacDonald, which included *The Poetry Review* in its list, and by mixing philanthropy with sharp practice. Ultimately Thring went for him in an article in the April 1918 issue of *The Author*. He reported that many members of the Society had cause to complain of Kyle, and that during 1917 the Society had taken up no less than 14 cases against him, mostly for non-payment of royalties. Thring also reproduced a letter from Kyle (as MacDonald) asking an author, who had sent him a MS, to subscribe for one year to *The Poetry Review* and purchase at least 'four volumes in my shilling series which indicates the quality of matter accepted, and the style of production, facilitating later discussion of terms'. Thring commented:

> It is impossible to conceive any of the better-known firms of publishers refusing to consider an author's MS until the author had purchased a certain number of books published by the firm.

He then flatly accused Kyle of shady behaviour by using his connection with the Poetry Society to get in touch with young poets, anxious for publicity; and then, as Erskine MacDonald, arranging to publish their work on highly unsatisfactory terms.

The article compelled Kyle to launch a libel action against the Society, the case being tried before Lord Hewart, Lord Chief Justice, and a special jury. Kyle made no bones about his activities, but attributed his troubles to inefficient assistance in the office, and hedged when, in cross-examination, it was put to him that there were some 30 or 40 instances where he never had any proper agreement, never kept proper accounts, never answered letters, and was involved in cases where he never paid sixpence until summonsed. Without leaving the box, the jury found for the Society, with costs.

It was a fine victory but an expensive one, for Kyle was unable to pay, and the Society had to ask members for a special contribution to settle the bill. As Ian Hay Beith, chairman of the Committee of Management at the time, said: 'to extinguish Galloway Kyle, the Society has temporarily extinguished itself'. The experience however was salutary for two reasons. First, it prompted the Society to set aside funds to fight large-scale actions in defence of principle. Secondly, it exposed more effectively than in any other fashion the related dangers of crooked agency and vanity publishing.

*   *   *   *

One of Heinemann's complaints against literary agents was that they demeaned literature by commercialising it. Similar accusations were levelled against the Society, whose spokesmen retorted sharply that if commercialisation meant paying a fair price for a book or an article, where was the cause for complaint? The servant was worthy of his hire, and authors had been hired for too little for too long. Moreover, who could seriously say that writers of the stature of Alexander Pope, Charles Dickens, George Eliot, or Alfred Tennyson, had lowered their artistic standards by keeping a strict eye on business? Edmund Gosse's remark to booksellers in 1895 that 'great authors by their unbridled greed are killing the goose on which they all live' was directed at Hall Caine—one of Heinemann's most profitable investments—but was generally written off as a piece of personal spite.

On the other hand it has been demonstrated time and again that good writing often sells badly, and that good writers have suffered neglect because they refused to compromise. Meredith suffered in this way and so did George Gissing, who characterised the problem in his novels, notably in *New Grub Street*, published by Smith Elder in 1891. His villain is the writer who deliberately 'writes down' to make a comfortable living, while his heroes are driven to the wall. Gissing was a depressive deeply concerned about artistic integrity. His attitude—sharpened by poverty and private unhappiness, duly reflected in his work—was actuated at a deeper level by awareness of social and cultural change. As a thinker he was both in advance of his age and astern of it. In advance because, despite the façade of national prosperity and stability, he recognised that Victorian society was becoming devalued as a consequence of the Industrial Revolution. Since the 1850s, when town dwellers began to outnumber country people, manufacturing industry and conurbia had displaced the traditional economy founded on the land, and was dehumanising personal relationships by sheer pressure of population and by the stultifying nature of industrial work. Fresh developments in mass communication deriving from these changes contributed, in Gissing's view, to the destruction of the artist; but instead of meeting the challenge—as John Ruskin and William Morris did—he confined himself to recording it and retreated into pessimism: in which sense he may be accounted 'astern' of his age. His life was short and sad. He struggled ceaselessly to make a living as a professional author, but never earned more than £300 a year, and in 1897 when already accepted in critical circles, his income fell to £101 13s 4d. He died in 1903 at the early age of 46.

*   *   *   *

Journalism—the mass communication which Gissing so deplored—had been transformed since the repeal of three restrictive measures, the Advertisement Tax in 1853, the Newspaper Stamp Duty in 1855, and the Paper Duty in 1861. The immediate result was a sharp drop in the price of newspapers, most dailies falling to 1d, some to $\frac{1}{2}$d, accompanied by a significant rise in circulations and a proliferation of provincial papers, many of them supplied with national news by syndicating agencies such as Tillotson's of Bolton. During the Franco-Prussian war the *Daily Telegraph* was selling 200,000 copies, far ahead of *The Times*, which before 1855 outsold all the other dailies put together. Evening papers came into their own, e.g. the *Pall Mall Gazette* (1865) launched by George Smith, the *Evening News* (1881) and the *Star* (1888); while weeklies and monthlies, some well established in the first half of the century, continued to find a ready public. Fiction magazines, such as the *Family Herald* and the *London Journal* appealed in large numbers to a public anxious to forget the realities of everyday life; while religion always made money. In 1881 it was said that the eight most popular religious weeklies sold almost 1$\frac{1}{2}$

million copies between them. Although the Education Act of 1870 failed to improve taste and morals to the extent hoped, it certainly increased literacy: one by-product being the success of 'juveniles', notably the *Boy's Own Paper* (1879), which enjoyed a circulation of 200,000, thanks to astute editing and the employment of first-class writers such as Jules Verne and Conan Doyle.

Although in the serious periodical field the *Cornhill* started with a dramatic sale of over 100,000 copies, it failed to hold that figure, and had to compete with *Macmillan's Magazine*, both founded in 1860, also with the older *Edinburgh Review*, *Quarterly* and *Maga*, and with a variety of new ventures including the *Fortnightly Review* (1865), the *Contemporary Review* (1866), and the *Nineteenth Century* (1877). Nor was that the sum of middle class leisure reading. Although part-publications (so favoured by Dickens) declined, the patronage of lending libraries, and the attractions of Christmas annuals, miscellanies, and railway bookstall literature, were fully sustained: so that between 1870 and 1900 the number of newspapers rose from 1390 to 2448, while magazines increased from 626 to 2446.

However the real explosion in print occurred in popular journalism, and was detonated principally by three men: by George Newnes in 1880 with *Tit-Bits*, a penny miscellany of 16 pages; soon followed by Alfred Harmsworth with *Answers to Correspondents*, and by Cyril Pearson with *Pearson's Weekly*. These and a crop of other publications in similar vein captured the mass market of literate but unintellectual readers, who were less interested in long stories and straight articles than in brief anecdotes, vivid serials, and short snappy paragraphs on all kinds of subjects, part-news, part-diversion, backed by competitions, prizes, and other circulation-boosting stunts. In 1894 Harmsworth, with his brother Harold, moved into daily journalism by revamping the *Evening News*. Two years later they launched the *Daily Mail*, a new 'morning' aimed at men and women in any section of society, too busy, too tired, or otherwise averse to concentrate on solid reading and pedestrian presentation. Within three years the paper was selling half-a-million copies and growing fast. It was the first of the mass-circulation dailies, setting the pattern for the future, and profiting from all the technological inventions and improvements then becoming available or already to hand—mechanical typesetting and rotary printing, news coverage by telephone and telegraph, and distribution by a first-class railway service, then at the peak of its efficiency.

The impact of the 'new journalism', as Matthew Arnold called it, was bound to be felt in the book trade, although it was not the only factor. Arnold, a pillar of popular education, had longed campaigned against the high prices of new books and accused the libraries of responsibility for these prices by providing publishers with a safe sale for small editions. 'It is a machinery for the multiplication and protection of bad literature, and for keeping good books dear.' While reprints were relatively inexpensive, they took a long time to appear after first publication, and Arnold rejected other cheap literature, 'hideous and ignoble of aspect, like the tawdry novels which flare in the bookshelves of our railway-stations'. Instead of new novels which had stuck at 10s 6d per volume for 50 years or more and issued in 3-volume editions ('three-deckers'), Arnold wanted the 3s book; and in 1904 Mudie's and Smith's libraries virtually obliged him by refusing to buy any more fiction except in single-volume editions at about half the current price. In the book trade the walls of Jericho fell like thunder all during the 1890s. The 'three-decker' vanished, and new novels—generally published at 6s—sold in thousands. In 1900 Marie Corelli's *The Master Christian* had a pre-publication printing of 75,000 copies. The price of reprints was slashed: cloth copies to 3s 6d and 2s 6d, paper copies to 6d and 7d. Abridgements also took the field. W. T. Stead, who had made history when editor of the *Pall Mall Gazette* by high-lighting the trade in the prostitution of young girls, and had gone to prison by 'buying' a sample girl, condensed favourite novels to about one-sixth of their original length, and sold them by the million at 1d each. George Newnes had similar success with unabridged texts. So reduced such books were cheap and nasty in appearance, closely printed with cut margins and difficult to read, but they did meet the demand by a fast growing population, determined to dissolve some of the barriers of education, and mentally on the make. Moreover the design of low-priced books was soon improved by J. M. Dent with his series of Temple Shakespeare and other classics selling at 1s each, followed by his famous Everyman Library, the most comprehensive investment in serious publishing for the masses before the advent of Penguins and Pelicans shortly before the second world war.[12]

Inevitably the dramatic fall in book prices had its effect upon the structure of the trade. It will be recalled that in 1852 the then Booksellers' Association (a combination of publishers and booksellers) had been defeated in its attempt to regulate retail prices, principally by 'free traders' (some prominent authors among them) who considered that control was an inadmissible interference with private enterprise. Since that date, retailers had commonly allowed customers up to 25 per cent discount off published prices—one reason why the latter had been inflated to compensate for this ruinous practice, which operated to the detriment of genuine booksellers competing with any sort of shop that undersold books to attract buyers for other goods. Of course publishers wanted stable and profitable bookselling, as much as booksellers themselves, but none seemed able to get rid of these retail discounts until Frederick Macmillan persuaded the trade otherwise.

Before describing the campaign that preceded the Net Book Agreement of 1899, I must refer to the remarkable efforts of John Ruskin to achieve the same goal. By 1870 Ruskin was in his fifty-first year, a distinguished critic, and an acknowledged authority on art and design. For some time however he had not been content to confine himself to aesthetics, but had been writing and lecturing on subjects revolving around the relationship of art and society: which led him to think about education, organisation of labour, function of money, and human incentives in industry. Hitherto, with George Smith as a friend, he had entrusted his books to Smith Elder & Co; but with the publication of *Fors Clavigera*, a monthly letter addressed 'to the workmen and labourers of Great Britain', starting in January 1871, he made a break. Disliking trade terms and discounts, he insisted that *Fors* be published at a fixed price (7d), but that the bookseller was free to *add* his own profit thereto. This proposition was not acceptable to Smith or to the booksellers, who promptly boycotted his works. Ruskin however was wealthy and could afford to ride the storm: which he did with the aid of one, George Allen, a carpenter and joiner, to whom Ruskin had taught drawing at the Working Men's College in the 1850s. Allen had become one of Ruskin's most ardent disciples and, as agent and distributor, agreed to handle all the business from his own modest home at Keston in Kent.

At first the going was hard. Nearly everything had to be sold by post, and for a time Ruskin toyed with the idea of disposing of all his earlier copyrights by auction. Allen dissuaded him, gradually took over all the previous titles from Smith Elder, and so expanded the business that the office and warehouse had to be moved—first to Orpington, and then to London. Meanwhile, in 1882, a break came in the boycott, and eventually Ruskin and the booksellers made peace: to the extent that, in exchange for selling his books over the counter, Ruskin made one concession. While the published price was to remain firm, a fixed trade discount might be deducted instead of the profit margin being added—which made it in effect one of the earliest examples of a net book agreement, though for a time it remained in isolation.[13]

Eight years later, in 1890, Macmillan proposed that books be divided into two classes: 'net books', i.e. those sold strictly at the published price, and 'subject books', on which discount might be given to the customer at the bookseller's discretion. The idea was broadcast in *The Bookseller* and the *Pall Mall Gazette*, but found little favour. Macmillan was not dismayed. He persuaded an eminent economist, Professor Alfred Marshall of Cambridge University, to allow his new work, *Principles of Economics*, to be priced at 12s 6d net and distributed to the trade on condition that the booksellers retailed it at that price and no less. At the same time Macmillan abolished the old anomaly of 25 copies for 24 (or 13 counting as 12 or $12\frac{1}{2}$). Any bookseller who contravened these terms had his account closed. The experiment succeeded. Most booksellers, and the most important wholesaler, Simpkin Marshall, conformed: so that Macmillan was able to issue an increasing number of net books—16 in 1890, 136 in 1897, and so on. Other publishers followed suit, though as yet the number of new net books remained small.

In January 1895 the entire outlook was altered by a resolution passed by the newly formed Associated Booksellers of Great Britain and Ireland to support the net scheme: a move which prompted the publishers to set up their own Association a year later (January 1896) as a means of advancing the proposal from their own side. The two organisations then drafted and redrafted the constituent clauses, keeping in touch with the Society of Authors as they went along, and finally arrived at the Net Book Agreement of 1899. The only serious objection sustained by the Society had been to the coercion of individual booksellers, who might be forced out of business if they refused to conform. This objection was disposed of however by the fact that 90 per cent of the booksellers in the UK (1,106 out of

1,270) accepted the basic provision whereby no discount would be allowed to customers on books priced above 6s.[14]

A new era had begun. For authors it proved a particular boon, since there was now a firm price for each book on which to base the royalty scale. For publishers and booksellers it was not always plain sailing, due to occasional difficulties that threatened the Agreement: for example the so-called 'Book War' caused by the exertions of *The Times* to halt its declining circulation. The main battle was fought round The Times Book Club, a new lending library that offered the public little used (library) copies of net books at heavy discounts. The Publishers Association regarded this as a contravention of the Agreement, and some fierce exchanges followed between the PA representatives and C. F. Moberly Bell, the business manager of *The Times*. Peace was not declared until September 1908, soon after the newspaper had passed into the hands of Lord Northcliffe (Alfred Harmsworth), but the Net Book Agreement remained intact.

*   *   *   *

While Gissing rejected the media explosion on the grounds that it lowered standards, few other writers could afford to take such a hard line, even if they believed it, nor did it always follow that quality was depreciated by quantity. Some highly talented writers, revelling in the openings offered by popular journalism and mass publishing, reached first rank; and, by the prospects before them, were inspired to do so. Two names illustrate the point—Arnold Bennett and H. G. Wells. Both came from lower middle class homes and had to endure hard beginnings. Both fought their way into the profession by concentrated effort and by seizing every opportunity that offered: to the extent that, in terms of sheer output, they bore comparison with almost any mass-manufacturer of words.

Arnold Bennett was born in 1867, eldest son of a solicitor in Hanley, one of the Potteries towns in Staffordshire. At the age of 21 he left his father's office to better himself in London, and abandoned the narrowly Methodist background of his youth. He found work in a lawyer's office in Lincoln's Inn Fields at 25s a week and became an efficient member of the staff, though he never passed a law exam. He did not want to. Instead he learned shorthand, read voraciously, dabbled in books, absorbed sights, sounds and facts like a sponge, and sidled into journalism by winning a *Tit-Bits* competition for £20. In 1893 he left the law to become assistant-editor of *Woman*, a mildly militant periodical, took shares in the business, and eventually ran the paper himself until his resignation in 1900. During that time he learned his trade as a journalist, in his own office and as a freelance, writing a mass of miscellanea at all literary levels—from hints on housekeeping to a story published in *The Yellow Book*. As a reviewer he got to know Wells, who became a lifelong friend, also Eden Phillpotts, who wrote an appreciative notice of Bennett's first novel, *A Man from the North*, published in 1898 by John Lane on a 5% royalty. Phillpotts, one of the most prolific novelists of any age, pouring out work at the rate of half-a-million words a year, set the pace for Bennett, who decided to write stories, produce them in quantity and sell them well. However it took him a little time to get into his stride. He let a serial, *The Ghost*, go for only £75 to Tillotson's, from whom he had been accustomed to buy work as an editor in the past; and he parted too cheaply with his next full-length work, *The Grand Babylon Hotel*, published in volume form by Chatto in 1903.

Even so by 1900 he was earning over £600 a year, and felt he was sufficiently established to give up staff journalism for full-time authorship; but he needed business advice. Two years earlier he had engaged W. M. Colles as his agent, but on Wells's advice had transferred in 1902 to Pinker, with whom he remained. Bennett was working at a furious rate, turning out two or three novels a year, serials, plays, articles, and other work, and sustained this flow at least until the outbreak of the first world war. For several years he treated Pinker—as some others did—as his banker, drawing £50 a month irrespective of earnings, and only paying interest (at 5%) when the 'overdraft' exceeded £1,000. But Bennett proved an excellent investment. In 1912 he earned £16,000 and later, in his best year, he attained £20,000. The relationship with Pinker was friendly and fruitful far beyond the strict confines of finance, although the assurance of a large income made everything else possible. It not only gave him the freedom to write without undue worry, though he always kept in close touch with Pinker's business propositions; but it enabled him to live a highly sophisticated life—to travel, take a flat in Paris, buy a yacht, cultivate a large and varied company of friends, and marry an unsuccessful French actress, to whom he proved a not very successful English husband, *qua* husband.

This is not the place to pursue the progress of his career which, by any standard, was a story of success, ably interpreted by his biographers, Reginald Pound and Margaret Drabble. His permanent contributions to English literature must include the Five Towns quartet, and other major novels such as *The Old Wives' Tale* and *Riceyman Steps*, which have prompted Miss Drabble to comment:

> Documentary reinforced by indignant emotion is his forte, and I at times find the protests about social conditions more moving than Dickens's, and his irony more delicately judged.[15]

He observed everything and wasted no experience; and in two early works it amused him to tell the world how to make money as a writer and how he himself had done it.[16] But his addiction to work and delight in the results, financial and literary, yielded a mass of ephemera which he generally recognised as such. With a few exceptions he was a failure as a dramatist and he had no feel for films, but he was a telling journalist and an influential critic, whose reputation withstood all assaults; so that, for example, he was able to command £5,000 a year for his regular column in the *Evening Standard*.

After his death in 1931, he left an estate valued at £36,600, exclusive of certain securities, copyrights and manuscripts: not as large a sum as had been anticipated, but then Bennett rarely stinted himself, his relations or his friends.[17] He was, in fine, an outstanding example of a dedicated artist in an era of literary boom, uninhibited by any consideration about the 'commercialisation of literature'.

* * * *

In the case of H. G. Wells this same attitude took a yet more positive form, since communication with the mass was an essential element in his make-up as an author. Wells was born at Bromley in Kent in 1866. His father was a shopkeeper and part-time cricket professional; his mother later became housekeeper at Uppark, the home of the Featherstonhaughs, near Midhurst in Sussex. Although Wells's family background and upbringing were less Puritanical than Bennett's, both men belonged to the same social stratum, and both had to work their way through years of drudgery as young men. For a time in the 1880s, after failing to qualify at the Normal School of Science in South Kensington, Wells was very poor indeed. Nonetheless he forced his way forward by intensive application and succeeded in supporting himself by a series of teaching jobs, supplemented by forays into journalism, writing science snippets for the popular press. Despite ill-health, his cerebral energy was phenomenal, and his speculations in the realm of science fiction made his name almost overnight. Whereas in 1893 he was publishing modest textbooks on biology, by 1897 works such as *The Time Machine, The Stolen Bacillus, The Island of Dr. Moreau, The Plattner Story*, and *The Invisible Man* had transformed him into the English counterpart of Jules Verne.

But where to place him in the literary universe? Was he a man of letters at all? Or simply a scientist with a vivid imagination who fascinated his readers without any pretensions of style? This was a question that he answered on his own by propelling himself into the literary world: partly through his natural ability to make friends (and enemies); and partly because 'the new journalism', popular and serious periodicals alike, was riding as high for him as for Bennett and other writers in fiction, especially in short stories.

Wells's income rose from £380 in 1893 to £792 in 1895, the year that W. E. Henley, editor of *The New Review*, paid him £100 for the series rights of *The Time Machine* (first called *The Time Travellers*), subsequently published in volume form by Heinemann on a royalty of 15% and an advance of £50; but these were still early days and modest terms for Wells. In 1896 he earned over £1,000 and began to employ Pinker as his agent. Unlike Bennett however Wells was a difficult client. He soon found fault with Pinker and discarded him, and then carried on intermittent campaigning against him and other agents for years. With publishers he took the line that the harder the bargain he drove, the harder the publisher would have to work to sell the book, *ergo* good business for both sides. In reality he suffered from a deep-seated suspicion of almost everyone with whom he had to do business, a characteristic that lasted all his life. It made him few friends in the book trade, and the number of his publishers was legion. The following extracts from correspondence in *The Author* tell the story: In May 1913 he wrote:

I never pay for advertisement or corrections, never allow an agency clause in my agreements (I generally don't do business through agents), always take 25 per cent upon a 6s book, always exact a big cheque on account of royalties (rather larger than what is caused by the certain sales), always reserve the right to publish a cheap edition at less than 1s 3d at the end of two years, and never suffer a 13 as 12 clause ... In the past I was not so wise as I am now; I left nearly all my business to an agent. I am still encumbered with his slovenly and disadvantageous agreements. Now I do business with an agent that suits me. None of them is good all round, and none can be trusted to 'handle' the whole of the author's affairs ... The ideal thing for an author to do is to fix up a standing agreement on the lines I have given above with a big honest solvent firm, give his books to an agent to serialise—and think no more of these things.

He followed this in June with

In the last month I have had three separate firms of agents 'butting in' to my business ... I know of no way of stopping this increasing nuisance of agents, except by proclaiming clearly that, like all sensible authors, I do not employ agents except for specific jobs.

This roused Bennett to reply in July.

So long as my friend Wells is content to speak for himself about agents I am ready to listen in respectful silence, but when he begins to speak for 'all sensible authors', I must protest.

As one 'sensible author' I wish to 'proclaim clearly' that I should not dream of employing agents only 'for specific jobs'. On the contrary I am absolutely convinced that every author of large and varied output ought to put the whole of his affairs into the hands of a good agent, and that every such author who fails to do so loses money by his omission.

Wells, my senior, once advised—nay, commanded—me to go to an agent. With my usual docility I did so ... I have never regretted it.

He was of course referring to Pinker.

The constant ferment of Wells's ideas and his restlessness as a person derived from two sources of energy. One was his belief in the inevitability of science, in its power to increase knowledge, dissolve dogma, and shape society; the other was his sex drive. After 1900 he became progressively interested in social problems. A natural Socialist, he joined the Fabian Society in 1903—on the proposition of Graham Wallas and Bernard Shaw—but his individualism made him an uncomfortable colleague and he was incapable of toeing any party line. Typically he did his utmost to convert the Fabians to his own brand of visionary humanism, and tried to take the Society over. He failed, but such was the stimulus of his ideas that he was soon accepted as a prophet—above politics, indeed almost above the ordinary standards of criticism.

His first marriage was a failure, and he was far from faithful to his second wife, to whom however he was devoted. Indeed he was sustained by a series of liaisons that led him, not merely to champion the rights of women, but to preach as well as practise the gospel of permissiveness. His novel, *Ann Veronica*, published by Fisher Unwin in 1909, was an historic defence of the independent woman; but it confirmed the judgement that Wells's novels were not works of art so much as 'vehicles for preaching' in thinly fictional form, and that his real role as an author was that of mass educator. This was clearly established between the two world wars with three encyclopaedic works, *The Outline of History* (Newnes 1920), *The Science of Life: A Summary of Contemporary Knowledge about Life and its Possibilities* (Amalgamated Press 1930), and *The Work, Wealth and Happiness of Mankind* (Heinemann 1932). All three were products of amazing industry and powers of comprehension, in the course of which Wells repeatedly drove himself and his collaborators right up to breaking point. They remain, even if rarely read today, monuments of his stature and the expression of his desire to reveal to the common man new vistas of thought and freedom. Later he lost faith in human ability to make creative use of opportunities once they had been realised; but *his* role had been to reveal them.[18]

Despite his awkwardness as a man of business. Wells made money and, like Bennett, enjoyed doing so and using it to live enjoyably. By 1914 he had saved £20,000, and when he died in 1946 he left nearly £60,000: not an astounding sum, but he too had been generous and spent largely on family and friends. The similarity to Bennett is striking, for Wells also demonstrated that prolificacy and popularity need be no bar to quality, nor—in his case—the absence of literary style. In the words of H. M. Tomlinson:

> He used only common speech. The words of the ordinary man were what he delighted in, and he gave them a novel sparkle and significance that has quickened discourse for nearly half-a-century . . .[19]

CHAPTER NINE

Bernard Shaw and the Society of Authors. His early life and activities—as his own publisher, champion of dramatists, and opponent of stage censorship. Fate of The Academy of Letters

WELLS JOINED the Society of Authors in 1895, Bennett waited until 1909. Although Wells was elected to the Council, neither he nor Bennett took an active part in the Society's affairs apart from occasional contributions to *The Author*.[1] Nonetheless they gave the Society their public support and enhanced it by their membership. It was however another, older, contemporary who—more than any other writer in the decade before the first world war—assumed the mantle of Walter Besant and promoted the interests of fellow authors, by marrying service to the Society to the momentum of his own dynamic career.

Shaw was born into a Protestant middle class family in Dublin in 1856.[2] His parents were unsuited and his mother removed to London in 1872, where she taught music and lived out the remaining forty years of her life in comparative comfort. Meanwhile the young Shaw had entered an estate agent's office, where he showed competence and promise 1871–6, but ultimately resigned because he was bored and saw no openings ahead. He then joined his mother in her house in Fulham Road, living with her for the next nine years while 'preparing to become a writer'. And, on his own terms, he did so prepare: picking up an occasional job in journalism, writing five rejected novels, exploring London on foot—he was a vigorous walker all his life—absorbing the arts, and studying a variety of exacting subjects, e.g. phonetics, harmony and counterpoint, and political theory. For him 'argument was entertainment'; and so he forced himself to become a fluent and articulate speaker, while acquiring a number of like-minded friends of great intelligence, all keenly aware of the need to reform society. By 1884 he was acknowledged as a rising radical and propagandist, and in the same year he joined the Fabian Society, for which he actively wrote and spoke. It was the beginning of a lifelong involvement in public causes.

Shaw was attractive to, and attracted by, women, and he sustained a string of liaisons, probably but not necessarily platonic: among whom was Annie Besant, the estranged wife, ironically, of Walter Besant's younger brother, Frank. Annie was a militant feminist, who took it on herself to serialise two of Shaw's novels in her journal, *Our Corner*, paying him out of her private purse until he discovered what she was up to, and stopped her. He was acutely sensitive about taking money from anyone, unless he had earned it. His dependence on his mother was not all one-sided. Although she supported him at first, he made ample amends in later life, and in those early years denied himself almost everything enjoyable for a young man. He was a vegetarian, teetotaller, and non-smoker. Of necessity his wardrobe was minimal, a fact that probably coloured his attitude to dress reform; and as noted he *walked* everywhere. He was sustained by a fundamental belief in his own abilities and, while waiting for his luck to change, tuned his brain and stored up knowledge.

As a writer he owed his real start to William Archer, the drama critic, who found him a niche as music critic on *The Dramatic Review*, his first article appearing on 2 February 1885. Later in the year, thanks again to Archer, he began reviewing books for *The Pall Mall Gazette*; he also wrote art criticism for *The World*: so that with these three regular and other occasional jobs, he was able to earn £117 in 1885. The pattern of his professional career was beginning to take shape. From 1889–90 he wrote music criticism regularly for *The Star*, an evening paper edited by T. P. O'Connor, at two guineas a week; and from 1890–4 for *The World*, edited by Edmund Yates, at five guineas a week. This was the time when he made his name as a music critic of startling individuality, a reputation enhanced by a flow of unpaid work for the Fabian Society: notably the publication in 1889 of *Fabian Essays*, of which he was both editor and a contributor. He was by now at ease (and on occasions at odds) with Sidney Webb and Beatrice Potter (she married Webb in 1892), Sydney Olivier, Hubert Bland and his wife E. Nesbit, and other leading Fabians—so that by the early 1890s he was renowned, not only as a music critic, but as a political journalist and pamphleteer as well. He was among the first to discount the Liberal Party or any Lib-Lab combination as an effective force for promoting social reforms; and he helped to draft the programme of the Independent Labour Party with Keir Hardie, the first Labour MP adhering—with the Webbs —to the belief that Socialists must have their own party in Parliament.

By now publishers were beginning to show interest in issuing Shaw's work in book form; but Shaw was not yet launched. His philosophical examination, *The Perfect Wagnerite*, was not published by Grant Richards until 1898, while his political writings remained Fabian pamphlets as before—even *The Quintessence of Ibsenism*, first delivered as a Fabian lecture in 1890 and issued by Water Scott in the following year. Although Shaw had been writing about plays alongside his music criticism, this was the first significant sign of his passionate interest in drama. His concern with Ibsen was associated with the initial reaction of the British public to Ibsen's social message, condemned by the majority as 'cancerous', but defended by a handful of critics—among them A. B. Walkley, William Archer, and Shaw himself, who was principally interested in the propaganda aspect of Ibsen's characters and plots. As St. John Ervine said, Shaw's book was 'a statement of what Ibsen would have thought had he been Bernard Shaw'.[3] Their link was their belief in the sanctity of the individual.

Shaw had further occasion to defend Ibsen when J. T. Grein, who founded The Independent Theatre for the encouragement of new drama, put on *Ghosts* at the Royalty Theatre in 1891, and suffered a storm of abuse for his pains. It was this that brought Shaw and Grein together, so that in the following year Grein staged Shaw's first play, *Widowers' Houses*, and published it in 1893. Its subject and treatment—slum landlordism —proved equally unpopular, and the play received only two performances. it was, however, the start of Shaw's career as a dramatist, and characteristically its reception failed to discourage him. However his next two plays did no better. He could find no management to present *The Philanderer*, while *Mrs. Warren's Profession* was banned, partly because it dealt with prostitution, and partly because it contained a reference to incest. His fourth play however, *Arms and the Man*, which made fun of militarism, ran for eleven weeks in the West End in 1894, thanks to a subsidy from Miss Annie Horniman.[4] It made no money and earned the author only £100, but it founded his reputation as a dramatist—albeit avant-garde and as yet unattractive to commercial managers. From that moment, plays flowed out of Shaw: *Candida* in 1894, *The Man of Destiny* in 1895, *You never can Tell* in 1896, though none of these reached the stage at the time they were written. Indeed it was the lack of performance that convinced Shaw of the need for prior publication, primarily to make his work known; and, by adding explanatory prefaces and detailed notes on the plot, to convey the full range of his thought—hence the origins of *Plays Pleasant and Unpleasant* published by Grant Richards in 1898.

Shaw owed his first popular success on the stage to Richard Mansfield's production in 1897 of *The Devil's Disciple* in America, where the run in New York alone yielded £2,500 in royalties, and where he first gained general recognition for his plays. At home however he found managements consistently reluctant—a disappointment not offset by a brilliant stint for $3\frac{1}{2}$ years (1895–8) as the regular dramatic critic of *The Saturday Review*, edited by Frank Harris. Nor was he any longer beset by poverty. In 1895 he earned £573 1s, in 1896 £1,089 4s, and by the time he married the wealthy Charlotte Payne-Townshend in 1898 his income from writing exceeded £2,000 a year, which confounded his own quip that he married for money. Nonetheless he was always serious about money, for he was convinced that without it creativity was crippled.

His next volume of plays, *Three Plays for Puritans* (*The Devil's Disciple, Caesar and Cleopatra,* and *Captain Brassbound's Conversion*), published by Grant Richards in 1901, proved the point. Its modest sale, and that of the previous volume, so added to his disenchantment with publishers, and with Grant Richards in particular,[5] that he decided to break away from the conventional system of publication. Instead of licensing a publisher to produce and market a book as best he might, the author to draw royalties on such sales as resulted, Shaw decided to set up on his own. Henceforward he paid for the entire production himself, employing R. & R. Clark of Edinburgh as his printers, and contracting with Constable to distribute to the trade in return for a commission.[6] This gave Shaw a free hand all round: in deciding the format, lay-out, type-face, and paper, and in overseeing the publicity. Indeed he was a master at promotion, as in other aspects of business, and he began the new régime with the publication of *Man and Superman* in 1903.

As to the stage, although his plays were now receiving

spasmodic performances at home and abroad, it was not until the 1904–7 seasons at the Royal Court Theatre in Sloane Square that Shaw finally came into his own. This was due to the inspired management of John E. Vedrenne, in association with Harley Granville Barker as producer, who devised a scheme for matinées whereby 'players could be persuaded to take part in them at small salaries because they were free to perform in other theatres in the evening'.[7] I quote further:

> The Vedrenne–Barker policy was to found a repertory theatre in which plays of quality, ancient and modern, should be performed for short runs, so that the players should not be staled by prolonged repetition of one part, and frequent revivals, ensuring the dramatist a more regular income than he would normally receive. Thirty plays, some of them short pieces, most of them long, were produced. Eleven of them were by G.B.S., who was, beyond doubt, the most profitable playwright whose work was performed. These were *Candida, John Bull's Other Island, How He Lied to Her Husband, You Never Can Tell, Man and Superman, Captain Brassbound's Conversion, Major Barbara, The Doctor's Dilemma, The Philanderer, Don Juan in Hell,* and *The Man of Destiny*.[8]

By this time Shaw was nearly 50 years old.

*   *   *   *

It will be seen from this narrative that, when Shaw joined the Society of Authors in 1897, he was already established as a critic and journalist, though not as a dramatist. His political stance was also well known; and he confounded all who regarded him solely as a theorist by a seven-year stint in local government in St. Pancras, 1897–1904.[9] To general surprise he proved an excellent committee man, both practical and progressive, concerning himself with the details of public health, housing, drainage, and other mundane matters. It added solid backing to the work he was beginning to do for fellow authors.

Shaw's contribution to the Society of Authors and the causes of authorship was of inestimable value. He was elected to the Council and to the Committee of Management in 1905, and served on the dramatic sub-committee from 1906 to 1915, when he diplomatically withdrew seeking characteristically to avoid any dissension in the Society due to his unpopular opinions about the war. He remained a member however, continued to provide advice and assistance privately to the Secretary, and kept in touch almost until his death in 1950. His principal characteristics were those he always displayed: unfailing in equanimity and detachment whatever the opposition, provocative but never spiteful, industrious, unyielding in the pursuit of a point at issue, and always humane. Thring could rely on Shaw absolutely to deal with correspondence and attend meetings, however laborious the commitment; and he could be sure that, even if Shaw said nothing new (which was unusual), he made everyone re-think the plainest propositions. For his part Shaw kept Thring at full stretch; and during the decade before the first world war, there was hardly an issue of importance in which both men were not involved.

Shaw's work for the Society was not confined to drama, although naturally it was his prime concern; and in his first article in *The Author* in December 1901, he argued vigorously in support of his own recent innovation—publishing plays without performance. But he was interested in everything, and he used *The Author*, committee and annual meetings and dinners to exercise his mind. For example, in a discussion on education, he though that boys cared nothing for books, 'and a very good thing too'. 'Why should boys be expected to read Wordsworth, one of the dullest men who ever lived?' In his view, the teaching of Latin and Greek was only supported by the fraud of pretending that they were necessary to the understanding of English, and the 'hallmark of a gentleman'. In his experience teachers were more demoralised than any other class, which he supposed to be due to their continual contact with defenceless minds.[10] In April 1902, by way of contrast, he commented on the Clarendon Press Rules for Compositors and Readers, and used the opportunity to air his views on simplified spelling—a subject that he developed later into reform of the alphabet, and a cause for which he made provision in his will.

As to fellow authors, he was often disarmingly and disconcertingly critical, mixing exhortation with taunts. He was especially contemptuous of those who bleated about bad treatment by publishers, failed to study their contracts or take advice before signing them, and then blamed the Society for not winning their battles for them. At the AGM on 5 March 1903 he asked whether no means existed for the punishment of literary blacklegs who might be responsible for defamatory statements [about the Society], i.e. 'adverse criticism and uninformed or wilfully mistaken obloquy in the Press'. In reviewing *A Publisher's Confession* by Walter H. Page[11] in the July 1905 issue of *The Author*, he hit out at the publishing scene:

> Confessions . . . as Dickens succinctly put it, are 'all lies'.
>
> A few simple principles furnish our professing penitent with a solid moral basis. Of these the chief is that Nature ordains ten per cent as the proper royalty for an author . . . a view strenuously combatted by theatrical managers, to whom the Voice of Nature whispers five per cent as seemly and sufficient.
>
> I shuddered as I read. For I too have a confession to make. I have not only exacted twenty per cent royalties; but I have actually forced the unfortunate publisher to adorn the dollar-and-a-half book with photogravures. It is quite true that the particular publisher whom I used thus barbarously actually did become bankrupt. But he broke, not because he paid too high royalties, but because his profits were so large that he acquired the habits of a Monte Cristo, and the ambitions of an Alexander . . . Three or four more bankruptcies, and he will settle down and become a steady millionaire.
>
> But the exaction of twenty per cent is not the blackest crime of which an author can be guilty . . . He [the publisher] forgives us everything, except DISLOYALTY . . . to prefer another's twenty per cent to his ten: this is human nature at its worst . . . I have done the very same thing myself.
>
> As for me, all I ask on the royalty system at six shillings [the published price] is a modest twenty per cent or so, a three years' trial, an agreement drafted by myself, and an unaffected bookseller.

This review roused the wrath of Andrew Lang, who rebutted him in the *Morning Post*, an incident recalled by Shaw many years later.

> Instantly a distinguished author, by reflex action, rushed to repudiate me and defend the shark. And he was a Scot, too: no less a person than Andrew Lang, whom I had never injured, and whose interests I was defending. At the next dinner of the Society I took advantage of the speechmaking to remonstrate with Andrew for betraying his profession for thirty pieces of silver (an understatement; but it pointed the moral). Andrew threatened to resign. As the sympathy was all

with him, I was expected to withdraw or resign. As I did neither, Andrew resigned. I crowned my infamy by remarking, whilst the Society was supposed in literary circles to be staggering from this blow, 'And a good job too'.[12]

Shaw had prefaced this piece with a paragraph which some of Thring's successors put up on their office notice boards:

What a heartbreaking job it is trying to combine authors for their own protection. I had ten years of it on the Committee of Management of the Society of Authors; and the first lesson I learnt was that when you take the field for authors you will be safer without a breastplate than without a backplate. They will not combine against the crook publisher and the sweating editor; but they will combine against you and the Society with the fervour of crusaders.

It was at the same Annual Dinner in 1906 that Shaw, in a speech not leavened by his customary wit, gave rein to his views about solidarity among writers.

Literature is also, unfortunately, a sweated trade. This is one of the reasons for the existence of our Society.

Those of you who, like myself, have studied sweating as an industrial phenomenon, are aware that it occurs at its very worst in those trades where the employer, instead of having the work done in his own factory, gives it out to workers who do it in their own homes. You can get at the factory through the factory inspector and your Factory Acts, but you cannot get at the private home.

Without union and collective action we are helpless. When we begin working, we are so poor and so busy that we have neither the time nor the means to defend ourselves against the commercial organisations which exploit us. When we become famous, we become famous suddenly, passing at one bound from the state in which we are, as I have said, too poor to fight our own battles, to a state in which our time is so valuable that it is not worth our while wasting any of it on lawsuits and bad debts. We all, eminent and obscure alike, need the Authors' Society. We all owe it a share of our time, our means, our influence.[13]

In other words Shaw was implying—though he never formally proposed altering the constitution and affiliating the Society to the Trade Union Congress—that the Society should in practice act as a trade union. This was in general consonant with his being a Fabian and a Socialist, and constituted a course of action that confronted the Society on several occasions during and after Shaw's life. In fact the majority of members long resisted it: partly because they disliked the face of trade unionism as displayed in industrial action; partly because they considered it impracticable in that any attempt to enforce a closed shop (as the ultimate sanction) would fail, since a number of writers would always disregard the ban; but at heart because they felt that to regiment writers was tantamount to dictatorship over the mind, and would result in the denial of a fundamental human right—that of freedom of expression.[14]

The alternative was a development of the policy begun by Besant—collective pressure and persuasion. In other words, backed by a strong membership (though never of course inclusive of everyone who wrote a book, article, play, or script), the Society conducted business by negotiation, by publicity, by lobbying in and out of Parliament, and when necessary by recourse to law. Its aims remained unchanged—to defend the rights of authors and improve the terms and conditions of writing in every medium available to the profession. Thus by 1950, when Shaw died, it had gained a position of authority that enabled it to combat, with cumulative effectiveness, the kind of exploitation to which Shaw referred in 1906. By following that policy, the Society did not succeed in solving the fundamental economic problem common to all the creative arts in a capitalist society: namely that every author of proved ability should be able to earn a living from his work. On the other hand, instead of pursuing demands based on a general withdrawal of labour, it turned the pyramid upside down; for it was the lead given by authors at the top, e.g. writers like Shaw, that raised the minima for all.

But Shaw was not narrow-minded about the rights of authors. Towards the end of his life, reflecting on his long experience of the business of writing and publishing books, and thinking back to the pioneer efforts of Besant and Thring, he had this to say:

Besant ... did not understand publishing as a business. He persisted in assuming that a publisher is an ordinary merchant who, like a baker or a dairyman, sells a certain article which everybody can produce with perfect certainty in unlimited quantities, and which everybody needs for use or consumption. He kept on citing quite irrelevant examples of books on which the publisher had made a big profit and the author a little one as damning proofs that the publisher who claims more than the cost of production of the book plus a reasonable profit, say 10 per cent, and does not give all the rest to the author, is a sharper and a robber.

This was an ignorant delusion. Publishing is not ordinary trade: it is gambling. The publisher bets the cost of manufacturing, advertising and circulating a book, plus the overhead of his establishment, against every book he publishes exactly as a turf bookmaker bets against every horse in the race. The author, with his one book is an owner backing his favorite at the best odds he can get from the competing publishers. Both are gamblers . . .

Besant and Thring would have had an easier time if they had understood this and allowed for the fact that a publisher must publish perhaps a hundred books to achieve ten best sellers. The remaining ninety may barely pay their way, or bring him prestige instead of money, or even flop completely. To keep his shop open he must keep on publishing whether the books he can get are promising or not.[15]

*   *   *   *

Shaw's practice of acting, in effect, as his own publisher made him keenly aware of the problems and shortcomings of booksellers. Writing in *The Author* of July 1903 he asserted that in the London borough of St. Pancras, with nearly a quarter of a million inhabitants, there was not a single bookshop. When challenged by reference to the London Directory, which listed sixteen booksellers in St. Pancras, he replied that they were at best stationers who stocked 'reprints of popular and classic literature, Bibles and prayer-books, photographs, picture frames, purses, artists' colors, and fancy goods of all cognate kinds'. In general he railed against the abysmal lack of bookshops worthy of the name, and the sheer inefficiency of book distribution. It was worse with plays.

> Suppose you have heard that one of my plays is called 'Caesar and Cleopatra', and you want to buy it. You go to the bookselling stationer. The moment he realizes that you do not want a photograph frame or five quires of notepaper for a shilling, his countenance falls. You ask for Shaw's 'Caesar and Cleopatra'. He has not got it, but can order it for you.

Good. You then call on him at intervals for three weeks or a month, and are assured each time that negotiations are proceeding. At last he tells you that there is no such book. You say you are sure there is. He replies that the wholesaler who supplies him could get it if there was; so it must be out of print. What can you do but apologize for having troubled him, and buy some stationery to console him? . . .

What we want above all things is not more books, not more publishers, not more education, not more literary genius, but simply and prosaically more shops.

Three years later he took issue with the Society's Committee of Management for supporting the publishers and booksellers against The Times Book Club, which was selling off library copies of new books at cut prices, soon after publication, in defiance of the Net Book Agreement (see pp. 179–80). In October 1906 the Committee passed a resolution condemning this practice, which found its way into the correspondence column of *The Times*: soon followed by a dissenting letter from Shaw who, though himself a member of the Committee, wrote over his own name.

As to all this pious horror about throwing new books at scrap price on the market, pray how many books do we see every year produced by publishers who, too languid to sustain interest in them, too poor to advertise them, and too incapable to distribute them, 'remainder' them at a few pence per copy, and leave the author penniless or out of pocket whilst the bookseller sells off the stock with a very fair profit at a large reduction on the published price?[16]

The matter came to a head at the AGM held on 20 March 1907, when Sidney Lee[17] proposed a motion critical of the Committee's action. He was supported by a large number of members, among them Professor Ray Lankester,[18] Sir Alfred Lyall,[19] and Israel Zangwill,[20] the latter attacking both the Committee and Shaw. The exchanges make lively reading, Shaw saying that he had taken his line simply in the interests of fellow authors, and that publishers had lost a lot of business by refusing large orders from a very large customer, without consulting the authors at all. In the vote that followed, the motion was lost by approximately 50 to 36, although no one seemed sure of the exact number, and Shaw—after protest—had to let it go at that.[21]

1907 was a fevered year for the Society. The row over the Times Book Club, particularly the 'failure' of the Committee of Management to consult the Council (although the Committee was absolutely within its rights to act as it did) generated a move, long overdue, to amend the constitution. Hitherto the Committee had been recruited solely from the Council (about 60, some of them old and no longer active as authors): thus preventing the bulk of the membership from nominating their own representatives and conducting an election by ballot. There was a general undefined feeling of dissatisfaction, not so much with the way in which things were being run, but that the Society was in the hands of a self-perpetuating clique, served by a Secretary (Thring) who kept far too tight a hold of the reins. This is a situation familiar to many organisations in the course of their history, and can be dangerous if ignored. It was not ignored.

A special committee was appointed, with representatives from the Council, the Committee, and the membership at large, including three women at the special request of Mrs. Humphry Ward.[22] Drafting was placed in the expert hands of Sidney Webb who, assisted by Anthony Hope Hawkins (the new chairman of the Committee of Management), made recommendations to a special general meeting of 23 January 1908. The document, like all Webb's work, was a model of painstaking preparation, and was examined in detail by a large company of members. Its main purpose, as Webb quietly stated, was to bring the organisation of the Society under the control of the subscribing members. In practice it meant that the Committee of Management (the real executive power) would consist of twelve members, four to retire each year, the vacancies to be filled—after due notice in *The Author*—by nomination and election (by postal ballot) if the candidates exceeded the number of vacancies. The meeting went off without undue trouble, despite tortuous amendments proposed by Bram Stoker,[23] Israel Zangwill, and a few others, all patiently handled by Webb and Hawkins. Shaw said nothing at all.[24]

*   *   *   *

In 1897, the year that Shaw and Somerset Maugham had joined the Society, a small dramatic sub-committee had been formed under the chairmanship of Henry Arthur Jones, one of the leading playwrights of the day. It happened that Jones invited Shaw to review his play, *The Liars*, opening at the Criterion on 6 October, Shaw's notice appearing in *The Saturday Review* three days later. Writing to Jones afterwards, on the 12th, Shaw referred to the dramatic sub-committee as follows:

> . . . it seems to me that we ought to try to work up some sort of an organization with a view to getting a *minimum* price established for plays, and putting a stop to the ridiculous jobbing of 'rights' that goes on at present through the silliness and ignorance of the authors . . . The difficulty is, of course, to find time for Trade Union work; but one feels that it ought to be done. It is all very well for you or me to pit our individual strength against Irving and Wyndham and the rest; but the small fry are bound to crumple up without an organization behind them. We also want to fight the system of forcing collaboration on authors, whereby some fool of an actor-manager spoils a man's play in order that he may collar half the percentage . . .
>
> Mansfield has just proved to me by figures that he must lose $300 on every performance of The Devil's Disciple unless I reduce my percentage from 10 to 4. I have replied in terms sufficient to stand him on his head for a fortnight.

The sub-committee lay low until 1899 when it was strengthened by the addition of Sydney Grundy and Arthur Wing Pinero, at a time when a number of other well-known dramatists were being recruited into the Society: among them, R. C. Carton, Haddon Chambers, W. S. Gilbert (rejoining after an absence), Clement Scott, Louis N. Parker and H. V. Esmond. These men were soon followed by a fresh intake which included Alfred Sutro, J. M. Barrie, John Galsworthy, John Masefield, and Harley Granville Barker. There was little doubt that, in terms of quality, virtually all the leading playwrights became members of the Society; while the total within the membership of those who had written plays, or who regarded themselves as connected with the theatre, was said to exceed 200.

This surge of recruitment reflected the widespread revival of interest in drama, already evident in the last quarter of the 19th century, when playwrights such as Grundy, Pinero and Jones were breaking away from Victorian melodrama with plots based on realistic situations, backed by better stage sets and more credible dialogue—however sentimental some of their work may seem today, And comedy, always a solvent when treating of serious themes, was also reaching a higher level: notably in the plays of Oscar Wilde, whose characters indulged in brilliant chatter that both challenged accepted values and concealed the triviality of the plots; while Shaw, in a different way, made the treatment of social problems (e.g. slum landlordism) an intellectual delight.

But—as Shaw soon found—good plays, whether psychological dramas by Ibsen or his own brand of assault upon society, needed far wider opportunities—receptive audiences, better theatres, and managers willing to find finance and take risks, let alone play fair with the authors. Some of these requirements were met by pioneers such as J. T. Grein who, as noted, put on Shaw and Ibsen; Annie Horniman who likewise helped Shaw, and started repertory at the Abbey Theatre, Dublin and (with Ben Iden Payne) at the Gaiety Theatre, Manchester; and Vedrenne and Granville Barker at the Royal Court. They were supported on the professional stage by Frederick Whelen's Stage Society and other theatre clubs, that put on special matinées or evening performances on Sundays; but even these enterprises would have been insufficient without the aid of amateur dramatic societies, which also offered openings for experimental and other work by young dramatists, unacceptable to commercial managers. Add to this the publication of plays in book form, decently printed and bound, by Shaw, Pinero, Jones, and others, which contributed to the revival through the reading public. At the same time no revival was likely to be permanent without the removal of certain legal anomalies which handicapped the dramatist. One was the continued necessity for a 'copyright performance', if an author was to guard against unauthorised presentation of his work:[25] another was the power of censorship as exercised by the Lord Chamberlain, of which more shortly.

Shaw's election to the dramatic sub-committee in 1906 was of course of great importance: not only because he was now recognised as a dramatist of the first rank, but because characteristically he got down to practical work. The first task, shouldered jointly by Jones and himself was to make a study of the methods of the French Société des Auteurs and Compositeurs Dramatiques—'on the possibility of applying them to English theatrical business'. Shaw and Jones rendered their report in March 1907, which was inserted as a separate typescript in the sub-committee minute book, with hand corrections by Shaw, and signed in person by both men. It was so cogent that I reproduce it in full at the Appendix on page 238.

This report should have been sufficient to assure members that the sub-committee was doing good work. Indeed it aroused prolonged scrutiny and comment, and was the first step towards drafting a model agreement on which Shaw and others worked assiduously until 1915, in an attempt to reach a settlement with West End managers. However these efforts were overshadowed by an explosion of anger against the whole system of stage censorship, as operated by the Lord Chamberlain under the Theatres Act 1843. Various attempts had been made in Parliament without success to alter the Act, the latest in 1906: and in October 1907 a protest was published in *The Times* signed by 70 dramatists (most of them members of the Society), followed in November by a deputation to the Prime Minister represented by Herbert Gladstone. These events were in train when drama came up for discussion at the AGM in April 1908, at which the chairman (Anthony Hope Hawkins) said unhelpfully that the dramatic sub-committee 'as a whole wanted livening up'. A member, H. M. Paull,[26] then took the floor and accused the Society of failing in its duty. It had taken no formal action when various plays had been banned, among them Granville Barker's *Waste*. It had not openly identified itself with the protest in *The Times* or the deputation to the Prime Minister. In consequence a body of at least 40 dramatist members were about to defect and form a separate Dramatic Authors Society, with Pinero as chairman.

Although Shaw replied forcefully that the Society had received no mandate to take formal action, and that no mandate was worth anything unless it had unanimous support, this did not satisfy the meeting, and a breakaway seemed inevitable. However, during the rest of 1908 and the early part of 1909, Shaw and Thring managed a series of manoeuvres which resulted in their completely outwitting the prospective defectors. They did this by strengthening the sub-committee, and by persuading Pinero to serve both parties concurrently. At the same time they prepared a special report of the Society's work for playwrights, 'explaining its nature, its costs, its difficulties, the extent to which it had been hampered by want of support from the dramatic authors themselves, the waste and inefficiency involved in breaking up the organisation of a profession so limited in numbers into two organisations, and the possibilities attainable by energy and unanimity'. This report went out to all the dramatists, asking them if they wanted one body or two. 'Out of sixty replies, none favoured secession, two were neutral, eight made suggestions as to extensions of our work. The remaining fifty gave unqualified support to union with the Society of Authors'.[27]

As usual Shaw was careful not to crow. On the contrary he saw to it that Pinero—who both admired and detested Shaw—was appointed chairman of the new united dramatic sub-committee early in 1909, and crowned it all by securing him a knighthood in the Birthday Honours of that year. Shaw's attitude and actions, and his imperturbability, were well exhibited in a letter to William Archer of 3 July 1908, in the very middle of the turmoil:

... In steering this Authors' Society business, you must bear steadily in mind that the thing we have got to do is to educate our men. . . . They have to be educated, not only in the economic and practical business they have to face, and in public procedure, of which, as you can see for yourself, they are all childishly ignorant, but above all in the impersonal habit of mind—the committee habit—without which every attempt to face and deal with the simplest hard fact leads to wounded feelings, squabbling, resignations, and, generally, the sort of baby stunt that Sutro treated us to the other day. Also, we must keep a perfectly open mind as to which body finally captures the position. I am at present applying all my driving force (which, you will observe, consists simply in sitting down and doing the work that nobody else will do) to make the Authors' Society Committee out-do, out-think, and out-goodmanner the other Committee . . . I have already done my best, by kindly and patronizing insolence, to make them feel that they be simply like infants in my hands and those of the Author's Society unless they really put their backs into the affair. The effect of this will be altogether good, because neither side can conceal its operations from the other. In a rash moment the new body invited me to attend one of their meetings; and five minutes after I had entered the room I had in an innocent manner raised the question of preliminary expenses and sent the hat round with a sovereign of my own in it. With that sovereign I purchased their souls: they can no more keep me out of their councils now than the Society of

Authors can keep them out. Each side will benefit by all the work the other does; and whether the result is a new Society or a complete regeneration of the dramatic committee of the old Society, all the intermediate work will be to the good . . .

In the Authors' Society in the old days (meaning in fact yesterday) we really did all we could to galvanise the dramatic committee into life; but the authors simply would not take any interest in it. When Pinero found that nothing was being done, instead of saying that something must be done and doing it, he acquiesced in the situation with a relief which was human and natural in the circumstances. Edward Rose and Grundy, like Jones, were driven to the same fatalistic acceptance of the uselessness of getting the dramatic authors to assemble and put in any work. At last, Hawkins and myself made the Executive Committee add us to the Dramatic Sub-Committee; and we did what we could until the censorship agitation gave us our chance. But we should collapse again tomorrow if the old apathy set in again.

The censorship row boiled up again in the summer of 1909, by which time Shaw was fairly in command of the dramatists' lobby and so intensified the agitation that the Government appointed a Select Committee of both Houses of Parliament 'to inquire into the Censorship of Stage Plays as constituted by the Theatres Act 1843 . . .' This Committee consisted of five peers and five commoners under the chairmanship of Herbert Samuel MP, and sat from 21 July until 28 October, fifteen meetings in all, during which time it examined 49 witnesses—a galaxy of critics, dramatists, actor-managers, and others connected with the entertainment world and public life. The Report[28]—a massive Blue Book 375 pages long—was published in November, and included verbatim reports of the evidence, together with introductory information about the history of stage censorship, and a considered explanation of the Committee's recommendations. It was a well presented and, in the circumstances of the time, an enlightened document.

The Report recorded that stage censorship had first been introduced in 1737 by Sir Robert Walpole under the Royal Prerogative, in order to control political and personal satire, largely directed against himself. It empowered the Lord Chamberlain to license theatres and censor plays, which had to be submitted before performance to an official known as the Examiner of Plays, who was paid £400 p.a. for doing the job.

Under the Theatres Act 1843 the law was revised. No plays were to be performed except in authorised places, as permitted by—in round terms—the Lord Chamberlain in London and the Justices of the Peace in the provinces (later the County Councils and other local authorities); but censorship remained firmly in the hands of the Lord Chamberlain, who exercised an absolute veto as before. No criteria were established beyond a suggestion by Lord Campbell that the Examiner 'shall be of the opinion that it [a play] is fitting for the preservation of good manners, decorum or of the public peace so to do'. That was the position in 1909, when it was found that—since 1895—out of 7.000 plays sumitted only 30 had been banned, but they included some notable examples, e.g. Shaw's two recent plays, *Press Cuttings* and *The Shewing-up of Blanco Posnet*.

Shaw prepared for battle by writing an 11.000 word statement which he intended to submit in evidence.[29] He had it privately printed and distributed to members of the Select Committee, to fellow dramatists and critics, and to other interested persons. He also wrote copiously to the press and lobbied a host of individuals, urging them to give evidence and briefing them as to what to say. In short he master-minded all the preliminaries with such energy that he probably confused rather than clarified the case. At all events, when he was examined on 30 July, the Select Committee refused to accept his printed statement in evidence, despite the precedent set in 1892 when Sir Henry Irving was allowed to submit a written memorandum of his views on the same subject. In the event much of the ground was covered under verbal examination on 30 July, and Shaw was not given a second opportunity to reply to questions. He was deeply disappointed and continued to labour the subject in private correspondence with Herbert Samuel and in statements to the press. All to no avail. The Select Committee completed the hearings, published the Report, and the Lord Chamberlain remained where he was, though with qualifications.

Strangely, it is not easy immediately to grasp Shaw's arguments, although once grasped they are clear enough. The confusion arises—and the Select Committee were certainly baffled for a time—from the fact that Shaw spoke and wrote at great length, and because he could not resist paradoxes and histrionics. Yet the essence of his case was clear, that:

i) censorship of plays was separate from the licensing of theatres.

ii) it was wrong to appoint a single individual to pass moral judgement on any work before performance. As he wrote many years later: 'My objection to censors is that in practice they mean appointing an ordinary official with a salary of a few hundreds a year to exercise powers which have proved too much for Popes and Presidents'.[30]

iii) if a play was performed that proved objectionable, then it was open to prosecution *before the law* on grounds of libel, obscenity, sedition, blasphemy, or whatever. In this matter the stage should be on the same footing as the press.

iv) as things stood, most theatre managers preferred to keep the censorship, since a licence helped to safeguard their investment in a play, at best always a risky venture. This held good for plays of all kinds, moral or immoral: in the latter case, however, it meant that a manager was free to circumvent the law if he was adept at the game (e.g. by tampering with the script or production), because he was protected by the Lord Chamberlain.

v) on the other hand, theatres should be licensed annually like public houses to control disorderly behaviour, prostitution, and other undesirable features: but such control should not be allowed to become synonymous with play censorship for the reasons stated.

Although the Select Committee did not accept Shaw's arguments as they stood, their force was reflected in the recommendations attached to the Report. These proposed *inter alia* that in future licensing be optional and that the power of veto be abolished; that unlicensed plays should take their chance with the law, but that in doubtful cases the matter be referred to a special committee of the Privy Council; and that music halls and theatres be placed on an equal legal footing. In the event no legislation was passed to implement these proposals, although in 1910 an advisory committee (which included representatives of the theatre) was appointed to assist the censor. Although stage censorship was not abolished until the Theatres Act 1968, the system was applied in the intervening years with far greater liberality and discretion; and as the dramatic sub-committee of the Society of Authors, and later Shaw himself, admitted, the whole exercise had yielded worthwhile results.

*   *   *   *

Hardly was this campaign at an end, when the Society found itself involved in the opening stages of the Copyright Bill, introduced in the summer of 1910 by Sydney Buxton MP, President of the Board of Trade. As will be understood from earlier chapters, copyright was the most important of all the Society's campaigns. It had been one of the original aims set out by Besant in 1884, it had absorbed more time and effort than any other subject ever since, and—as will be described in the next chapter—it was to prove the Society's outstanding achievement in the thirty years of its existence before the outbreak of the first world war. Even so, important as drama was as a component element of the Bill, Shaw was only peripherally involved and found time to pour cold water on a half-baked proposal to establish an Academy of Letters. This was a familiar subject raised at intervals by English pedants and eccentrics ever since the 17th century, following the foundation of the Académie Française by Cardinal Richelieu in order to regulate the language and protect standards of speech and literature. The idea had never taken root in England, not even inside the Royal Society of Literature (founded 1823), one of whose declared objects had been 'to preserve the purity of the English language'. As for the Society of Authors, Besant had dismissed the subject as irrelevant from the start. In his view, as of most writers, the essence of English as a language and literature lay in its power to assimilate fresh words and usages, and to enrich itself in the process. And who would ever observe the dictates of an Academy of Letters?

Nevertheless the subject recurred. In July 1890 Oswald Crawfurd[31] suggested in *The Author* that the Society ought to be involved. While he doubted whether 'the *ex cathedra* pronouncements of an official Board of Letters would ever carry much weight', he thought that 'in a humble way some useful work might be done', e.g. 'to resolve the doubts and uncertainties that exist on many points in syntax, spelling, prosody and phraseology'; also to encourage 'the admission of useful provincial words into general usage'. He quoted the example of *backword*, common in the west and north of the country, meaning 'a refusal to comply with a promise made or to fulfil some intention declared'. A telegram had lately been handed into a London post office which ran, 'Dine with me on Saturday, A- sends me a backword'. The clerk refused the message, not finding 'backword' in the dictionary.

Herbert Trench[32] reverted to the subject in October 1902, arguing on different grounds.

The lower forces of literary productiveness are amply organised. The higher are without representation. There is no council at the head of literature to control or keep order, or by example to discountenance the indecencies of advertisement... Our Society of Authors—admirable body that it is—exists only to protect literature as an article of commerce, not with literature as an art, and as more than art.

He referred to other professions which

...all have their societies, to influence, to keep order, to recognise rank and confer honour. Pure literature ... has no society whose aim is to sustain the name, and publicly to represent to foreigners and to the community the power of English intelligence and imagination.

His articles generated a lively response in subsequent issues of *The Author*. One idea was to form a committee—George Meredith, William Lecky,[33] John Morley,[34] James Bryce,[35] James Frazer,[36] Algernon Swinburne, Thomas Hardy, and others—to take the matter further. Rider Haggard wanted an Academy of Imaginative Literature. Morley Roberts[37] thought that 'an academy is nothing if not academic ... it ends in imposing senility'. H. G. Wells surprisingly was favourably disposed, if it could place a 'hall-mark' on good writing. But who would bother to take on the job? Meredith confined his reading to the literature of France, John Morley was engrossed in politics, and how could Frazer, an anthropologist, sift contemporary fiction? Thinking no doubt of himself, Wells added

The Good Outsider, that Intrusive Bounder, who is the living soul of literature, will be left outside anything Mr. Trench and his fellow workers can possibly invent, and the Uninspired Respectability will be in—from the very beginning.

Max Beerbohm compared Trench to a man on a beach 'looking for forty fossils', and concluded, 'I, like Mr. Trench himself, prefer to devolve the task of naming *them*.'

William Archer quoted the story of Thackeray who, when

asked by an American, 'What do you in England think of Martin Tupper?', replied 'We don't think of Martin Tupper'.

Nothing further was heard of all this again until February 1910, when the Royal Society of Literature asked the Society of Authors to help form an Academic Committee, 14 names to be proposed by each organisation, the 28 to elect a further 12 to make up the magic total of 40. The Committee of Management responded by asking Maurice Hewlett,[38] Anthony Hope Hawkins and Douglas Freshfield[39] to draw up a list—which they did, which the Committee was too stunned or bored to alter or reject, but which they forwarded with relief to the Council, where Mrs. Humphry Ward—always on the look-out for slights on her sex—protested *inter alia* that no woman's name was on the list. Shaw solved the problem by suggesting that the Academic Committee, if it ever got off the ground, should look after its own elections and that the matter be dropped. It was.[40]

However the Royal Society of Literature proceeded with the plan and set up the Academic Committee by resolution later in 1910. The 40 members were to be elected at the AGM, but its objects and functions hardly varied from those of the RSL itself. It thus became an *imperium in imperio* but a totally purposeless one; and as in due course it was discovered that the roll contained none of the leading members of the parent organisation, the Committee was allowed to wither into oblivion.[41]

Shaw wrote on a postcard: 'What a lot of rubbish'.

CHAPTER TEN

Problems of authorship in the decade before 1914—theatre contracts, taxation, library lending, prices of novels. Hardy succeeds Meredith as President of the Society of Authors. The Copyright Act 1911

STAGE CENSORSHIP was not the end of theatre politics for Shaw. In December 1909 he was at Shavian war over the membership of the Dramatists' Club, founded by Pinero earlier in the year. In a letter to his biographer, Hesketh Pearson, dated 20 February 1939, he said that the Club

> began as a clique of old stagers who insisted on excluding everyone who was not 'a dramatist of established reputation' which was their definition of one of themselves. They invited me to join in the sure and certain hope that I would refuse; but as I was for years trying to get them to organise the profession—any sort of organisation being better than none—I joined and made a duty of attending their lunches for quite a long time.[1]

Characteristically Shaw made himself felt at once by trying to get several 'non-established' playwrights, including women, elected to the Club, but without much success; and ultimately he was expelled because certain members took affront at his attitude to the war. In reality, as he openly implied, Shaw wanted to use the Dramatists' Club as a weapon; in particular to support the dramatic sub-committee of the Society of Authors in its campaign for a minimum terms agreement, or Managerial Treaty as it was called, with the Society of West End Managers. The struggle was protracted and exhausting, and after four years (1911–15) came to a dead stop; the managers rejecting three specific conditions upon which the dramatists insisted:

i) the author's right to a voice in the selection of the cast.

ii) the author's right to coach individual members of the cast.

iii) the author's right to cancel the contract in case of bankruptcy of the manager.

209

At a meeting held in November 1915, open to all dramatist members of the Society, it was decided to break off negotiations. It was however felt that the Society was now strong enough to deal effectively with the different managers, treaty or no treaty; and with dramatists such as Barrie, R. C. Carton, Galsworthy, Pinero, and Shaw in the lead, the future looked reasonably rosy. It was however the signal for Shaw's resignation from the dramatic sub-committee after nearly ten years' consistent and, at times, electrifying service.[2]

Looking back over the records of seventy or so years ago, i.e. during the decade before the first world war, and working as I have done at the Society of Authors since the early 1960s, I find no difficulty in spotting subjects of current and prophetic interest. Taxation, for example. As early as 1904, authors were asking why the sale of copyright, a capital asset, should be liable to income tax. As things stood, an author was taxed on his receipts, whatever their nature, everything being treated as income. When the Inland Revenue was asked about copyright sales, the reply was as negative as it was illogical, for the validity of the point was virtually admitted in the Report of the Departmental Committee on Income Tax, 1905, Section IV, paragraph 46, which concluded:

> There is much to be said for this view [that copyright sales should be treated as capital transactions] which, in fact, is in accordance with the principle adopted in dealing with other transactions of a similar character. But in practice it has become the well-established rule to treat such payments for copyright as income to the author, and to assess them in accordance with the rules of Schedule D.

On 22 June 1909 Robert Harcourt MP, a member of the Society, put the same question to the Chancellor of the Exchequer, but to no effect.

In November 1915 Shaw and Charles Garvice[3] were asked by the Society to look into the matter again. They compared an author to an inventor, whose sale of a patent was treated as capital; but they discovered that, for the purposes of tax, invention was regarded not as a profession but as 'a scarce and happy accident', while authorship was a continuing chore. It was not until after the second world war that the Society succeeded in getting the rule altered.[4]

Another subject concerned public libraries. In 1911 a correspondent was complaining that several librarians were buying in job lots of cheap Tauchnitz and Colonial paperback editions of popular novels (the sale of these editions being illegal in the UK), and binding them up to prolong their library use. In 1913 another author reported that in one town the librarian had purchased several copies of a newly published novel, and by operating a short-term system of lending to eager borrowers, succeeded in killing the sale of the book in local shops. In other words public money was being used to deprive the author of his rightful return.[5] The phrase, 'Public Lending Right', had not been framed in 1913.

Yet another subject was the price of novels, hotly debated during 1909, when the Society[6] circulated a questionnaire among authors, publishers and booksellers, asking

a) should new novels be priced at less than 6s (the reigning figure, based on an average sale of 3,000 copies bearing a 10% royalty), in the hope of securing larger sales and thus a better return to the author, although the royalty rate would be less?

b) would authors refuse to authorise the issue of a cheap edition within two years of original publication?

The consensus of replies to the first question was 'No', to the second 'Yes'. Statistics showed that, if an author was to receive an improved or a comparable return to the 6s formula, then it would be necessary to print and sell 9,000–12,000 copies at 2s, 8,000 at 2s 6d, and 6,000 at 3s. The conclusion was that it was safer to stick to the *status quo* and be reasonably sure of selling 3,000 copies at 6s.

*   *   *   *

In that same year, 1909, the Society lost its President, George Meredith, shortly after the death of Algernon Swinburne, who had been his runner-up in the previous presidential election in 1892. The choice for a successor fell, almost without discussion, on Thomas Hardy, long established as a novelist and more recently as a poet. For Hardy to succeed Meredith was an odd quirk of fate, for it was Meredith—as reader to Chapman & Hall—who, while recognising Hardy's potential, advised him to put aside his first MS and try again, which he duly did. Strangely he did not return to Chapman & Hall but went to Tinsley, a grasping publisher of the old sort who, in 1871, issued

Desperate Remedies, Hardy's first published work, on the basis of a contribution of £75 and half-profits thereafter—at a time when Hardy had no more than £123 in the world. In the event Hardy was repaid £60 and thought he had done rather well. Tinsley then paid him £30 outright (plus £10 later for the continental copyright) for *Under the Greenwood Tree*, published in 1872: such an obviously bad bargain that the author asserted he promptly bought a copy of *Copinger on Copyright* and tried his hand at better terms for *A Pair of Blue Eyes*. To little effect however for, when offered serial rights only, Tinsley made a face and said he would only accept if Hardy threw in the volume rights as well—which he weakly did; but the price was better, £200 on advance. It was not however until he let Leslie Stephen[7] serialise *Far from the Madding Crowd* in the *Cornhill* magazine (first instalment in December 1873), and so came to do business with the publisher, George Smith, that he began to get fair terms.

When approached by Maurice Hewlett about the presidency, Hardy at first refused on the grounds that, whereas it had been appropriate for the Society to have in its early years a purely ornamental figure at its head, the time had come to elect someone willing to take a part in its affairs and who, if possible, lived in London. That he could never do. He was 69 years old and lived at Max Gate, the house he had built near Dorchester, where he proposed to remain. In his place he suggested John Morley. However Hewlett managed to persuade him to change his mind, and so Hardy became the Society's third President until his death in 1928, when he was succeeded by J. M. Barrie.

*　　　*　　　*　　　*

Looking back again at the Society's records—the correspondence, minutes and publications—I am always astonished at the volume and variety of work sustained by the Secretary and the small permanent staff. Thring himself was being paid less than £1,000 a year before 1914, and that included an extra fee for editing and producing *The Author* (ten numbers a year). The offices resembled those of a modest solicitor—indeed Edmund Gosse had described the Society as a 'firm of solicitors acting solely for literary clients'; and apparently, it was not until March 1913, when the Society moved from Storey's Gate[8] to 1 Central Buildings, Tothill Street, in Westminster nearby, that there was enough elbow room in which to administer this eccentric organisation. Fifteen months later the title was altered to The Incorporated Society of Authors, Playwrights, and Composers—an indication of the growth of its work.[9] Indeed 'Filmwriters' might have been added, for the cinema was already becoming a factor in authors' contracts.[10]

With 2,500 members, each paying £1 1s a year, a Council, a Committee of Management, five or six permanent sub-committees (including finance, copyright, drama, music, and cinema), several *ad hoc* ones (price of novels, censorship, etc), a Pension Fund started in 1900, a Collection Bureau as from 1912 (which collected royalties for members, though each issue of *The Author* was careful to state that the Bureau was 'in no sense a literary or dramatic agency for the placing of books or plays'), a reading service, and provision for registering scenarios and stamping sheet music, and with correspondence of the order of a thousand outgoing letters a year, personally dictated and signed by Thring himself—all this might have seemed sufficient for a guinea subscription. Yet by the very nature of the Society, fresh demands were constantly being heaped upon it. It should set up a co-operative publishing enterprise, act as a clearing house for the book trade (including disposing of members' unwanted remainders), loan money, train beginners, run a register of titles, and take in allied workers such as illustrators and photographers. All this makes familiar reading. Yet the Society's principal role in this pre-1914 decade has yet to be described.

*   *   *   *

It will be recalled that in 1901—despite formal notice in the King's Speech and further frenzied exertions by authors and publishers acting together—the copyright campaign had died of 'senile decay'. This was one of those occasions when failure after intensive and prolonged pressure (23 years since the Report of the Royal Commission published in 1878) might, through sheer despair, have called a total halt. Yet the protagonists never lost heart, and already fresh impulses were at work—in music for example.

Unlike authors, composers had done virtually nothing to assert their rights by corporate action, notwithstanding repeated invitations by Walter Besant 'to combine with the authors and band themselves together to protect their own property'.[11] A few prominent composers did join the Society and form a sub-committee as early as 1899 but, with the exception of Charles Villiers Stanford, they failed to pursue 'a virile and energetic policy'; so this initial effort petered out and had to be replaced by a more vigorous body after 1911. Publishers dominated the music world. Although the royalty system was belatedly finding its way into music contracts, it was still customary for composers to dispose of their copyrights (both publication and performance rights) to their publishers, who made most of their money from the sale of sheet music: for which purpose they promoted public concerts and subsidised artistes to perform new works.

Unlike the French[12] however, British music publishers paid little or no attention to performing right; indeed they considered that to charge a fee for the right to perform a work acted as a deterrent on the sale of sheet music. Moreover performing right had had an unfortunate history in Britain, due to the activities of Thomas Wall and the legislation of the 1880s,[13] which involved sticking a printed notice on all published music in copyright in order to reserve the right of performance.[14] In fact, since most composers assigned this right to their publishers, almost all public performances were free of copyright restrictions.

By the 1890s however the situation was showing signs of change. For one thing public concerts, even the 'pops', were losing money, and so music publishers gave up promoting them.[15] Another factor was the escalation in the early 1900s of pirate music publishing and sale by street hawkers, especially of songs: a practice that required two Acts of Parliament and a temporary embargo by music publishers on all new music in order to control it.[16] A third factor was the rapid growth of the pianola and gramophone industries and doubts as to whether 'mechanical music', i.e. reproduction of music by 'mechanical contrivances', constituted an infringement of copyright. These events induced a change of attitude towards the enforcement of performing right as a source of income, and ensured its inclusion—together with mechanical right—in the Copyright Act 1911. Thereafter followed the formation in 1914 of the Performing Right Society Ltd, a collecting organisation to which composers, lyric writers, and publishers assigned their performing rights and agreed to share in the resulting income according to carefully calculated proportions.[17] The exploitation of mechanical rights was similarly, but not identically, controlled by two organisations, which amalgamated in 1924 to form the Mechanical Copyright Protection Society Ltd.[18]

Another impulse for reform derived from the periodical revisions of international copyright. The first revision of the Berne Convention of 1886 had taken place in Paris in 1896. It had opened the door to non-signatory countries, and enlarged or altered a number of clauses, providing—for example—improved protection for translations and serialised works and —in a separate Declaration—it covered the conversion of a novel into a play and vice versa. Britain ratified only part of the Paris revision, and it was not until the next conference held in Berlin (14 October–14 November 1908) that such far-reaching changes were made that it became imperative to conform in domestic law.

The Berlin conference was attended by representatives of a large number of countries, including 20 that had so far stayed outside the Convention; while the USA sent an observer, Thorvald Solberg, the renowned Register of Copyrights. The British delegation was led by Sir Henry Bergne, one of the unsung heroes of authors' rights, who tragically died the day after the conference had closed.[19] For most of his life he had worked in the Treaty Department of the Foreign Office; had represented Britain at Berne, Paris and Berlin; and had also applied himself to the problems of copyright in the colonies and dominions, notably Canada, always an area of difficulty. He was far more than an expert civil servant, for he felt deeply about the authors' condition: so much so that he joined the Society of Authors in 1890, became a member of the Committee of Management, and then chairman in 1907–8, when he was brought at an early stage into the preparations for Berlin and revision of domestic copyright.

The Berlin Convention defined afresh, in unmistakeable terms, all original literary, dramatic, artistic and musical works covered by copyright—from leaflets to pantomimes—however published or performed. It took account of the new media—pianola rolls, gramophone records, cinematograph films, etc—and provided protection for the creator even if his work was first issued in a country other than his own, a point of great value to the Americans.[20] Most important it fixed the period of copyright as the life of the author plus 50 years.

In Britain the Liberal Government of the day wasted no time. In March 1909 Sydney Buxton MP, President of the Board of

Trade, assembled a Departmental Committee of 16 members representing the various copyright interests, and examined 45 witnesses in 16 sittings, before publishing its Report at the end of the year. The chief technical representative of the Society of Authors was E. J. MacGillivray, copyright counsel, closely supported by Thring. Their combined contribution to the framing of the Bill was critical, since it comprehended all the knowledge, effort and experience accumulated by the Society since its foundation in 1884. Moreover, as all their most important recommendations were accepted, the 1911 Copyright Act—in its literary aspects—was predominantly the Society's work, and a fitting climax to 27 years of campaigning.

There were of course some anxious moments. It was a Government measure, and the Government had to face two General Elections during 1910. Thus the first Copyright Bill introduced in that year had to be replaced by a second in 1911; but it finally reached the statute book on 16 December, the law to take effect as from 1 July 1912. Hailed as the greatest single advance in the history of domestic copyright, the Act repealed 17 previous Acts absolutely and considerable portions of certain others. It also replaced Common Law in respect of unpublished material. All the anomalies were swept away. Henceforward the copyright owner—be he author, artist, or composer—possessed the sole right to produce or reproduce his work in any form, or to authorise others to do so, e.g. by publication, performance, or mechanical recording, including film. The law vested in the author once and for all the right to dramatise his novel or to novelise his play, and it protected his lectures and speeches. This right of copyright was his for life, and then belonged to his heirs for 50 years after his death.[21] The principal flaw, in the eyes of both authors and publishers, was the continued obligation to deliver no less than six free copies of each new work to 'deposit libraries', viz., one to the British Museum (which all agreed was right), and one each to the Universities of Oxford and Cambridge, Trinity College, Dublin, Advocates' Library, Edinburgh,[22] and—with certain exceptions—to the National Library of Wales. That provision still sticks in the gullets of the producers.

The euphoria generated by the passing of the Act was fairly quickly absorbed, so far as MacGillivray and Thring were concerned, by problems arising out of its adoption by the colonies and dominions. Meanwhile it was a time for jubilation, and the Society's Annual Dinner on 8 December 1911, a week before the Royal Assent, was held to celebrate the event. The speeches are of no particular interest now, indeed mutual congratulations make the most boring kind of reading. What was interesting, for historical reasons, was the presence at the Dinner of three people. One was Squire Sprigge, who had succeeded Maurice Hewlett as chairman of the Committee of Management, and who had served as Secretary of the Society before Thring. Another was Sprigge's uncle, 'Robbie' Ross, friend of Oscar Wilde, whose brother Alexander Galt Ross had been Sprigge's predecessor. Their attendance therefore was a visible reminder of the long struggle for the Act. The third person was Ezra Pound. That was just extraordinary.

*   *   *   *

As I have written in the Introduction, the 1911 Act—a visionary piece of legislation in its own right—was important for another reason, for it could be regarded as the end of an era in which literary communication was restricted to print and the stage. I quote:

> It is true, of course, that both these media continued to play a vital role, and have themselves experienced significant changes since 1911. It is also true that the Act took account of film rights (and for the composer, mechanical music rights); but these new media were still in their beginnings, and were to make no critical impact until after the 1914–18 war, when they were joined by radio, talkies, television and, later still, by tapes, cassettes, and all the new technical resources for storage and communication.

Two years after the Act came into force in July 1912, Austria–Hungary declared war on Serbia. The outbreak of the first world war was an historical boundary, not only in the determination of military, economic and political power throughout the world, but in the dynamics of society. In Britain it took time to register the depth of change, for the 'normality' of the 1920s was barely skin deep. It bore no relation to the reality of decline in national strength and self-confidence, nor to the cracks in the social structure propped up by privilege and wealth. It took the General Strike of 1926 and the economic collapse of 1930 to reveal the full impact of events, and to link the consequences of the first war to the beginnings of the second.

For authors, the changes was no less far-reaching. For four centuries they had been recruited from the broad stream of the middle class in all its reaches. Most had had the benefit of a secondary education, and all had looked to a market dependent on aristocratic patronage or middle class money. Theirs, in short, was still a restricted company in a restricted world. After 1918, but particularly in a society turning turtle after 1939, it was not only the terms of authorship that altered, but the origin and outlook of authors themselves.

NOTES

Introduction
1. The Arvon Foundation has two centres for courses: one at Totleigh
   Barton, Sheepwash, Beaworthy, Devon; the other at Lumb Bank, Hebden
   Bridge, West Yorkshire.
2. *The Book Writers, who are they?* by Richard Findlater. Society of
   Authors 1966. Findlater has written several studies of authorship, based
   on his own knowledge and experience as a professional journalist, notably
   as a member of the staff of *The Observer*, and as editor of *The Author*
   since 1961; also as the author of a number of books on the theatre. His
   studies include two pamphlets, *What are Writers worth?* and *The Book
   Writers, who are they?*, published respectively in 1963 and 1966 by the
   Society of Authors. The last two titles were based on findings of an
   independent postal survey carried out for the Society by Research
   Services Ltd.
3. 'The chief glory of every people arises from its authors'. Samuel Johnson.
4. See Note 2 above.
5. Hansard Vol. 369, No 57, Col 1431. Lord Paget also said: 'I should think
   it extremely doubtful as to whether Shakespeare was a professional
   author'.
6. Lectures and speeches might arguably be added to the list. Both were fully
   protected by the 1911 Copyright Act.

Chapter One
1. This paragraph is based on 'Copyright in a Dramatic Work', contributed
   by M. Elizabeth Barber to *The Oxford Companion to the Theatre*, edited
   by Phyllis Hartnoll, pp. 201–2. OUP 1967.
2. From 'Copyright and Society', contributed by Ian Parsons to *Essays in
   the History of Publishing*, edited by Asa Briggs, p. 32. Longman 1974.
3. From *The Profession of English Letters* by J. W. Saunders, p. 50.
   Routledge 1964.
4. Saunders, p. 72.
5. Information by courtesy of Dr. A. L. Rowse, and Professor David
   Daiches who, however, makes the point that *Titus* was almost certainly
   printed from the author's draft and is now held to be the first
   Shakespearean play to be published from an authoritative MS.
6. 'An Act for the Encouragement of Learning by vesting Copies of printed
   Books in the Authors or Purchasers of such Copies during the Times
   therein mentioned.'
7. One reason was that the effective life of many books was so short that
   only a few titles remained in demand after the first flush of publication:
   which meant that normally neither author nor publisher considered
   arrangements, other than outright sale, worth while.
8. Shakespeare was 'shared' by several publishers. Jacob Tonson I died in

1736, having retired several years earlier and handed over business to his partner and nephew, Jacob II.

9. Robert Walker.

10. Saunders, p. 96.

11. Richardson was Master of the Stationers' Company in 1754.

12. Issued as the third of three volumes of *Miscellanies*.

13. Drury Lane and Lincoln's Inn Fields (whence it descended in 1732 via Dorset Garden to Covent Garden). See *The Oxford Companion to the Theatre*, p. 722. See pp. 22 and 203 re. the Licensing Act 1737.

14. Apart from, say, Goldsmith's *She Stoops to Conquer* (1773), and Sheridan's *The Rivals* (1775) and *The School for Scandal* (1777), no new plays of any quality were written until the advent of Pinero, Wilde, Shaw, and Henry Arthur Jones, at the end of the 19th century.

15. Jacob Tonson I drove a hard bargain whenever he could. One of his authors was Aphra Behn (1640–89), the first professional woman writer of note, who had some success as a dramatist and also tried her hand at novels, translations and lyric poetry. She is on record as having pleaded with Tonson for an advance on a book of poems, 'good deare Mr. Tonson, let it be £5 more . . . I have been without getting so long that I am just on ye poynt of breaking'. Information from Cynthia Hollie. See also *The Incomparable Aphra* by George Woodcock. Boardman 1948. Also *The Passionate Shepherdess* by Maureen Duffy. Cape 1977.

16. Johnson dedicated his *Dictionary* to Lord Chesterfield, who gave him only £10 by way of patronage. In a letter (February 1755) to Chesterfield, Johnson wrote: 'Is not a Patron, my Lord, one who looks with unconcern on a man struggling for life in the water, and, when he has reached ground, encumbers him with help? The notice which you have been pleased to take of my labours, had it been early, had been kind; but it has been delayed until I am indifferent, and cannot enjoy it; till I am solitary, and cannot impart it; till I am known, and do not want it.'

17. See *Oliver Goldsmith: His Life and Works* by A. Lytton Sells, who takes a more optimistic view of Goldsmith's deals. Allen & Unwin 1975.

18. Strahan was then in partnership with Andrew Millar; after the latter's death in 1768, with Thomas Cadell.

19. From *Authorship in the Days of Johnson* by A. S. Collins, p. 43. Robert Holden 1927. James Lackington (1746–1815) was a highly successful bookseller, referred to later in the chapter.

20. For information on share publishing, see A. S. Collins, pp. 18–20, and Chapter XI of *The English Book Trade* by Marjorie Plant. Allen & Unwin 1965.

21. See *Grub St. stripped bare* by Philip Pinkus, Constable 1968.

22. James Thomson, author of *The Seasons* was a member; but he did not take the title away from his friend and publisher, Andrew Millar.

23. Plant, pp. 66–7. John Murray II is said to have been one of the first publishers, who abandoned bookselling.

24. *The Autobiography of John Britton*, two volumes, privately printed and subscribed, 1849–50. The information here derives from Volume I, pp. 200–258.

25. From *The English Common Reader* by Richard D. Altick, pp. 51–2. University of Chicago Press 1963.
26. From *The Minerva Press, 1790–1820* by Dorothy Blakey, p. 18. Printed for the Bibliographical Society at the University Press, Oxford, 1939.
27. *Calamities of Authors: including some inquiries respecting their Moral and Literary Characters* by Isaac d'Israeli. Murray 1812.

Chapter Two
1. From *History of Elementary Education* by Charles Birchenough, p. 251. University Tutorial Press 1931.
2. Leading members included Thomas Babington, Zachary Macaulay, John Newton, James Stephen, Lord Teignmouth, Henry Thornton, and William Wilberforce.
3. From *Hannah More and her Circle* by Mary Alden Hopkins, p. 211. Longman 1947.
4. Altick, p. 129.
5. From *Samuel Smiles and his Surroundings* by Aileen Smiles, p. 88. Robert Hale 1956. John Murray II had offered half-profits.
6. Dr. Thomas Bowdler (1754–1825) edited the *Family Shakespeare* in ten volumes in 1818, 'in which nothing is added to the original work, but those words and expressions are omitted which cannot with propriety be read aloud in the family'.
7. Altick, pp. 272–3.
8. The four names generally associated with the founding of the *Edinburgh Review* were Sydney Smith, Francis Jeffrey, Francis Horner, and Henry Brougham.
9. This quotation and most of the information about the *Edinburgh Review* is taken from the chapter contributed by John Clive to *Essays in the History of Publishing*. Longman 1974.
10. For a discerning account of literary journalism and its practitioners from 1800 onwards, see *The Rise and Fall of the Men of Letters* by John Gross. Weidenfeld and Nicolson 1969.
11. Thomas Longman III bought the copyright, after the first edition, for £500, to which his partner, Owen Rees, added £100. See *Publishing and Bookselling* by F. A. Mumby and Ian Norrie, p. 189. Cape 1974. Longman had also bought the copyright in the third volume of *The Minstrelsy of the Scottish Border*. See also *At the Sign of the Ship, 1724–1794*, a short account of the Longman family and firm, by Philip Wallis. Longman 1974.
12. The first series of *Tales of My Landlord* were published by Murray and Blackwood.
13. Saunders, p. 178.
14. The Society of Literature was founded in 1823 at the suggestion of Thomas Burgess, Bishop of St. David's (later of Salisbury), and received its Royal Charter in 1825. Its objects were:
    The advancement of literature by the publication of inedited remains of ancient literature, and of such works as may be of intrinsic value, but not of that popular character which usually claims the attention of publishers; by the promotion of discoveries in literature; by

endeavouring to fix the standard as far as is practicable, and to preserve the purity of the English language; by the critical improvement of English lexicography; by reading at public meetings of interesting papers on history, philosophy, poetry, philology, and the arts, and the publication of such of those papers as shall be approved of; by the assignment of honorary awards to works of great literary merit, and to important discoveries in literature; and by establishing a correspondence with learned men in foreign countries for the purpose of literary inquiry and information.

See *The Royal Society of Literature of the United Kingdom: A Brief Account of its Origin and Progress* by Edward Brabrook. Asher 1897. Also a leaflet issued by the RSL, 1 Hyde Park Gardens, London W2 2LT.

15. John Hookham Frere (1769–1846), diplomat and author; one of the founders of the *Quarterly Review*.

16. In 1810 the civil remedy of damages was made available in cases of infringement of copyright.

17. From a letter to J. Forbes Mitchell, 21 April 1819. In reproducing these references to perpetual copyright by Southey and Wordsworth, I acknowledge my debt to Ian Parson's chapter, 'Copyright and Society', in *Essays in the History of Publishing*. Longman 1974.

18. John Cam Hobhouse, a college friend at Cambridge, had had a small volume of Byron's poems, *Fugitive Pieces*, privately printed in 1806. This same work was re-issued, with alterations, by Byron in 1807 under the title of *Hours of Idleness*.

19. Cantos VI–XIV of *Don Juan* were published by John Hunt, and XV–XVI by John and his brother Leigh Hunt. Byron's *The Vision of Judgment* was published in the first issue of *The Liberal*, edited by Leigh and published by John Hunt in 1822. Byron gave the copyright to Leigh.

20. *The Late Lord Byron* by Doris Langley Moore. Murray 1961. See also *A Publisher and his Friends: Memoir and Correspondence of the late John Murray, with an Account of the Origin and Progress of the House, 1768–1843*, by Samuel Smiles. Two volumes. Murray 1891.

21. Thomas Moore (1779–1852), Irish poet. He was appointed Admiralty Registrar at Bermuda in 1803, but left the business in the hands of a deputy, who incurred debts of £6,000 which Moore had to pay. Longman paid Moore an advance of £3,000 for his epic *Lallah Rookh*, which, published in 1817, proved a great success. The Bermuda debt was eventually discharged in 1822.

22. The rights in the Cantos first published by the Hunts were secured after the auction.

23. It was first called the *Edinburgh Monthly Magazine*, then *Blackwood's Edinburgh Magazine*, Blackwood himself taking over the editorship.

Chapter Three

1. The authorities were still liable to panic, as shown by the savage treatment meted out to those desperate countrymen who, when denied wages of half-a-crown a day, burned ricks and smashed machinery in the riots of 1830–1. Three years later six Dorset labourers were sentenced to transportation for trying to form a trade union.

2. My own forebears, the Carters, controlled Portsmouth in this fashion, for some seventy years. See my *In a Liberal Tradition*. Constable 1960.
3. This ended the Speenhamland system, which subsidised wages out of the rates, and was costing over £10 million per annum in public assistance.
4. In Ireland tithe was particularly resented, being imposed by a Protestant establishment on a Roman Catholic majority. In 1838 the trouble was submerged by absorbing tithe in rent—in short by transferring the odium from the incumbent to the landlord. The situation was exacerbated seven years later by the failure of the potato crop, expulsion of tenants and a massive wave of emigration to America.
5. The limitations of high book prices and a relatively small buying public were only partly offset by the activities of book clubs, circulating libraries, and organisations such as the Society for the Diffusion of Useful Knowledge. Most cheap books were reprints.
6. G. L. Craik 1798–1866. Historian and man of letters.
7. For example Thomas Tegg, a remainder publisher of doubtful honesty, James Catnach, and the 'sensation-mongers of Salisbury Square and Holywell Street'. See Altick, p. 284 *et seq.*
8. I am obliged to R. M. Cooper, archivist of Longmans, for this information. I have purposely omitted any reference to Longmans' publication in 1880 of Benjamin Disraeli's *Endymion*, for the copyright of which the publisher paid £10,000, the highest sum for a work of fiction up to that date. This episode is fully recounted by Annabel Jones in a chapter contributed to *Essays in the History of Publishing*, edited by Asa Briggs. Longman 1974.
9. In his article in *Studies in English Literature*, Volume X, No. 4, autumn 1970, Robert L. Patten of Rice University, Houston, Texas, states that *Vanity Fair* lost money as a serial. 'It did not earn enough to pay the publishers their contractual £1,200 until mid-1850. On the other hand bound volumes and the cheap edition (1853) sold well; by 1859 Thackeray had received over £1,700 for his novel'. Patten supplies a detailed table of returns, June 1847–December 1858, and adds the following note on the publisher's side of the contract. 'Bradbury and Evans were to deduct all expenses, including their 10% commission on gross sales [plus revenue from space sold to advertisers], and were then supposed to take an equivalent £60 for themselves, during the serial run. The remainder was to be divided equally, and the copyright owned jointly'.
10. Thackeray's income from journalism at this time was in excess of £700 p.a. He ended his regular connection with *Punch* in 1851.
11. See Chapter Four, p. 85.
12. Dickens sold the copyright of the original series to Macrone for £150, but it has been estimated that this total had increased to nearly £400 by 1839.
13. Edward Chapman and William Hall set up their publishing house in 1830.
14. Dickens resigned from the *Morning Chronicle* in 1837.
15. Richard Bentley began his publishing business in 1829 in partnership with Henry Colburn, whom he bought out in 1837.

16. I am advised that, for all practical purposes, the terms 'part' and 'number' are interchangeable.
17. *American Notes* was published by Chapman & Hall to whom Dickens gave a quarter share of the copyright and profits.
18. See p. 598 of Volume One of the Pilgrim Edition of *The Letters of Charles Dickens*, edited by Madeline House and Graham Storey. Clarendon Press, Oxford, 1965. See also *Charles Dickens* by Una Pope-Hennessy, pp. 287–8. Pelican 1970.
19. Successive Christmas books all did well. *'The Chimes* (1844) sold at least 20,000 yielding £1,400 to £1,500 profits; *The Cricket on the Hearth* (1845) "at the outset doubled the sales of both its predecessors"; *The Battle of Life* (1846), sold 24,450 by the end of the year, £1,281 15s 4d as Dickens's share; *The Haunted Man* (1848), 17,776 to 31 December, £793 5s 11d profits to Dickens.' See Appendix 1 contributed by Robert L. Patten to *Dickens: The Critical Heritage*, ed. Philip Collins. Barnes and Noble, New York, 1971.
20. *op. cit.*
21. *op. cit.* It should be emphasised that the figure of £2,900 referred only to Dickens's writings, exclusive of income from *Household Words* and *All the Year Round*, and from his public readings.

Chapter Four
1. Altick, pp. 253–4.
2. See *Free Trade in Books: A Study of the London Book Trade since 1800* by James J. Barnes, Chapters II–V. Clarendon Press 1964. This work is referred to as Barnes (1). Most publishers were still known as 'booksellers', hence the title of the 'Booksellers' Association'.
3. Routledge, for instance, contracted to pay Bulwer-Lytton £2,000 p.a. for ten years' rights. Altick, p. 299. See also Note 5.
4. See Chapter Three of Gavin McFarlane's *Copyright: The Development and Exercise of the Performing Right* (thesis submitted to the University of London in 1975 for the degree of Doctor of Philosophy), which describes in detail the ways in which dramatists' works were exploited before the 1833 Act.
5. Bulwer-Lytton was born Edward George Earle Lytton Bulwer (1803–73), created baronet 1837, 1st Baron Lytton 1859. His mother, Elizabeth Barbara Lytton extended the surname after the death of her husband, General William Bulwer, and on inheriting her property at Knebworth. Thus Edward was referred to as Lytton Bulwer or Bulwer-Lytton at different times in his life. He combined an active public career with a prodigious output of novels, plays, essays, poems, and other works which gained great popularity during his lifetime. It was he who asked for a Select Committee (1831–2) to inquire into legislation affecting dramatic literature and performance—which preceded the 1833 Act.
6. From *The Oxford Companion to the Theatre*, edited by Phyllis Hartnoll, p. 202. Third Edition, OUP 1967.
7. *op. cit.*, p. 202. The official title was the Copyright Amendment Act 1842.
8. Thomas Noon Talfourd (1795–1854), miscellaneous writer, barrister,

serjeant 1833, justice of the common pleas 1849. MP for Reading 1835–41.

9. Hansard, 5 February 1841.
10. Brougham had not held office since being Lord Chancellor 1830–4, but he was still a powerful advocate in the House of Lords.
11. See *Copyright: its History and its Law* by R. R. Bowker, p. 28. Houghton Mifflin 1912.
12. From *International Copyright and the Publisher in the reign of Queen Victoria* by Simon Nowell-Smith, p. 22 and footnote. Clarendon Press 1968. An important source of information for this chapter.
13. Harriet Martineau (1802–76) wrote mainly on social and economic subjects and was highly esteemed in public life. See later in this chapter and in Chapter Five. She visited USA 1834–6 and published two books on her experiences which were eagerly read but, owing to the absence of a copyright treaty, she never received a cent from her American sales.
14. Quoted from p. 118 of *Authors, Publishers and Politicians. The Quest for an Anglo-American Copyright Agreement 1815–54* by James J. Barnes. Routledge 1974. Referred to later as Barnes (2). An important source of information for this chapter.
15. The British possessions in North America were not at that date united; and consisted of Canada, New Brunswick, Nova Scotia, Newfoundland, and Prince Edward Island.
16. This Act applied chiefly to the treaty with France signed the previous year, and intended as much to protect authors of French farces against the depredations of British adaptors, as British novelists whose works proved popular in translation abroad.
17. Barnes (2), p. 153. However a music case, *D'Almaine* v. *Boosey* in 1835, and a book case, *Bentley* v. *Foster* in 1839, established that foreign authors were protected if a work was published in Britain 'prior to or simultaneous with its appearance abroad'. Ironically, by introducing the concept of reciprocity, the International Copyright Act 1838 confused the issue, so that—despite the 1839 decision—most lawyers then took the view that copyright was only valid for authors whose countries had concluded treaties with Britain under the Act; but since no such treaties came into being before 1846, the whole matter was thrown into limbo.
18. Barnes (2), Chapter III, p. 49 *et seq.*, traces the history of voluntary copyright payments by US publishers: e.g. by Carey and Lea of Philadelphia who made small payments for advance sheets of some of Walter Scott's novels, and by Harper Brothers of New York who made similar arrangements with Bulwer-Lytton. Eventually the latter's London publishers, Saunders and Otley, opened an office in New York in 1836 in an attempt to forestall their rivals and issue American editions of British copyright works themselves; but competition—particularly by Harpers—proved too strong and the venture had to be abandoned within a few years.
19. Although refused an injunction in the Court of Chancery, mainly due to doubts about the dates and origins of first publication in the UK, Murray and Bentley decided to take proceedings further. Their cause was greatly strengthened when, on 20 May 1851, in the same court, Lord Campbell reversed a previous ruling in respect of a music case, *Boosey* v. *Jefferys*,

and upheld the right of a foreign author to British copyright protection. Soon afterwards Murray and Bentley settled with their opponents out of court and sold them the copyrights as mentioned. But that was not the end of the story for, two years later, Lord Campbell's decision was altered yet again. Thanks to the energy of Henry Bohn, who formed a group calling itself 'The Society for Obtaining an Adjustment of the Law of Copyright', recruiting Bulwer-Lytton and other authors in support, the question was referred to the House of Lords as described.

20. Barnes (2), p. 172.
21. *op. cit.* Chapters IV and IX–XII describe in detail the protracted efforts (including bribery) to secure an International Copyright Act in USA at this time.
22. The petition is reproduced in Bowker, pp. 341–4.
23. Edward Everett (1794–1865), US Minister to Great Britain 1841–5.
24. See Note 18.
25. From footnote, p. 86 of Volume Three of the Pilgrim Edition of *The Letters of Charles Dickens*, edited by Madeline House, Graham Storey, and Kathleen Tillotson. Clarendon Press 1974. Referred to later as *CD Letters III*. I have drawn on this work for all the quotations and most of the information about Dickens's visit to America in 1842 and his activities on his return.
26. *op. cit.*, footnote, p. 59.
27. *op. cit.*, footnote, p. 238. 'A memorial against international copyright . . . forwarded to Congress by a convention of printers, publishers, and others engaged in the book trade, after a meeting in Boston on 26 April 1842 . . . concluded with statistics showing that 41,000 people were employed in the American book trade, and that the capital invested was almost 15 million dollars.'
28. Dickens pictured Scott in highly emotional terms, broken by debts that might have been met, had he received the income due from his American sales.
29. *CD Letters III*, pp. 82–3.
30. *op. cit.*, footnote, p. 84.
31. *op. cit.*, footnote, p. 85.
32. The memorial, printed on pp. 621–2 of *CD Letters III*, was dated 28 March 1842, and signed by Edward Bulwer-Lytton, Thomas Campbell, Alfred Tennyson, T. N. Talfourd, Thomas Hood, Leigh Hunt, Henry Hallam, Sydney Smith, J. J. Milman, Samuel Rogers, John Forster, and Barry Cornwall. The letter from Thomas Carlyle, dated 26 March, is printed on pp. 623–4.
33. From a letter to John Forster of 3 May 1842. *CD Letters III*, p. 231.
34. *op. cit.*, pp. 256–9.
35. Earlier and contemporary attempts of which I have found evidence include:
    i) The Society for the Encouragement of Learning, 1736–48. See pp. 28–9 of this book.
    ii) Unnamed society, no date or details, proposed by Richard Cumberland, the dramatist, (1732–1811). Referred to by Horace Smith, see Note 53.
    iii) Society for the Encouragement of Literature. Prospectus published

in *John Bull*, 6 March 1825, and in the *Courier*, 11 March. Its main aim was to purchase the copyright of works 'which may be deemed worthy of public approbation'. Capital to be £100,000 in shares of £25. Colonel Nugent, chairman. SoA archives.

iv) Thomas Campbell's Literary Union Club, 1831. Its object was to raise capital so that members could co-operate in publishing their own works. *CD Letters III*, footnote, p. 287.

v) William Jerdan's National Association for the Encouragement and Protection of Authors, 1838. This had aims similar to those of Campbell's Club. *op. cit.*, footnote, p. 287.

vi) Charles Mackay's Milton Institute, 1842: proposed as an association of men of letters for 'mutual support and assistance', with club facilities. *op. cit.*, footnote, p. 287.

vii) The Literary and Dramatic Fund Association, a benevolent fund, established late in 1842, first meeting 6 June 1843, Benjamin Bond Cabbell, President; William Carpenter, Secretary. *op. cit.*, footnote, p. 435.

viii) The British and Foreign Institute, 1843, founded by James Silk Buckingham, who may have thought of the idea as early as 1825. The Prospectus proposed 'a centre of Personal Intercourse' for gentlemen of all countries, and 'a permanent home and resting-place' for Mr. Buckingham himself. Apparently over a thousand members joined, some of them possibly from the still-born Society of British Authors (described in this chapter). The Institute was formally opened in Hanover Square on 2 February 1844 by the Prince Consort, but the organisation collapsed in 1846. *op. cit.*, footnote, p. 508.

ix) Also published in 1843 was John Petheram's *Reasons for Establishing an Authors' Publication Society*, which advanced proposals for co-operative publishing. Nothing came of the idea, which—with some of the other schemes mentioned—is discussed by James Hepburn in his *The Author's Empty Purse & The Rise of the Literary Agent*, p. 37 *et seq.* OUP 1968.

36. Walter Besant (1836–1901). His life and work are described later in this chapter and in Chapters Six to Eight. He had researched the history of the Society of British Authors in some depth, having acquired an important collection of correspondence and other papers (including some belonging to Wilkie Collins) which have unfortunately disappeared. The information here derives from Besant's article and *CD Letters III* (especially the footnote on pp. 442–3).

37. *CD Letters III*, footnote, pp. 442–3.

38. *op. cit.*, footnote, pp. 477–8.

39. A proof of this Prospectus, with a copy of the covering letter dated 3 May 1843, signed by John Robertson, is in the possession of the Rare Book Department, Free Library of Philadelphia, USA. It is of interest that, in this version of the Prospectus, it was proposed to use the title 'The Society of Authors' instead of 'The Society of British Authors'.

40. From p. 13 of Besant's article, from which succeeding quotations are taken.

41. An earlier covering letter, signed by John Robertson.

42. It is suggested that Dickens was thinking of Samuel Carter Hall, a journalist, and James Silk Buckingham, see Note 35 (viii).
43. *CD Letters III*, pp. 477–8.
44. *op. cit.*, pp. 478–9.
45. See Barnes (2), p. 129 *et seq*, and p. 281, Note 33 on that page.
46. See Nowell-Smith, pp. 41–63.
47. Information from The Royal Literary Fund, 11 Ludgate Hill, London EC4.
48. Pope-Hennessy, p. 393.
49. *op. cit.*, p. 570.
50. *CD Letters III*, footnote, pp. 478–9.
51. These letters formed part of the collection acquired by Besant. See Note 36.
52. She was commenting on the original draft, not the revised version of the Prospectus.
53. Horace Smith (1779–1849), friend of Richard Cumberland, see Note 35 (ii), and joint-author with his brother James of *Rejected Addresses*, a best-selling collection of parodies.
54. George Henry Lewes (1817–78), man of letters, Common Law husband of Mary Ann Evans ('George Eliot'). See Chapter Five.
55. All was virtually over by June 1843.
56. *CD Letters III*, footnote, pp. 478–9.

Chapter Five
1. My principal authority in all that follows about Charles Reade is *Charles Reade* by Malcolm Elwin. Cape 1931. Russell and Russell, New York, 1969.
2. Tom Taylor (1817–80), dramatist, journalist, barrister, and Secretary to the Royal Board of Health, 1850–71.
3. Dion Boucicault (1820?–90), actor and dramatist, retired to America in 1876 and died there.
4. Charles John Kean (1811?–68), son of a famous father, Edmund Kean (1787–1835), both actors.
5. Nicholas Trübner (1817–74), born at Heidelberg, clerk at Longmans before setting up on his own as a publisher.
6. For a discussion of the royalty system, see pp. 135–8 and p. 180.
7. Elwin, pp. 109–10.
8. *op. cit.*, p. 117.
9. Edouard Brisebarre and Eugene Nus.
10. Registration at Stationers' Hall was voluntary, but provided essential evidence in cases of infringement.
11. 'Thou shalt not steal'.
12. Elwin, p. 139.
13. 'Another cumbersome institution brought into being by ambiguous phrasing in the [1842] Act was the "copyright performance". It was generally believed, though the belief seems to have had no clear legal support, that if a play was published before it was performed, the performing right in it was irretrievably lost. Actors were therefore hired to give what amounted to public readings of manuscript plays. Normally no costumes were worn and no scenery used.' From *The Oxford*

Companion to the Theatre, pp. 202–3. Third Edition, OUP 1967. See also the remarks by John Hollingshead on pp. 139–41.

14. Published in three volumes on commission by Sampson Low.
15. For an account of this *cause célèbre*, see *The Tichborne Claimant* by Douglas J. Woodruff. Hollis and Carter 1957.
16. For example, Wilkie Collins, Charles Dickens, W. S. Gilbert, and other less eminent authors.
17. See *Justice for Authors*, contributed by William Moy Thomas (1828–1910) to the *St. James's Magazine*, Vol. 1, 1875.
18. The Letters were published Sept–Oct 1875 simultaneously in these two journals, and may be regarded as an Appendix to *The Eighth Commandment*. See Elwin, p. 281.
19. Sir James Fitzjames Stephen (1829–94), author, barrister, and judge.
20. Bowker, p. 30.
21. See *The Brontës* by Phyllis Bentley. Home and Van Thal 1947; *The Brontës: The Creative Work* by Winifred Gérin. Longman 1974; and *The House of Smith Elder* by Leonard Huxley. Privately published 1923.
22. *The Autobiography of Harriet Martineau*. Two Volumes. Smith Elder 1877. This passage is from Vol. 1, pp. 249–50. All the information and quotations in this chapter derive from the same work.
23. All the information in this chapter about George Eliot derives from one particular biography, *George Eliot*, by Gordon S. Haight. OUP 1968. But see also *Victorian Novelists and Publishers* by J. A. Sutherland. The Athlone Press 1976, an authoritative study of the contractual arrangements of Eliot, Dickens, Thackeray, Trollope, and other successful writers of the time.
24. John Chapman (1822–94), head of the business, led the revolt against price control which caused the downfall of the Booksellers' Association in 1852, see Chapter Four. He is not to be confused with Edward Chapman of Chapman & Hall.
25. The finances of the *Westminster Review* were always precarious. The contributors cost £250 per issue, of which only 650 copies were printed, selling at 5s. Chapman had acquired the periodical with the help of an eccentric benefactor, Edward Lombe, who unfortunately died before the publication of the second number. Thereafter others made loans, including Harriet Martineau, who recorded her relations with Chapman in this matter in Vol. II of her autobiography, p. 425 *et seq.*
26. Although Harriet Martineau and Mary Ann Evans remained friends, Harriet took a dislike to Lewes from the first.
27. Haight, p. 370.
28. *An Autobiography* by Anthony Trollope. The World's Classics. OUP 1974. All the information and quotations used in this chapter derive from this edition.
29. *Can You Forgive Her?* earned £3,525, and several other works exceeded £3,000.

Chapter Six
1. Sir William Frederick Pollock Bt (1815–88), Queen's Remembrancer and author, was the father of Frederick Pollock (1845–1937) and Walter

Herries Pollock (1850–1926), who were both barristers and authors, and active in the affairs of the Society. Sir William Frederick was Chairman of the Committee of Management 1886–7, Sir Frederick (his son) held the same post 1893–4, while Walter Herries also served on the Committee.

2. All the information and quotations about the formation and progress of the Society of Authors (SoA) derive from SoA archives, unless otherwise stated.

3. Paternoster Row, where many publishers had their offices.

4. A protracted examination of the constitution was conducted 1973–8.

5. In his autobiography (p. 197), Besant wrote: 'The novel or story first appeared in a magazine or journal; it was then published in three-volume form; after a year or so it came out in a single volume at 3s 6d; and finally as a "yellow-back" at 2s.'

6. The sequence of events was described on 2 March 1887 at the meeting at Willis's Rooms (see p. 139) by Sir Francis Adams, Minister at Berne and a Vice-President of the Society of Authors. He said that the International Literary and Artistic Association (founded in 1878 under the presidency of Victor Hugo, thanks to the initiative of the French Société des Gens de Lettres) had met at Berne in 1883 and drafted the Convention which the Swiss agreed to submit to various interested Governments in Europe and America, inviting them to send representatives to a diplomatic conference. This duly led to the first International Conference on Copyright held at Berne in 1884, which Adams attended as an observer, without power to speak or vote. On a visit to England shortly afterwards, Adams impressed on the Council of the Society of Authors the great importance for the representative of Britain, as one of the first literary countries of the world, to be allowed in any future Conference to play a full part and vote. He put the same point to the Foreign Office and the Board of Trade, with the result that he and Henry Bergne (a civil servant at the Foreign Office and a later Chairman of the Society's Committee of Management) attended the 1885 Conference at Berne with full powers. This meant that, following the March deputation and the passage of the International Copyright Act, the British representatives were authorised to sign the International Copyright Convention in September 1886. The Order in Council was signed in November 1887. Britain thus became an original member of the Berne Union, together with France, Germany, Italy, Belgium, Spain, Switzerland, and Haiti. The USA had sent an observer but did not sign the Convention. For a detailed account of these events, see *The Law of International Copyright* by William Briggs, p. 234 *et seq.* Stevens and Haynes, London 1906.

7. Report in the *Daily News*, 16 March 1886. SoA representatives were Frederick Pollock, Comyns Carr, Basil Field, Walter Besant, J. Lely, Charles Leland, James Martineau, John Hollingshead and E. M. Underdown QC.

8. Of the £285 0s 6d, life subscriptions accounted for £115 10s, annual subscriptions and miscellaneous income for £169 10s 6d. Valentine intimated that if the life subscriptions were capitalised, the balance of income would stand at £10 16s 11d: in which case he would make no

charge, since he had agreed to forgo any payment until the subscription income exceeded £200 p.a. If however the life subscriptions were to be treated as income, then his bill for handling members' cases would be £90 6s 0d. His forecast for 1885 was most pessimistic. Since a recent recruiting drive had yielded only 9% in terms of 'favourable replies' and many subscriptions remained unpaid from the previous year, he did not see how his future charges were to be met. Valentine continued to badger the Society, and in May 1885 submitted a claim for £221 11s, when the Society had less than £100 in the bank. By this time however Besant had recruited a new solicitor, Basil Field, senior partner of Field Roscoe & Co, of Bedford Square, a firm that was to serve the Society for the next 80 years or so. It is not recorded how Field finally dealt with Valentine, but it is understood that a settlement of about £100 was duly reached. It is likely that Field's own charges remained practically invisible for the next few years.

9. In January 1885 the Society had taken a single room on the ground floor of 6 Queen Anne's Gate at a rent of £35 p.a., and authorised the expenditure of a maximum of £21 on the purchase of 'a table, chairs, and other necessary articles'.

10. Little served in this capacity January 1887–c. August 1888.

11. On giving up the post of Secretary, Sprigge joined the Committee of Management and was Chairman in 1911 and 1912. He was a qualified doctor of medicine and edited *The Lancet* for many years.

12. Edward Thring is an honoured name in the history of education. He transformed Uppingham into one of the foremost public schools, was an original and progressive teacher, and founded the Headmasters' Conference in 1869.

13. Re-issued as a separate pamphlet. SoA archives.

14. Actually 24 Salisbury Street, Strand.

15. While remaining Chairman of the Council, Besant retired as Chairman of the Committee of Management, though he continued to attend as a member. Besant was succeeded by James Cotter Morison in 1885, and he in turn by Sir William Frederick Pollock Bt in 1886–7. The latter fell ill in 1887 (and died in 1888), and Besant was voted back as Chairman 1888–92. He also edited *The Author* 1890–1901, see Note 16.

16. *The Author*, July 1901, p. 23. *The Author* was launched as the journal of the Society in May 1890 as a monthly and 'conducted', i.e. edited by Walter Besant. It later became a quarterly.

17. In his paper Besant omitted any reference to the type of arrangement favoured, for example, by George Eliot and John Blackwood, i.e., the limited licence or lease of copyright per edition or term of years. The omission was however corrected in the Society's booklet, *The Methods of Publishing*, written by Squire Sprigge and published in 1890. Further information on the various systems current in the 18th and 19th centuries is provided by James Hepburn in his book, *The Author's Empty Purse*, pp. 10–14. OUP 1968. He refers particularly to two essays entitled *Publishers and Authors*, printed at his own expense in 1867 by James Spedding, and devoted to a study of half-profits and royalties.

18. Besant conceded that the publisher was entitled to make a handling charge, not however calculated as a percentage of the cost of production, but an outright fee not exceeding £50 per book.
19. Both Smith's letter to *The Times* and Putnam's statement were published as Appendices to *The Grievances between Authors and Publishers*.
20. Quoted in *Grievances*.
21. John Hollingshead, 1827–1906, journalist and theatre manager.
22. Herman Charles Merivale, 1839–1906, playwright and novelist.
23. See Note 13, Chapter Five.
24. Mrs. Henry Wood (née Ellen Price) published *East Lynne* in the *New Monthly Magazine* 1861.
25. 'Ouida', pen name of Marie Louise de la Ramée, 1839–1908, wrote 45 novels on military and fashionable subjects.
26. John Lawrence Toole, 1830–1906, actor and theatre manager.
27. Little's account was intended for publication in *The Author*, spring issue 1928; but it never appeared, possibly owing to being crowded out by an obituary of Thomas Hardy, lately President of the Society.

Chapter Seven
1. Quoted from the Resolution passed in the House of Commons on 18 February 1834 and adopted by the Select Committee of 1837.
2. Published by Chatto & Windus in 1888.
3. *op. cit.*, pp. 334–8.
4. Between December 1888 and February 1889.
5. For information about Nicoll, see *A Living Memory* by John Attenborough. Hodder 1976.
6. The Associated Booksellers of Great Britain and Ireland was founded on 23 January 1895, the Publishers Association on 23 January 1896. The former changed its title to The Booksellers Association in 1948.
7. For information about Tennyson I am indebted to *Alfred Tennyson*, the biography written by his grandson, Sir Charles Tennyson. Macmillan 1949; and to notes by his great-grandson, Hallam Tennyson.
8. *Memories* by C. Kegan Paul, p. 294. First published in 1899, new edition by Routledge in 1971.
9. For information about Meredith, I have drawn on *George Meredith* by Jack Lindsay. Bodley Head 1956.
10. SoA archives.
11. *The Author, the 'Ghost', and the Society* by Hume Nisbet. Greening and Co., 1904.
12. *The Art of Authorship*, compiled and edited by George Bainton. James Clarke 1890.
13. *The Author*, June 1890, pp. 44–5.
14. *op. cit.*, July 1890, pp. 83–4.
15. For example, the views of Richard D'Oyly Carte, the opera impresario, were sought on dramatic copyright.
16. G. H. Putnam, the American publisher and a staunch crusader for international copyright, commented: 'The conditional measure for securing American Copyright for aliens . . . a measure which is the result of fifty-three years of effort on the part of individual workers and of successive Copyright Committees and Leagues, brings the United States

to the point reached by France in 1810 and by Great Britain and the States of Germany in 1836–1837'. Quoted on p. 642 of *The Law of International Copyright* by William Briggs. Stevens and Haynes 1906.

17. This Act laid the foundations of Canada as a self-governing Dominion, consisting of a federation of the provinces.
18. Gilbert Parker (1862–1932) wrote poetry, plays and novels. Member of SoA Council and Committee of Management. MP for Gravesend 1900–18.
19. By the Customs Tariff Act 1894, Canada abolished the duty levied under the Foreign Reprints Act 1847. By the Copyright Act 1900 she prohibited the importation of copies of British works, when the exclusive rights of publication had already been secured in Canada.
20. This was to be a Government Bill.

Chapter Eight
1. OUP 1968.
2. The validity and scope of authors' rights are still not fully understood. As late as November 1976, the Public Lending Right Bill—a Government measure, supported by all parties—was defeated by a filibuster on Third Reading in the House of Commons; and this, after 25 years' strenuous campaigning.
3. Quoted from Notices regularly appearing in *The Author*, from 1892 onwards.
4. From *William Heinemann* by Frederic Whyte, p. 123. Cape 1928.
5. Reported in *The Author*, January and February 1910.
6. See Hepburn; also *A. P. Watt: The First Hundred Years* by Hilary Rubinstein in *The Bookseller*, 3 May 1975; also *Literary Agents come of age* by the same writer in *The Times Literary Supplement*, 12 December 1975.
7. See *The Letters of Arnold Bennett: Volume 1, Letters to J. B. Pinker*, edited by James Hepburn. OUP 1966.
8. See *Contacts* by Curtis Brown. Cassell 1935.
9. It was said that Heinemann's dislike of agents in general, and of A. P. Watt in particular, stemmed from the allegation that Watt had taken Kipling away from him. It should be added that Heinemann spoke out no less forcefully against the Society of Authors at times. In December 1892 in the *Athenaeum*, he described the Society as 'a trades union more complete, more dangerous . . . more determined in its demands than any of the other unions—conducted, besides, with intelligence, with foresight, with purity of purpose, but unquestionably and avowedly against the publisher'.
10. From *The Commercialisation of Literature* by Curtis Brown in the *Fortnightly Review*, August 1906.
11. In 1932 the Society published a discussion in *The Author* about the pros and cons of literary agency, concluding that the best thing for agents was to set up an organisation of their own.
12. Most of the information about the 'new journalism' is taken from Herd and Altick.
13. For information about Ruskin's publishing enterprise and subsequent history of the firm of George Allen & Sons, see *Facets of Ruskin* by J. S.

Dearden. Charles Skilton 1970; and *From Swan Sonnenschein to George Allen & Unwin Ltd* by F. A. Mumby and Frances H. S. Stallybrass. Allen & Unwin 1955.

14. See *The Net Book Agreement 1899* by Frederick Macmillan. Robert Maclehose 1924.

15. From *Arnold Bennett* by Margaret Drabble, p. 278. Weidenfeld and Nicolson 1974.

16. *The Truth about an Author*, Constable 1903; and *How to become an Author*. Pearson 1903.

17. One anecdote about Bennett's attitude to authorship is particularly revealing. On being asked in 1922 for a contribution to a fund to subsidise T. S. Eliot, so that he could give up his work as a bank employee to write poetry, Bennett replied: 'It irks me to refuse an appeal from you; but I do not think that this kind of appeal can be logically justified. According to my gospel, the first duty of a man is to earn his living; he must be an artist afterwards'. From *Ottoline: The Life of Lady Ottoline Morell* by Sandra Jobson Darroch, p. 250. Chatto 1976.

18. For much of the information about Wells, I have drawn on *The Time Traveller: The Life of H. G. Wells* by Norman and Jeanne Mackenzie. Weidenfeld and Nicolson 1973. *The Outline of History* and *The Science of Life* were first issued in fortnightly parts; and for the latter work Wells depended heavily on the help of his son, G. P. Wells, and Julian Huxley. For an account of his row in 1929–30 with Hugh P. Vowles, one of his collaborators in *The Work, Wealth and Happiness of Mankind*, see pp. 359–63 of the Mackenzies' book. This is of particular interest as it involved G. Herbert Thring, Secretary of the Society of Authors, and in due course most of the Committee of Management, Bernard Shaw playing a prominent part as peacemaker. The original correspondence and papers, including two pamphlets which Wells had privately published by Stanley Unwin, form part of the Society of Authors' archive in the British Museum.

19. Quoted from an article in *The Author*, autumn 1946, p. 2.

Chapter Nine
Note. Unless otherwise stated, quotations from letters by Shaw are taken from *Collected Letters*, edited by Dan H. Laurence. See SELECT BIBLIOGRAPHY.

1. This disregards Wells's row with Hugh P. Vowles in 1929–30, which involved most of the top brass of the Society. See Note 18, Chapter Eight.

2. The following summarised account is based on information in two biographies of Bernard Shaw: one by St. John Ervine (Constable 1956); the other by Hesketh Pearson (Collins 1942, re-issued by Macdonald and Jane's 1975).

3. St. John Ervine, p. 231.

4. See p. 200.

5. Grant Richards went bankrupt in 1905.

6. The relationship with R. & R. Clark dated back to 1896–7, when Shaw declined to let Richards work with a non-trade union shop on his book, and opted for Clark's which *was* unionised and had carried out printing

234

for Webb. The connection lasted until Shaw's death. The firm of Constable was founded in 1890 by Archibald Constable, grandson of the great Edinburgh publisher and friend of Walter Scott. Three years later he retired in favour of his nephew, H. Arthur Doubleday, the latter being joined in 1895 by Otto Kyllmann and W. M. Meredith (son of George Meredith).

7. St. John Ervine, p. 342.
8. *op. cit.*, pp. 336–7 fn.
9. Vestryman 1897–9, and after the Local Government Act of 1899, Borough Councillor 1899–1904.
10. *The Author*, February 1902.
11. Doubleday, Page & Co, 1905.
12. *The Author*, Winter 1932.
13. *op. cit.*, June 1906.
14. This was the same issue fought in a running battle over the Press Charter 1975 onwards, involving publishers, editors, journalists and authors. In 1978, after active consultation of members, the Society organised a Referendum which yielded a 2 : 1 majority in favour of applying for trade union status. This action was regarded as necessary in view of the changed political climate, following the passage of the Trade Union and Labour Relations Act 1974, and the Employment Protection Act 1975. No mandate however was given for affiliation to the Trade Union Congress.
15. *The Author*, Summer 1945. Shaw had expressed the same view in a letter to Daniel Macmillan of 11 September 1943. See *Letters to Macmillan*, edited by Simon Nowell-Smith. Macmillan 1967.
16. Letter to *The Times* of 17 November 1906.
17. Sidney Lee, 1859–1926, editor of the *Dictionary of National Biography*.
18. Professor Ray Lankester, 1847–1929; zoologist.
19. Sir Alfred Lyall, 1835–1911, Indian administrator and historian.
20. Israel Zangwill, 1864–1926, author and philanthropist.
21. Shaw practised what he preached by issuing, in August 1907, a special edition (500 copies) of a new volume of plays over the imprint of The Times Book Club. Sales went very well. He had earlier justified his intentions to Constable, in a letter dated 26 March 1907 addressed to Otto Kyllmann, prefacing his remarks with the sentence, 'The first thing to grasp in this matter is that you are hopelessly and entirely in the wrong, and that I am absolutely and solidly in the right'.
22. Mrs. Humphry Ward, 1851–1920, popular novelist.
23. Abraham Stoker, 1847–1912, novelist, author of *Dracula*.
24. It is likely that Shaw had given Webb much help in the drafting behind the scenes, but said nothing publicly in order to avoid arousing personal opposition.
25. This was not corrected until the Copyright Act 1911.
26. H. M. Paull later acted as Hon. Secretary to the Dramatists' Club, founded by A. W. Pinero on 17 March 1909.
27. Annual Report of the Society of Authors for 1908.
28. *Report from the Joint Select Committee of the House of Lords and the House of Commons on the STAGE PLAYS (CENSORSHIP) 1909.* (214) 3s 6d. Shaw's evidence was also reprinted by the Shaw Society in

Shavian Tract No. 3, February 1955, under the title, *Shaw on Censorship*.

29. This statement is included in the Preface to *The Shewing-up of Blanco Posnet*.
30. Miscellaneous paper dated 17 May 1948.
31. Oswald Crawfurd, 1934–1909, essayist and poet.
32. Herbert Trench, 1865–1923, poet and playwright.
33. W. E. H. Lecky, 1838–1903, historian, President of the Royal Literary Fund.
34. John Morley, 1838–1923, politician, editor and biographer.
35. James Bryce, 1838–1922; jurist, politician, and historian.
36. James Frazer, 1854–1941; anthropologist, author of *The Golden Bough*.
37. Morley Roberts, 1857–1942, novelist and biographer.
38. Maurice Hewlett, 1861–1923, novelist, poet and essayist.
39. Douglas Freshfield, 1845–1934, explorer and geographer.
40. Members nominated to the Academic Committee were listed in the December 1910, June and October 1911 issues of *The Author*.
41. Information from The Royal Society of Literature.

Chapter Ten

1. Hesketh Pearson, p. 283.
2. The next collective move occurred in 1920, when the Society sought to form a Union of Dramatic Authors. This was followed ten years later by the foundation of the League of British Dramatists.
3. Charles Garvice 1833–1921, novelist, journalist and dramatist.
4. See *Quick Guide No. 4*, issued by the Society of Authors, which covers Income Tax, Capital Gains Tax, and Sale of Copyright.
5. In both cases, of course, the interests of publishers and booksellers were also affected.
6. This operation was managed by a sub-committee consisting of S. Squire Sprigge, chairman, Mrs. Belloc Lowndes (1868–1947, novelist), Charles Garvice, E. W. Hornung (1866–1921, journalist and novelist) and W. W. Jacobs (1863–1943, short story writer and playwright).
7. Leslie Stephen 1832–1904, first editor of the *Dictionary of National Biography*.
8. The Society had left Portugal Street in September 1901.
9. Approved by the Board of Trade on 12 June 1914.
10. The Screenwriters' Association was formed by the Society in 1937.
11. Report on p. 11 of *The Author*, October 1902.
12. La Société des Auteurs, Compositeurs et Editeurs de Musique (SACEM) had been founded in 1851 to license and collect performance royalties. Since the Berne International Copyright Convention 1886, it had employed an agent in the UK to collect fees due on the performance of French musical copyright works in this country.
13. See Chapter Five, p. 99–100.
14. This was a chore carried out for composer members by the Society of Authors for a charge of 6d per 100 copies.
15. The reasons are explained on pp. 38–40 of *The Composer in the Market Place* by Alan Peacock and Ronald Weir. Faber 1975. This book and

Gavin McFarlane's thesis are my main sources of information for this part of the chapter.

16. The Music (Summary Proceedings) Act 1902 and the Music Copyright Act 1906. In 1905 the 19 members of the Music Publishers Association formed the Musical Defence League and persuaded T. P. O'Connor MP to take charge of the Bill that passed into law in 1906. These two Acts were eventually repealed by the Copyright Act 1956.

17. William Boosey was the driving force behind the formation of the Performing Right Society, whose object was to license and collect royalties on the public performance of non-dramatic musical works. This did not cover operas, music dramas and similar stage works, for which the composer would make a separate contract. Considerable friction existed for several years between the Society of Authors' composers' sub-committee and the PRS. The sub-committee, mainly made up of heavyweight composers took exception to the fact that the PRS was publisher inspired, and held the view that composers ought to collect their own royalties, and share them with no one. This was not a realistic attitude. Relations gradually improved and in 1944 the Society helped to set up the independent Composers' Guild.

18. The two original organisations were The Mechanical Copyright Licences Company Ltd and The Copyright Protection Society Ltd. It is of interest that, under the Copyright Act 1911, a compulsory royalty was established once permission for recording had been given. In other words, after the composer and the recording company had agreed terms, any other company might reproduce the music on payment of a statutory rate. Moreover, in contrast to the PRS, neither the MCPS (nor its predecessors) ever monopolised the market. A number of music copyright holders have always collected their own royalties direct from the recording companies.

19. Other copyright stalwarts who died in the early 1900s, and who thus failed to see the completion of their labours, included F. R. Daldy, Secretary of the Copyright Association, and Lord Thring who had drafted the 1899 Copyright Bill—both these men died in 1907. Three years later came the death of Lord Monkswell, who had piloted the Society of Authors' Copyright Bill 1890–1 and the 1899 Bill through the House of Lords. Walter Besant had died in 1901.

20. The USA passed a new Copyright Act in 1909. This Act repealed all previous legislation and provided comprehensively for the whole subject of copyright. It proved however a disappointment to foreign, especially British authors, since it not only retained the manufacturing clause but extended it to require printing and binding as well as typesetting within the United States. The period of copyright was fixed at 28 years after first publication or performance, with a renewal term of 28: thus 56 in all.

21. The Act introduced a curious restriction whereby, after 25 years following the author's death, the reproduction of any of his works was not deemed to be an infringement of copyright, if a statutory royalty of 10% was paid to the then copyright owner.

22. Now the National Library of Scotland.

237

APPENDIX

La Société des Auteurs et Compositeurs Dramatiques
Report by G. Bernard Shaw and Henry Arthur Jones

10th March 1907.

Dramatiques

At a meeting of the Dramatic Sub-Committee of the
Society of Authors at 39 Old Queen Street on the
1907, we were requested to confer and report on the methods
of the Societe des Auteurs et Compositeurs and on the possibility of applying them to English theatrical business;
also on the subject generally of organizing the business
interests of the profession of dramatic authorship in
the English speaking countries.

We now beg to report our conclusions as follows:-
The system of the Société des Auteurs has one feature
unknown in England. In addition to the usual separate agreements between manager and author for each play, there is a
standing general treaty (traité générale) between the
Société and the theatres. The ostensible effect of this
general treaty is to place the manager so completely at the
mercy of the Société that little is left to be settled by
the ordinary agreements except time, place, duration of contract and rate of author's fees. The Société is empowered
to forbid the performance of any of its members plays without
notice; and it is expressly declared that if the manager
produces any play by an author who remains outside the
Société this power will be exercised. Various privileges
are stipulated for the agents of the Société, including
the right to receive six tickets for each performance, and
to sell those tickets if they desire to do so. On paper,
therefore, the French Société is completely master of the
situation, and can at any moment compel any theatre in
France either to close its doors or confine its performances
to non-copyright plays.

Our first obvious comment on those clauses is that no
sane manager in England would sign such a treaty. This
raises the question, why do the French managers sign it?
The answer is that it is found in practice to be better
policy to give the Société a weapon so formidable that it
dare not use it than to make a reasonable and practicable
agreement with it. The power of the Société to close the
Français and the Odéon may exist on paper; but it is clear
that in practice the traité générale would not survive the
first serious attempt to enforce it. An attempt to have it
enforced by the courts would not only rouse public opinion

strongly against its arbitrary character, but might quite
possibly raise questions as to whether the Societe may
not have overstepped the laws against conspiracy, or lead to
legislation, analogous to our Factory Acts, for restraining
abuses of the monopoly established by the institution of
copyright.. We are agreed as to the inexpediency of copying
the provisions of the traité générale in England. We note,
however, one provision as worth further consideration. The
French manager, under the traité, agrees to pay the author
for all seats occupied at a performance, whether they are
paid for or not. Whether he actually does so or not we cannot
say. But as we are agreed that the papering system, difficult as it is to resist it under long-run conditions, is on
the whole disastrous, being in economic effect a dumping
system, we make a special note of the clause for the consideration of the Committee.

Our rejection of the provisions of the French traite does
not, however, imply any condemnation of the principle of
general treaties. It seems to us that the Society of
Authors might well aim at making a general treaty with
the managers which would leave nothing to be settled except
the two or three variable factors which might be set out on
a half sheet of notepaper, thereby saving a good deal of
trouble to both author and manager. This, however, cannot
be attempted until the Authors' Society is in a position
to approach the Managers' Association with a conclusive
majority of the dramatic authors behind it . For the present
we must proceed in the way hitherto customary by separate
agreements.

It is not possible to draw up a single form of agreement
which will fit all the cases. There are half a dozen clauses
which should form part of practically all agreements between
authors and managers; and these the Committee will have no
difficulty in modelling. In addition to these a number of
model clauses shpuld be drawn up dealing with conditions which
vary from one agreement to another. By adding such of these
as may be suited to the particular case, to the clauses which are
common to all cases, it will be easy at any moment to draw up
an agreement without any fresh drafting. We suggest that the
next business of the dramatic Sub-Committee should be to draw
up such a series of model clauses.

There are some matters, of great importance to authors,
such as the control of the author over the casting of his play,
and over those parts of the business handling of it which cannot be reduced to figures, or to definite terms, which must
always remain outside the written contract. At least we are
unable to suggest any practicable clauses which would make the
author independent of his personal influence with the Manager,
fortified by a strong professional organization at his back.
No doubt a good deal could be done by a well-drafted agreement,
and especially by the resolute limitation of these agreements
to short periods of time and to the actual places in which the
play is to be produced. The recklessness with which agreements are at present made for unlimited periods, and literally
whole quarters of the globe, when there is not the slightest
likelihood of the manager making any use of the play in more
than a couple of dozen towns, is only mitigated by the fact that
the agreements are for the most part so absurdly drawn up by
managers who are ignorant of law and solicitors who are ignorant

239

of copyright and theatrical business, that the courts would
make short work of them if any attempt were made to take them
seriously. But this consideration is as unsatisfactory to the
author as to the manager; and it is extremely desirable that a
typical agreement, with alternative clauses to deal with the
variable factors, should be prepared at once by our Society.

We have also considered the proposals to circularise all
the dramatists of England with a view to establishing closer
combination between them. We are heartily in favour of such a
step; but it is clear to us that the first condition of its
success is that we should approach authors with a completed
scheme for their assistance and defence. We therefore recommend
that nothing be done in this direction until we have prepared
our model clauses and elaborated our plan of campaign.

G. Bernard Shaw
Henry Arthur Jones

SELECT BIBLIOGRAPHY

All the sources used in this book, published and unpublished, are referred to in the Notes and Acknowledgements. The following therefore is not a comprehensive list, but more in the nature of a general guide.

Reference Works

The British Book Trade by Robin Myers. Deutsch 1973.

The New Cambridge Bibliography of English Literature. Volumes 1–3 edited by George Watson. Volume 4 edited by I. R. Willison. CUP 1969–74.

The Dictionary of National Biography. The Compact Edition. Two Volumes. OUP 1975.

The Oxford Book of Literary Anecdotes, edited by James Sutherland. Clarendon Press 1975.

The Oxford Companion to the Theatre, edited by Phyllis Hartnoll. OUP 1967.

The Society of Authors. Relevant publications issued by or for the Society include:

> *The Grievances between Authors and Publishers.* Leadenhall Press 1887.
> *The History of the Société des Gens de Lettres* by S. Squire Sprigge. 1889.
> *Literature and the Pension List* by W. Morris Colles. Glaisher 1889.
> *The Cost of Production* by S. Squire Sprigge and Walter Besant. 1889.
> *The Methods of Publishing* by S. Squire Sprigge. Glaisher 1890.
> *The Literary Handmaid of the Church* by Walter Besant. Glaisher 1890.
> *The Author.* The Society's Journal. 1890 onwards.
> *Copyright Law Reform* by J. M. Lely. Eyre and Spottiswoode 1891.
> *The Society of Authors. A Record of its Action from its Foundation* by Walter Besant. 1893.
> *Addenda to the Methods of Publishing* by G. Herbert Thring. Cox 1898.
> *What are Writers worth?* by Richard Findlater. 1963.
> *The Book Writers, who are they?* by Richard Findlater. 1966.

See also the 'Bibliography on the Conditions of Authorship' contained in *The Author's Empty Purse* by James Hepburn. OUP 1968.

Special and General Studies

Allen, Walter	*The English Novel.* Phoenix House 1954.
Altick, Richard D.	*The English Common Reader.* University of Chicago Press 1963.
	The Sociology of Authorship. Bulletin of the New York Public Library. Volume 66, No. 6. June 1962.
Attenborough, John	*A Living Memory.* Hodder 1976.
Barnes, James J.	*Free Trade in Books. A Study of the London Book Trade since 1800.* Clarendon Press 1964.

	Authors, Publishers and Politicians. The Quest for an Anglo-American Copyright Agreement 1815–54. Routledge 1974.
Beljame, Alexandre	*Men of Letters and the English Public in the Eighteenth Century.* Edited by Bonamy Dobree. Routledge 1948.
Bentley, Phyllis	*The Brontës.* Home and Van Thal 1947.
Bennett, Arnold	*The Letters of Arnold Bennett.* Volume 1: Letters to J. B. Pinker. Edited by James Hepburn. OUP 1966.
	The Truth about an Author. Constable 1903.
	How to become an Author. Pearson 1903.
Besant, Walter	*The Pen and the Book.* Burleigh 1899. This book contains a chapter on *Copyright and Literary Property* by G. Herbert Thring.
	Autobiography. Hutchinson 1902.
	Essays and Historiettes. Chatto 1903.
Birrell, Augustine	*The Law and History of Copyright in Books.* Cassell 1899.
Blakey, Dorothy	*The Minerva Press, 1790–1820.* OUP 1939.
Bowker, R. R.	*Copyright: its History and its Law.* Houghton Mifflin 1912.
Brabrook, Edward	*The Royal Society of Literature. A Brief Account of its Origin and Progress.* Asher 1897.
Briggs, William	*The Law of International Copyright.* Stevens and Haynes 1906.
Britton, John	*Autobiography.* Two volumes. Privately printed 1849–50.
Brown, Curtis	*Contacts.* Cassell 1935.
Bryant, Arthur	*Macaulay.* Peter Davies 1932.
Campbell, Ian	*Thomas Carlyle.* Hamish Hamilton 1974.
Carey, John	*Thackeray: Prodigal Genius.* Faber 1977.
The Cornhill Magazine	Numbers 1057/8, autumn/winter 1968/9 contain *1768: The Literary Background* by Peter Quennell and *The Rewards of Writing over the Centuries* by Maurice Temple Smith. Murray.
Collins, A. S.	*Authorship in the Days of Johnson.* Holden 1927.
Dearden, J. S.	*Facets of Ruskin.* Skilton 1970.
Dickens, Charles	*The Letters of Charles Dickens.* The Pilgrim Edition.
	Volume 1, edited by Madeline House and Graham Storey. Clarendon Press 1965.
	Volume III, edited by Madeline House, Graham Storey and Kathleen Tillotson. Clarendon Press 1974.
Drabble, Margaret	*Arnold Bennett.* Weidenfeld 1974.

242

Duffy, Maureen	*The Passionate Shepherdess.* Cape 1977.
Dyer, Isaac Watson	*A Bibliography of Thomas Carlyle's Writings and Ana.* Southworth Press, Portland, Maine 1928.
Elwin, Malcolm	*Charles Reade.* Cape 1931. Russell and Russell, New York 1969.
Ervine, St. John	*Bernard Shaw. His Life, Work and Friends.* Constable 1956.
Findlater, Richard	*Banned. A Review of Theatrical Censorship in Britain.* MacGibbon and Kee 1967.
Fuller, Jean Overton	*Shelley: A Biography.* Cape 1968.
Gerin, Winifred	*The Brontës: The Creative Work.* Longman 1974.
Gissing, George	*New Grub Street.* Smith Elder 1891.
	The Rediscovery of George Gissing. A Reader's Guide by John Spiers and Pierre Coustillas. National Book League 1971.
Gittings, Robert	*Young Thomas Hardy.* Heinemann 1975.
	The Older Hardy. Heinemann 1978.
Gosse, Edmund	*The Life and Letters of Edmund Gosse.* Edited by Evan Charteris. Heinemann 1931.
Gross, John	*The Rise and Fall of the Man of Letters.* Weidenfeld 1969.
Haight, Gordon S.	*George Eliot: A Biography.* OUP 1968.
Hardy, Florence Emily	*The Life of Thomas Hardy.* Macmillan 1962.
Hepburn, James	*The Author's Empty Purse and the Rise of the Literary Agent.* OUP 1968.
Herd, Harold	*The March of Journalism.* Allen and Unwin 1952.
Hopkins, Mary Alden	*Hannah More and her Circle.* Longman 1947.
Howe, P. P.	*The Life of William Hazlitt.* Hamish Hamilton 1947.
Hunt, Leigh	*Autobiography.* Edited by J. E. Morpurgo. Cresset Press 1949.
Hurrell, Henry	*Copyright Law and the Copyright Act 1911.* Waterlow 1912.
Huxley, Leonard	*The House of Smith Elder.* Privately printed 1923.
d'Israeli, Isaac	*Calamities of Authors.* Murray 1812.
James, C. F.	*The Story of the Performing Right Society.* PRS 1951.
Laurenson, D. F.	*A Sociological Study of Authorship.* The British Journal of Sociology. Volume XX, No. 3. September 1969.
Mackenzie, Norman and Jeanne	*The Time Traveller: The Life of H. G. Wells.* Weidenfeld 1973.
	The First Fabians. Weidenfeld 1977.

McFarlane, Gavin — *Copyright: The Development and Exercise of the Performing Right.* Thesis for the University of London 1975.

McLaren, Moray — *Sir Walter Scott. The Man and the Patriot.* Heinemann 1970.

Macmillan, Frederick — *The Net Book Agreement 1899.* Maclehose 1924.

Marchand, Leslie — *Byron: A Portrait.* Murray 1971.

Moore, Doris Langley — *The late Lord Byron.* Murray 1961.

Mumby, F. A., and Norrie, Ian — *Publishing and Bookselling.* Cape 1974.

Mumby, F. A. and Stallybrass, Frances H. S. — *From Swan Sonnenschein to George Allen and Unwin Ltd.* Allen and Unwin 1955.

Nicoll, Allardyce — *British Drama.* Harrap 1962.

Nowell-Smith, Simon — *Letters to Macmillan.* (Editor). Macmillan 1967.

International Copyright and the Publisher in the Reign of Queen Victoria. Clarendon Press 1968.

Patten, Robert L. — *Vanity Fair versus Dombey and Son.* Studies in English Literature. Volume X, No. 4, autumn 1970.

The Sale of Dickens's Works. Appendix contributed to *Dickens: The Critical Heritage*, edited by Philip Collins. Barnes & Noble 1971.

Pickwick Papers and the Development of Serial Fiction. Rice University Studies. Volume 61, No. 1, winter 1975.

Paul, C. Kegan — *Memories.* Kegan Paul 1899/Routledge 1971.

Peacock, Alan and Weir, Ronald — *The Composer in the Market Place.* Faber 1975.

Pearson, Hesketh — *Bernard Shaw.* Collins 1942/Macdonald and Jane's 1975.

Pinero, A. W. — *The Collected Letters.* Edited by J. P. Waring. University of Minnesota Press 1974.

Pinkus, Philip — *Grub St. stripped bare.* Constable 1968.

Plant, Marjorie — *The English Book Trade.* Allen and Unwin 1965.

Poole, Adrian — *Gissing in Context.* Macmillan 1975.

Pope-Hennessy, Una — *Charles Dickens.* Chatto 1945.

Pound, Reginald — *Arnold Bennett.* Heinemann 1953.

Publishing, Essays in the History of — Edited by Asa Briggs. Longman 1974.

Ray, Gordon N. — *William Makepeace Thackeray.* Two Volumes. OUP 1955/8.

Saunders, J. W. — *The Profession of English Letters.* Routledge 1964.

Sells, A. Lytton   *Oliver Goldsmith: His Life and Works.* Allen and Unwin 1975.

Shaw, George Bernard   *Collected Letters.* Edited by Dan H. Laurence. Volume I, 1874–1897. Volume II, 1898–1910. Max Reinhardt/Dodd Mead & Co 1965/72.

The Complete Bernard Shaw Prefaces. Paul Hamlyn 1965.

Skone James, E. P.   *Copinger and Skone James on Copyright.* Sweet and Maxwell 1971.

Smiles, Aileen   *Samuel Smiles and his Surroundings.* Hale 1956.

Smiles, Samuel   *A Publisher and his Friends.* Two Volumes. Murray 1891.

Sutherland, J. A.   *Victorian Novelists and Publishers.* Athlone Press 1977.

Tennyson, Charles   *Alfred Tennyson.* Macmillan 1949.

Thring, G. Herbert   *The Marketing of Literary Property.* Constable 1933.

Trollope, Anthony   *An Autobiography.* Edited by Michael Sadleir. OUP 1974.

Wain, John   *Samuel Johnson.* Macmillan 1974

Whyte, Frederic   *William Heinemann.* Cape 1928.

Williams, David   *George Meredith.* Hamish Hamilton 1977.

Williams, Keith   *The English Newspaper.* Springwood Books 1977.

Williams, Raymond   *Culture and Society, 1780–1850.* Chatto 1958.

The Long Revolution. Chatto 1961.

Woodcock, George   *The Incomparable Aphra.* Boardman 1948.

INDEX

This Index is divided for convenience into *General Subjects* and *Principal Personalities*.

General Subjects

Principal Personalities

Allen, George 178–9, 233–4
Archer, William 97, 188, 189, 202, 207–8
Arnold, Matthew 63, 121, 177
Austen, Jane 45, 48–9, 100

Bainton, George 160–1, 232
Ballantyne brothers 40–1
Barker, Harley Granville 191, 199, 200, 201
Barnes, William 44
Barrie, J. M. 141, 150, 199, 210, 212
Beerbohm, Max 156, 207
Behn, Aphra 220
Beith, Ian Hay 174
Bennett, Arnold 167, 171, 180–2, 183, 184, 185, 187, 233, 234
Bentley, Richard 66, 67, 77, 91–3, 94, 103, 116, 133, 223, 225
Bergne, Henry 215, 230
Besant, Annie 188
Besant, Walter 26, 80–1, 82–3, 86, 88–9, 106, 119, 121, 125–8, 129, 130, 131, 132, 134–9, 143, 145–51, 155, 156, 157, 164, 167, 169, 171, 195–6, 206, 213, 227, 228, 230, 231, 232, 237
Blackmore, R. D. 121, 160
Blackwood family 26, 39, 48–9, 110–14, 222, 231
Blake, William 25
Bohn, H. G. 77, 226
Boucicault, Dion 96, 228
Britton, John 30, 81, 220
Brontë sisters 100, 229
Brougham, Henry 35, 36, 37, 44, 74, 221, 225
Brown, Curtis 169, 170, 171, 233
Browning, Elizabeth Barrett 63, 100
Bryce, James 128–9, 142, 207, 236
Buchanan, Robert 157
Buckingham, James Silk 227, 228
Bulwer-Lytton, Edward 63, 64, 72, 75, 77, 78, 80, 84, 85–6, 107, 121, 224, 225, 226
Burnett, Frances Hodgson 97, 142
Burns, Robert 25, 44, 45
Buxton, Sydney 206, 215
Byron, Lord 40, 45–8, 50, 52, 54, 222

Caine, Hall 141, 160–1, 163
Campbell, Lady Colin 143
Campbell, Lord 72, 225–6
Campbell, Thomas 45, 226, 227
Carlyle, Thomas 39, 54, 56–8, 60, 61, 80, 86, 107
Carr, J. Comyns 124, 230
Cave, Edward 24
Caxton, William 9, 11
Chambers brothers 55–6
Chapman, John 109, 229
Clay, Senator Henry 75, 77, 78
Cobbett, William 34
Colburn, Henry 104, 223
Coleridge, Samuel Taylor 41–3, 45, 52, 53, 106
Colles, William Morris 145–7, 155, 167–8, 181
Collins, Wilkie 121, 142, 160, 162, 169, 227, 229
Constable, Archibald 26, 38, 39–41, 48, 71, 234
Copinger, Walter 121, 212
Corelli, Marie 141, 177
Cottle, Joseph 41, 43
Cowper, William 25
Crabbe, George 44, 48
Craik, G. L. 56, 81, 223
Croker, J. W. 49

248

249

251